I0803130

IMAGES
of America

KENTUCKY'S STATE CAPITOL

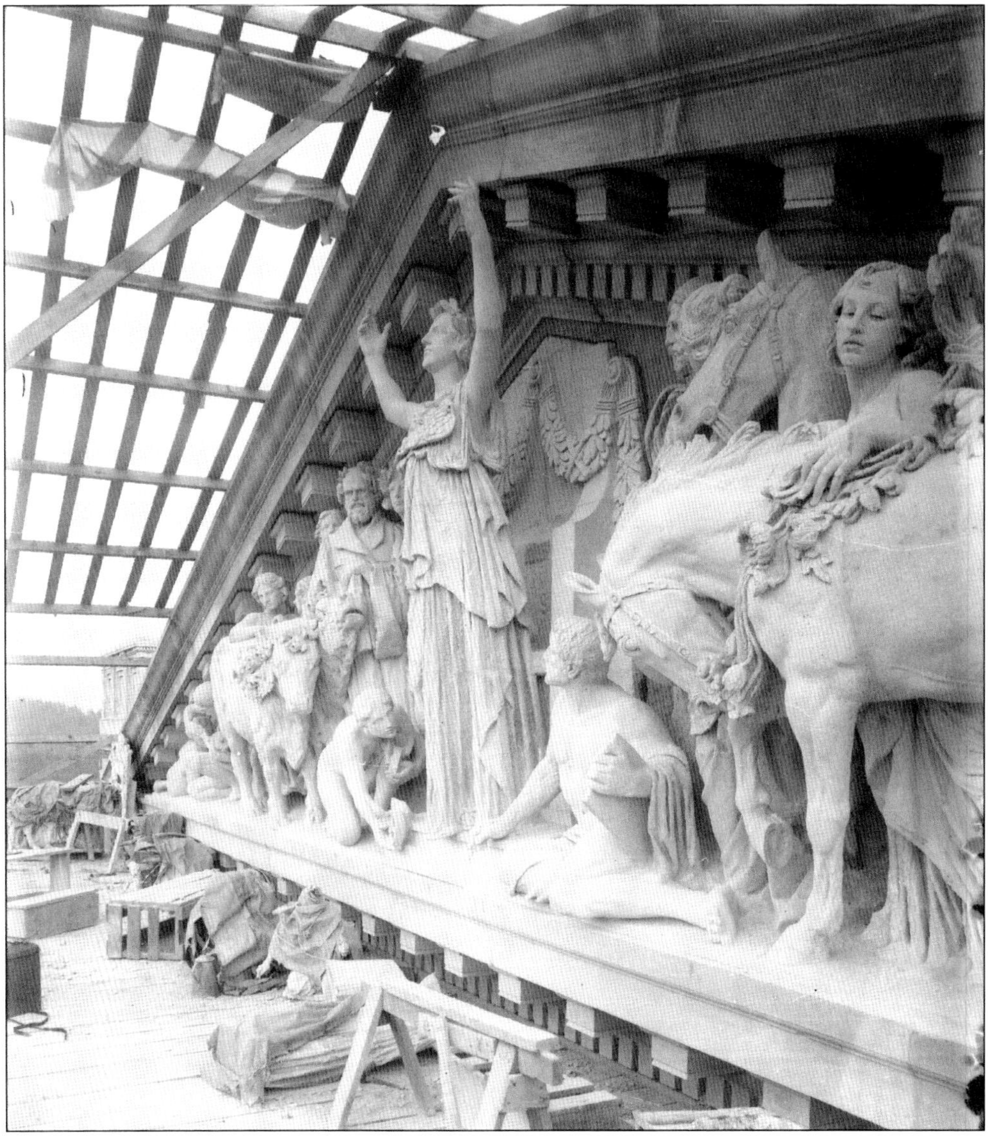

Capitol Sculpture. This is a 1907 photograph of the scaffolding used for sculpting the unfinished pediment. Situated over the north entrance, the pediment is richly sculpted and defines the appearance and architectural lines of the imposing building. Noted sculptor Charles Henry Niehaus received $40,000 for the work. He was assisted on the project by Peter Rossack from Austria. (Courtesy of Kentucky Historical Society.)

On the Cover: The sweeping aerial photograph chosen for the cover was taken between 1920 and 1930 by Bowman-Park Aero Company of Louisville, Kentucky, and is thought to be one of the earliest known aerial photographs of the Kentucky Capitol building. The historic image in sepia tone beautifully captures the harmonious relationship between the bluegrass landscape designed by the Olmsted Brothers landscape architecture firm and the symmetry of the graceful capitol building. Many visitors and architectural historians alike have noted Kentucky's Capitol campus next to the sinuous Kentucky River as one of the most picturesque settings in America for a seat of government. (Courtesy of Ekstrom Library Special Collections, University of Louisville.)

IMAGES
of America

KENTUCKY'S STATE CAPITOL

David L. Buchta

ARCADIA
PUBLISHING

ISBN 978-0-7385-8578-9

Published by Arcadia Publishing
Charleston SC, Chicago IL, Portsmouth NH, San Francisco CA

Printed in the United States of America

Library of Congress Control Number: 2009940079

For all general information contact Arcadia Publishing at:
Telephone 843-853-2070
Fax 843-853-0044
E-mail sales@arcadiapublishing.com
For customer service and orders:
Toll-Free 1-888-313-2665

Visit us on the Internet at www.arcadiapublishing.com

To Allyson, my faithful wife and perfect partner in the kaleidoscope of life. I would not be who I am without your unwavering love and support. Thank you for always inspiring me to reach my endeavors.

Contents

Acknowledgments

An architectural and cultural history of a building with the importance of the Kentucky Capitol would not be very effective without images and illustrations, but it would be difficult if not impossible to capture over 100 years of the Kentucky State Capitol's history without the guidance of archived photographs. I would like to thank the staff of the Kentucky Historical Society (KHS) for their assistance in making the nearly 200 photographs included in *Kentucky's State Capitol* available. Unless otherwise noted, all images are courtesy of the Kentucky Historical Society. Particular thanks to my KHS colleagues Marilyn Zoidis and Kent Whitworth for their recognition and support of the importance of this endeavor for the capitol's centennial anniversary. Many of the images have never been mass-marketed in print, and KHS is proud to make them available in this forum for all to enjoy. The wonderful historic postcards in the book were graciously provided by the extensive collection of local Frankfort architect Scot Walters. The libraries and special collections at the University of Kentucky and the University of Louisville were also instrumental in discovering resources and photography references for this book. Thank you to Amy Perryman, my editor at Arcadia Publishing, who recognized as I did the value of a pictorial book dedicated to this great building and had faith we would have the publication ready for the 2010 centennial anniversary. Special recognition is reserved for my Kentucky Division of Historic Properties senior assistant, Sommer Torabi, for her invaluable time spent working with photographs for this book.

I feel that this book should play an instrumental role in celebrating the centennial anniversary of the capitol building. Therefore, all of my proceeds from Images of America: *Kentucky's State Capitol* will be contributed to the Kentucky Division of Historic Properties Endowment Fund. The fund's purpose is to provide for the conservation and acquisition of historic artifacts for the commonwealth's most significant buildings, including the capitol.

INTRODUCTION

Kentucky was the first territory to be organized west of the Appalachian Mountains. Historically the region had been home to several Native American tribes, which included ancestors of the Sioux, followed by invasions of the Iroquois, and pockets of Shawnee. Exploratory trips were begun by white settlers in the late 1600s, and more extensive colonizing missions occurred in the mid–1700s. Much of this interest was related to the territorial gains won during the French and Indian War from 1755 to 1763, which resulted in the elimination of France as a political and military force in the Mississippi Valley. After the war, many settlers ventured into the region now known as Kentucky, despite a proclamation from King George III forbidding settlement west of the Appalachian highlands. Among these early adventurers was Daniel Boone, who made several trips to the Kentucky region in the 1760s and 1770s.

Numerous speculative land companies promoted the settlement of Kentucky. The colonies of North Carolina and Virginia were rivals for the territory of Kentucky, with Virginia-based land companies eventually securing the region. Following the American Revolution, settlers in Kentucky began to consider separate statehood under the Articles of Confederation. After 10 conventions met to consider the question, a proposed state constitution was ratified in Danville in April 1792. On June 1, 1792, Kentucky was admitted as the 15th state to the newly formed Union under the U.S. Constitution. Inauguration of state officers, including Gen. Isaac Shelby as governor, took place in Lexington on June 4, 1792. Five commissioners were selected to choose a suitable location for a permanent capital. In several meetings held between August 6 and December 5, 1792, the commissioners selected Frankfort over Leestown, Lexington, Petersburg, and Louisville. In exchange for donating the land to build a capitol building, the state government entered into a contract with the City of Frankfort to "fix the seat of government" there unless moved by a two-thirds majority.

Frankfort is centrally located in the bluegrass region of Kentucky, where the Kentucky River forms an "S" caused by the shifting of the drainage channel. The site of Frankfort was first surveyed by adventurers in 1773, when Hancock Taylor claimed the land on behalf of Robert McAfee of Virginia. This claim was not properly recorded, and after a legal battle among subsequent claimants, Gen. James Wilkinson of Virginia organized the town in 1786. The first capitol building was constructed between 1793 and 1794 on the public square, the site of all subsequent capitol buildings until the new capitol of 1905–1910. This first capitol, a rough-hewn stone building three stories in height, was destroyed by fire in 1813. The second capitol was constructed in 1814–1816 on the same site. This two-story brick building also burned in 1824. In 1827, an elegant new capitol building, now known as the old capitol, was designed by Gideon Shyrock (1802–1880) in the Greek Revival style. Shyrock's architectural lineage can be traced to Benjamin Latrobe and William Strickland, two of the earliest and most significant architects in the United States. Other important architecture commissioned to Shyrock is the Jefferson County Courthouse in Louisville, Morrison Hall at Transylvania College in Lexington, and the Arkansas Old State Capitol in Little Rock.

The arrival of the Civil War had detrimental effects on the state's development. The state was the sixth most populous in the union, but one fourth of its population was slaves. Kentucky followed the path of other border states. Family members fought on opposite sides of the war, despite or perhaps because of the state's neutrality. In 1862, Confederate forces led by Braxton Bragg invaded Frankfort and set up a Confederate state government. The occupation was short-lived, as Union forces soon retook the city. On the future site of the new capitol building, a tragic event occurred on November 2, 1864. Four Confederate prisoners of war, all Kentuckians, were executed in reprisal for the murder of a Union supporter.

In 1869, the state government determined that the 1827 capitol building was inadequate to meet its needs. The legislature appropriated $100,000 to begin the construction of a new building designed by Bradshaw, Vodges, and Company. This budget amount, along with later appropriations, allowed a new east wing to be constructed. However, no further appropriations were made due to the economic conditions in the state and the continued fight between Lexington and Louisville for Kentucky's state capital. The lower south had been Kentucky's best market for agricultural goods before the war, and industry, confined to larger cities like Louisville, was limited in comparison to the northern states.

Kentucky has more counties than any other state except for Georgia and Texas. Counties were divided and subdivided, often in order to name the county for a particular politician whose favor was desired. Eventually, Kentucky would have 120 counties. This led to factionalism, complicated by the rise of political organizations in Louisville and other cities. In 1891, the fourth state constitution permanently settled the question of the location of the state capital. However, this document, written in an atmosphere of distrust and contempt, defined and limited government rather than guiding it.

The tragic episode surrounding the 1899 election for governor shows the intensity of political feuds at the time. The state's first Republican governor was elected in 1895 due to a dispute that divided the normally dominant Democratic Party. In 1897, the Kentucky General Assembly passed the Goebel Election Law, setting up the board of election commissioners to oversee elections and decide disputes. Named for the bill's sponsor, William Goebel, the board was to have three members, almost guaranteeing an unfair advantage to one political party or the other. When Goebel ran for governor in 1899, factional divisions again divided the Democrats, and a Republican was elected governor, but by a very narrow margin. The board of election commissioners ruled in favor of Republican candidate W. S. Taylor, but passed ultimate authority over the election over to the Kentucky General Assembly. During legislative committee hearings on the matter, William Goebel was shot outside the old capitol, becoming the only U.S. governor to be assassinated in office in history. He died four days later, although in the meantime the heavily Democratic general assembly had voted in Goebel's favor, naming him the victor in the gubernatorial election. In the years following this historic scandal, the decision was made to construct a new capitol building for the commonwealth.

One

A New Capitol for a "New" Commonwealth

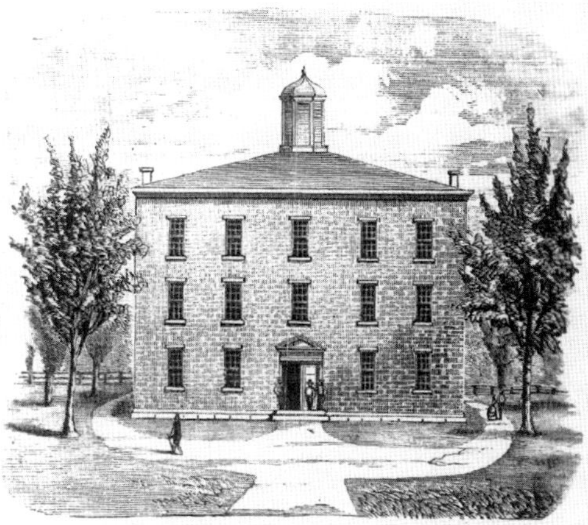

FIRST (PERMANENT) STATE HOUSE, FRANKFORT, KY.
(Built, 1793-94; and Destroyed by fire, Nov. 25, 1813.)

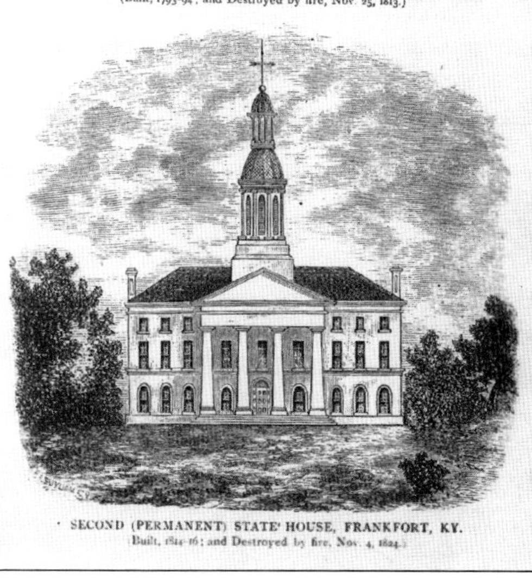

SECOND (PERMANENT) STATE HOUSE, FRANKFORT, KY.
(Built, 1814-16; and Destroyed by fire, Nov. 4, 1824.)

Two Original State Houses. The commonwealth's first two permanent statehouses are represented in this early engraving. Both buildings were said to have been constructed on the square where the current old capitol sits. The first one, a simple three-story stone structure built in 1793–1794 with a small cupola, burned in 1813. The second statehouse, more decorative with a columned portico and three-story tower finished between 1814 and 1816, was also destroyed by flames in 1824. The next capitol building would be built by Gideon Shyrock as the oldest Greek Revival structure west of the Allegheny Mountains. The Kentucky River marble building was started about 1827 and completed by 1832.

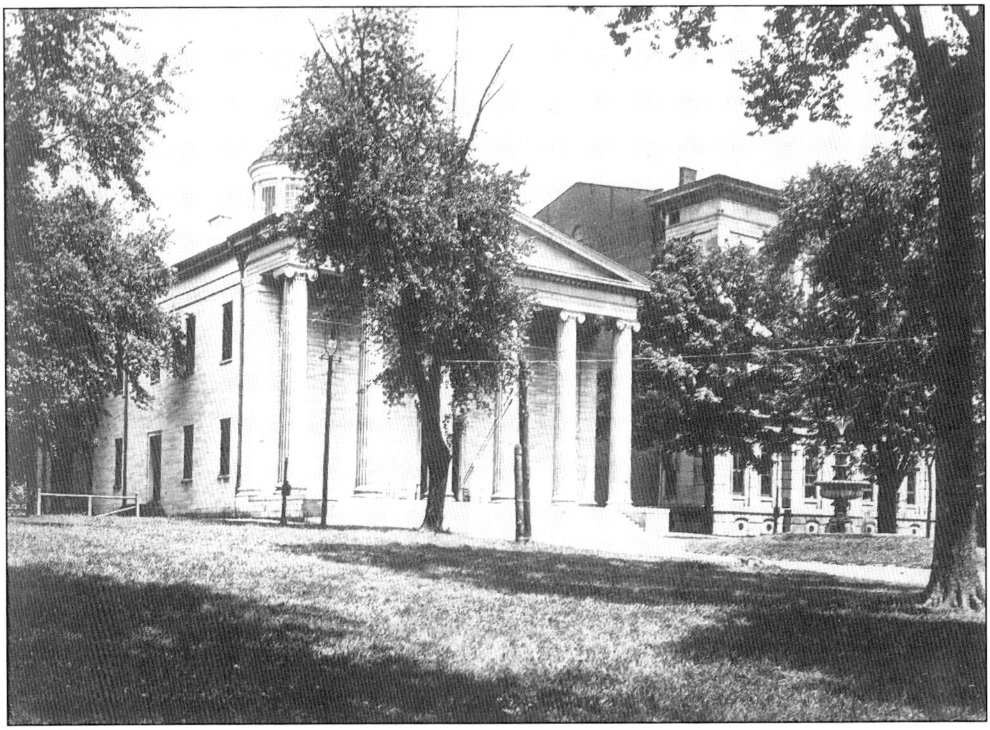

Old Capitol (1827). This photograph, taken just after the end of the 19th century, shows the old capitol. The third capitol of the commonwealth was reported to be in deteriorated condition as early as 1886, "making it possible that at any time the massive pillars may come crashing down on the heads of the passersby." The building was heated by fireplaces, increasing the risk of fire. Adjacent buildings, including the east wing or 1869 annex, were also overcrowded. During the legislative session, the state assembly members would meet in any available space, including taverns and local residences. (Courtesy of Division of Historic Properties.)

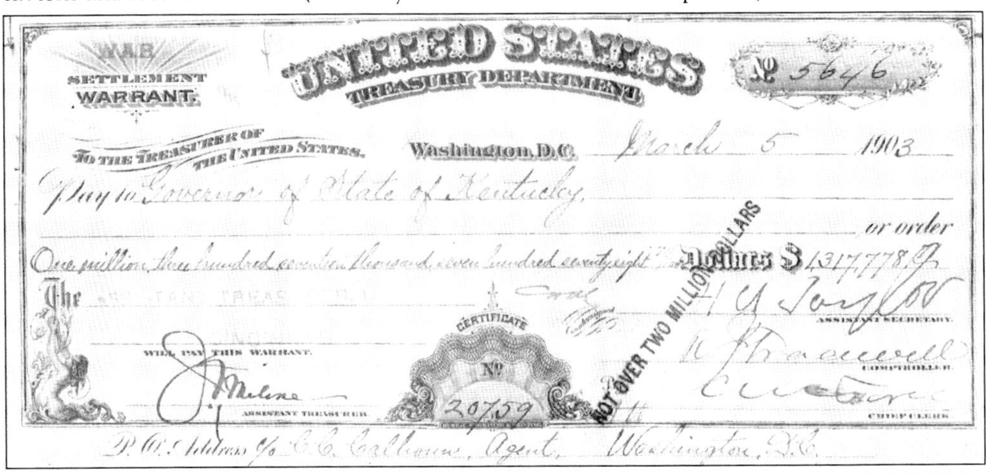

Check for Capitol. This photograph is of the 1903 check that Kentucky received for $1,317,778.71 from the federal government for damages sustained during the Civil War and for services provided in the Spanish-American War of 1898. Gov. J. C. W. Beckham was celebrated for his efforts in requesting the funds from the government. The legislature session of 1904 also voted to appropriate an additional million for the construction of a new capitol building.

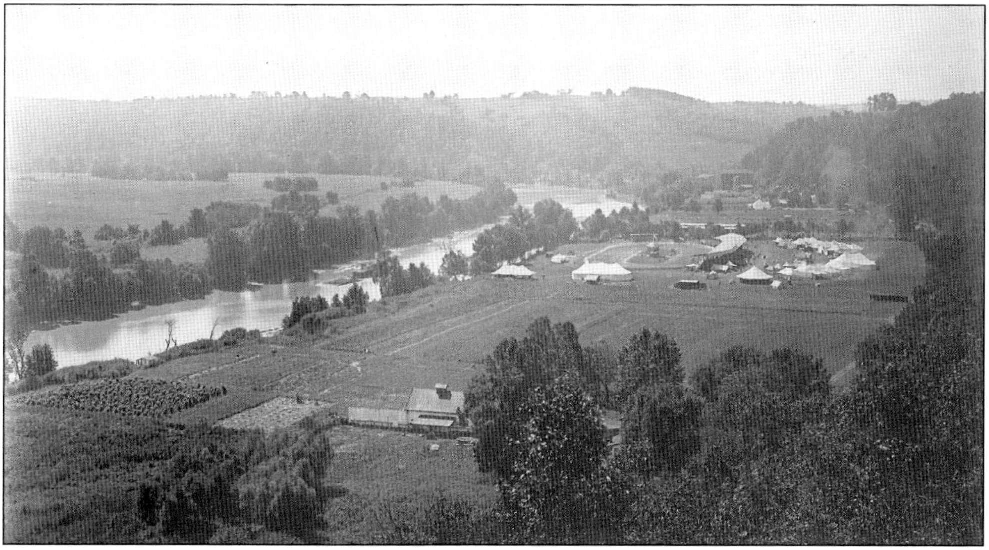

Hunt Property. The initial $1-million appropriation for the new Kentucky capitol required that the new building be built on the site of Frankfort's square and the 1827 capitol; however, the beaux-arts design submitted by architect Frank Mills Andrews was much too large in scale for the square. A special legislative session held in January 1905 appropriated $40,000 for the purchase of appropriate land. The most favored site was the Hunt property shown in these early 1900s photographs, located at the southern end of South Frankfort. The Hunt property location was one of four locations considered at capitol commission meetings in March and April 1904. (Courtesy of Division of Historic Properties.)

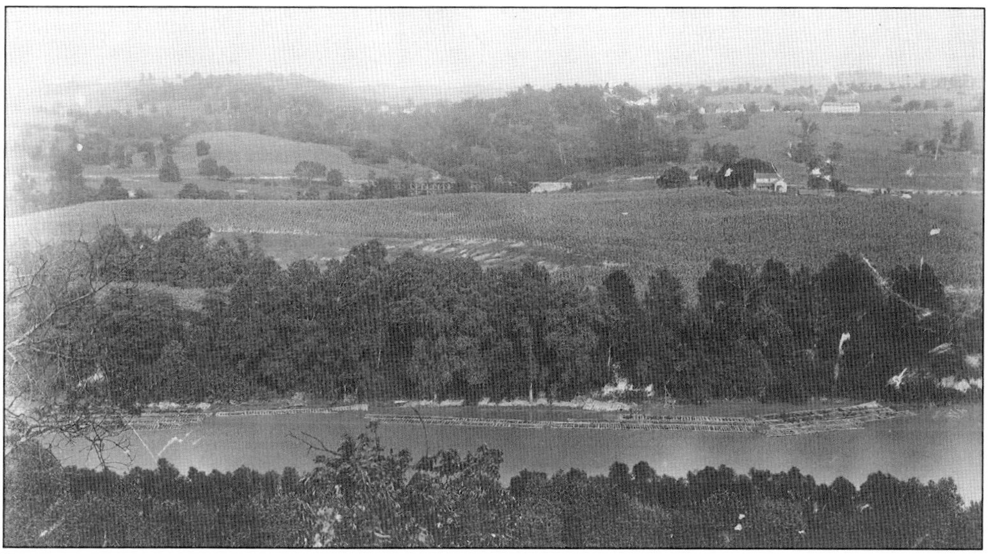

South Frankfort or Downtown. There were four possible sites considered for a new capitol in Frankfort. The first was the site of the 1850 state arsenal on a bluff overlooking the Kentucky River. This location was criticized because, although large enough for the proposed design, it was feared that erosion of the site may undermine the foundations of a large building in the future. The grounds of the Kentucky Feeble-Minded Institute were considered, but moving that structure to a new site would need to be included in the cost of the new building. The third site, known as the Rodman property, was not seriously considered. (Courtesy of Division of Historic Properties.)

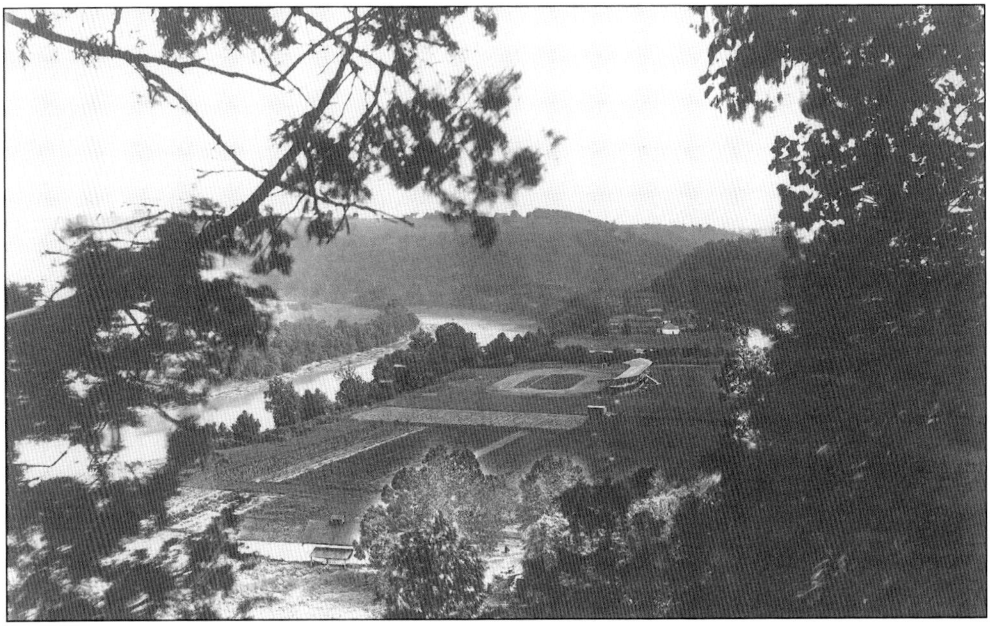

PERFECT SITE. Few state capital cities can boast the picturesque setting of Kentucky's capitol. Visitors often note it seems as though the imposing site on which it sits was made for it. In actuality, the landscape was built up with several hundred thousand pounds of fill and excavated to embrace the building's mass. This early-1900s photograph verifies that the Hunt property was flat and not the undulating landscape that appears today. (Courtesy of Division of Historic Properties.)

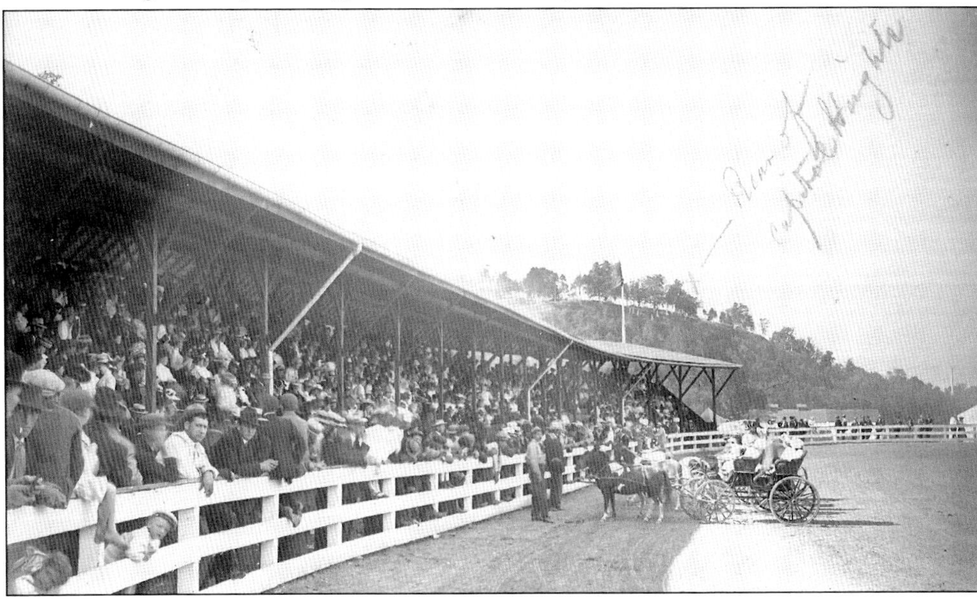

DAY AT THE RACES. As noted on this early photograph labeled "Capitol Heights," South Frankfort expansion was planned in 1909 with the development of Capitol Heights, a suburban subdivision with 111 plots on the bluff to the south and west of the almost-complete new capitol. However, the plots failed to sell, and development would not occur until the 1920s. The photograph was taken prior to the Hunt property becoming the grounds of the new capitol. (Courtesy of Division of Historic Properties.)

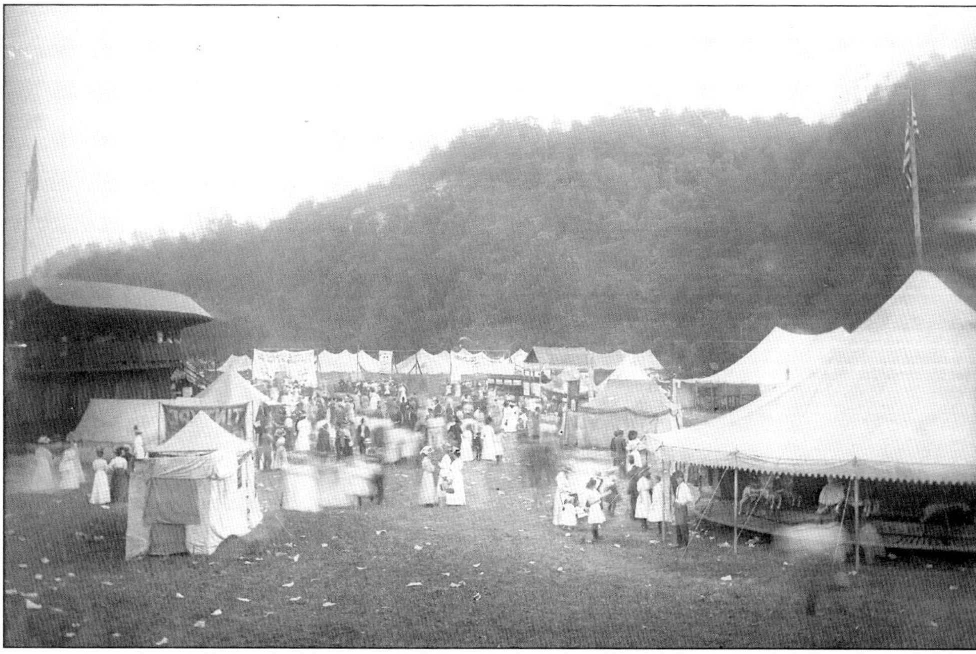

CARNIVAL ATMOSPHERE. Before the construction of the new capitol, the Hunt property was known for horse racing, rides, and amusements. This photograph shows the subjects enjoying the atmosphere of an early 1900s fair. The blur of motion evident above was often mistaken for ghosts in early photography. (Courtesy of Division of Historic Properties.)

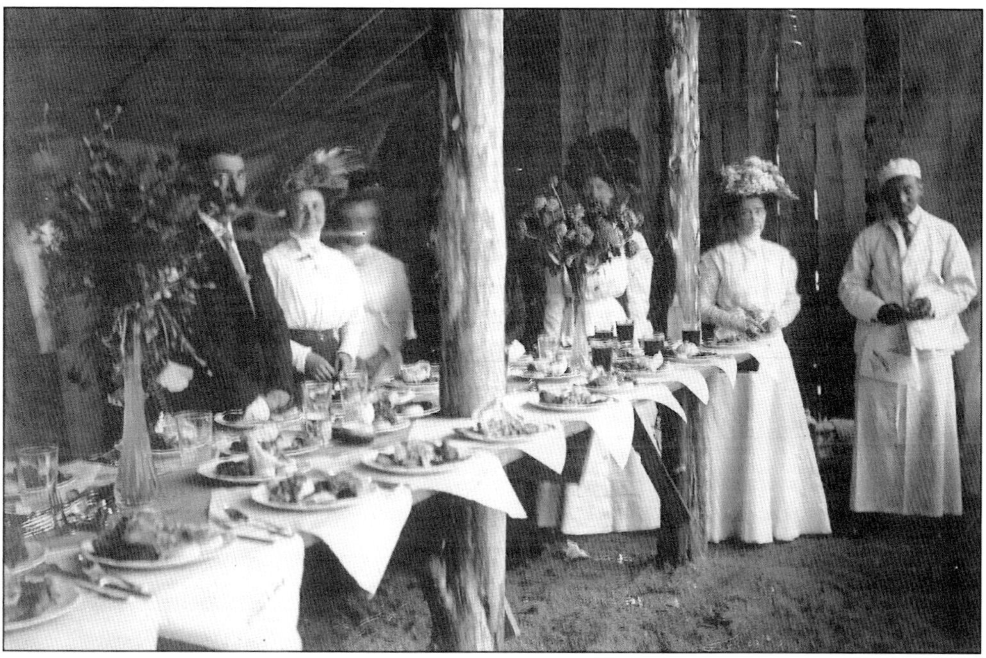

FANCY FEAST. Frankfort's social history is well chronicled, and this scene is reminiscent of many early gatherings in the capital city. This early photograph, taken on the Hunt property before the capitol was constructed, gives a glimpse of unidentified socialites enjoying a meal in the improvised dining room tent. (Courtesy of Division of Historic Properties.)

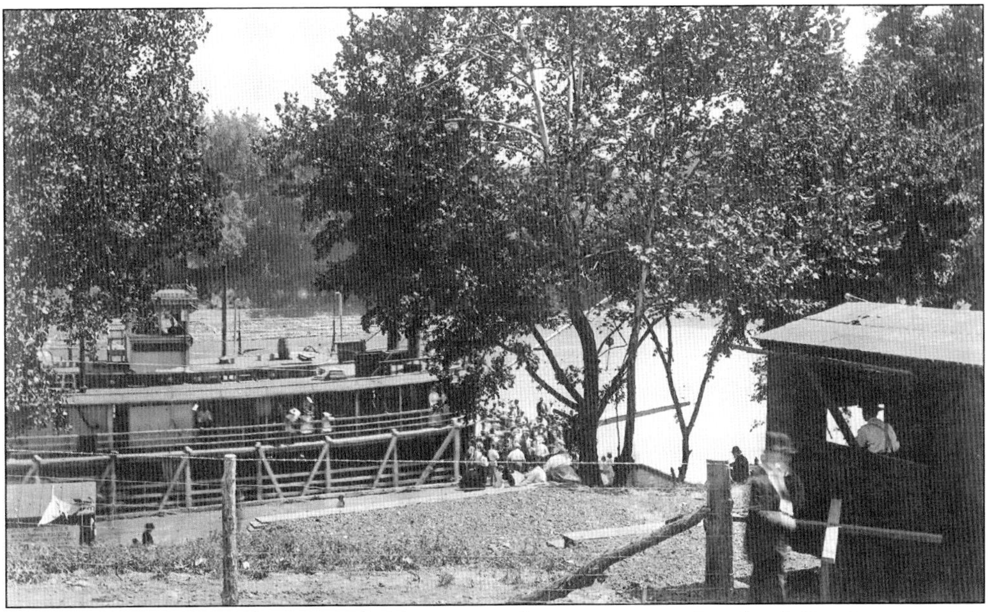

FRANKFORT'S RIVER. The Kentucky River served as a major conduit for delivering materials from all over the United States to the new capitol site. Records indicate that some construction shipments traveled on riverboats from ports on the Ohio River such as Cincinnati and Pittsburgh to Frankfort. This undated photograph was taken near where riverboats and barges would have unloaded materials for building the capitol. Note the simple wooden turnstile in the lower right-hand corner allowing the man in the small building to record riverboat passengers. (Courtesy of Division of Historic Properties.)

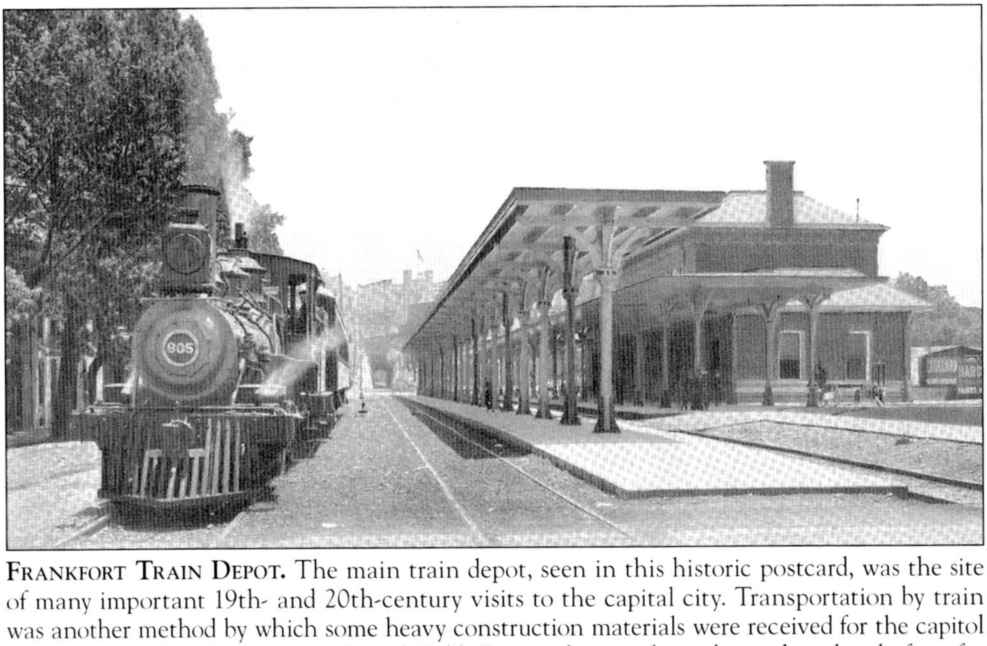

FRANKFORT TRAIN DEPOT. The main train depot, seen in this historic postcard, was the site of many important 19th- and 20th-century visits to the capital city. Transportation by train was another method by which some heavy construction materials were received for the capitol building. Presidents Harrison, Taft, and Teddy Roosevelt were also welcomed on the platform for their visits to Frankfort. The rolling luggage cars from the old depot are still used for transporting heavy objects in the capitol today. (Courtesy collection of Scot Walters.)

Two

Building a Landmark

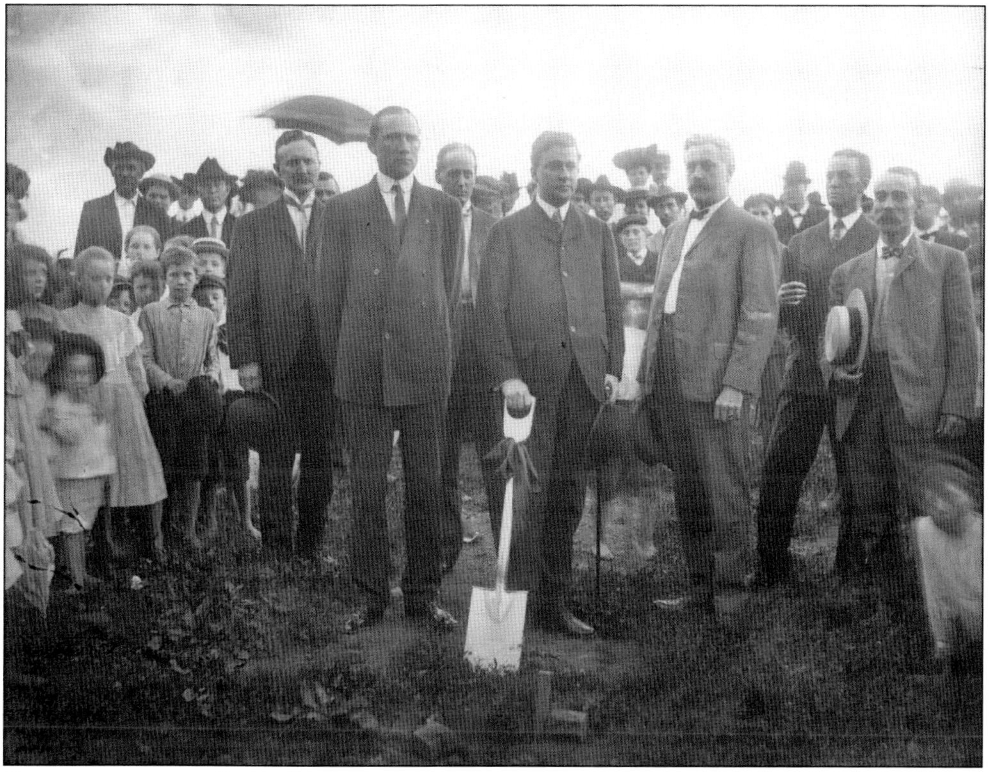

Ground-breaking Ceremony. On May 30, 1905, Gov. J. C. W. Beckham shoveled the first ceremonial spade of dirt for the new state capitol. Governor Beckham was instrumental in securing the funds for building the capitol by traveling to Washington and lobbying on behalf of the commonwealth. The capitol commission board concluded to have simple ceremonies on the grounds, and it is reported that the hour was hand-set to exactly 5:00 p.m. to meet the contractor and any citizens of Frankfort desiring to be present. Promptly at 5:00 p.m., the first shovel of dirt was thrown by Gov. J. C. W. Beckham with some officials present and what appear to be many school-age children in this photograph. The official ground-breaking for the new capitol's construction was on August 14, 1905, four days after the contract was officially given to the General Supply and Construction Company.

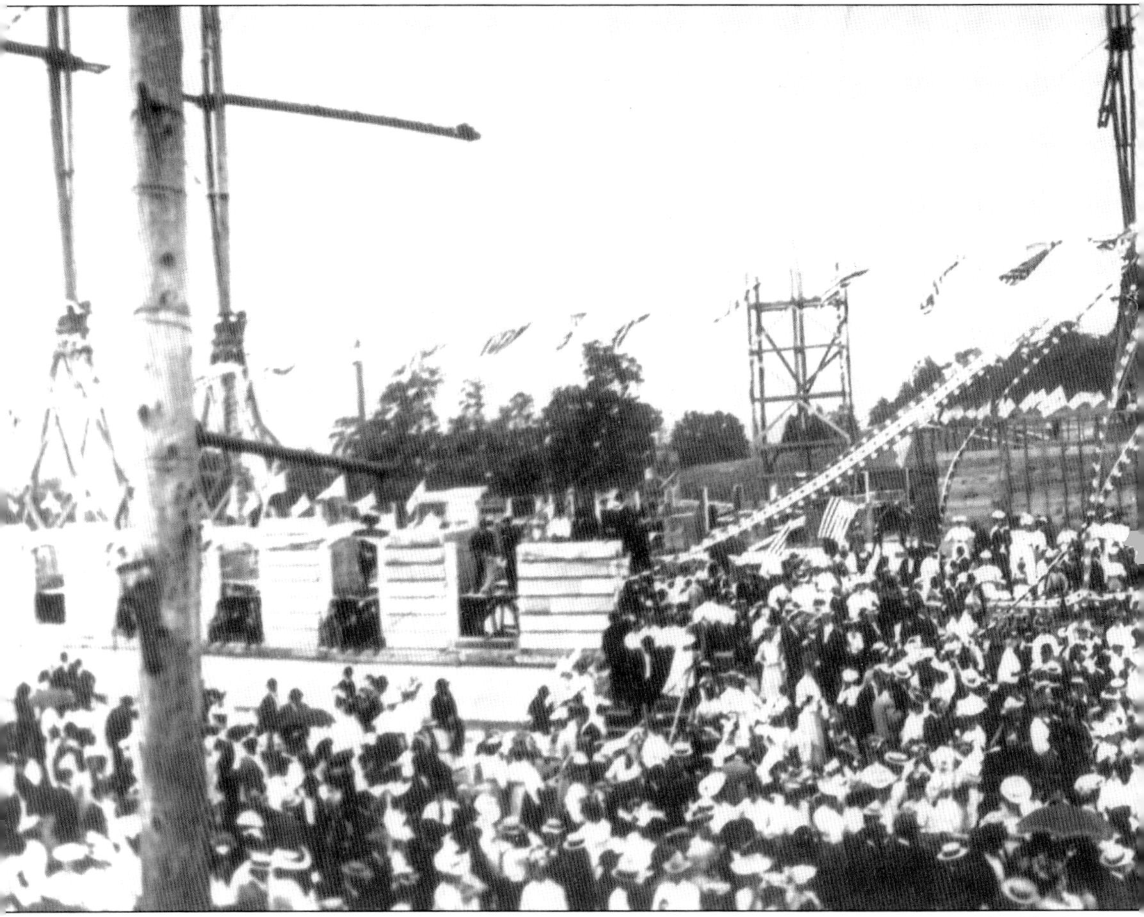

Laying the Cornerstone. On June 16, 1906, the cornerstone of the new capitol was laid before a throng estimated at 20,000. The ceremony began with a procession from the old capitol, across the Kentucky River, and up Capitol Avenue to the building site. The laying of the cornerstone was followed with an address by Gov. J. C. W. Beckham and the placing of items in the cornerstone by Frankfort mayor E. E. Hume. This historic photograph of the event shows the throng of onlookers

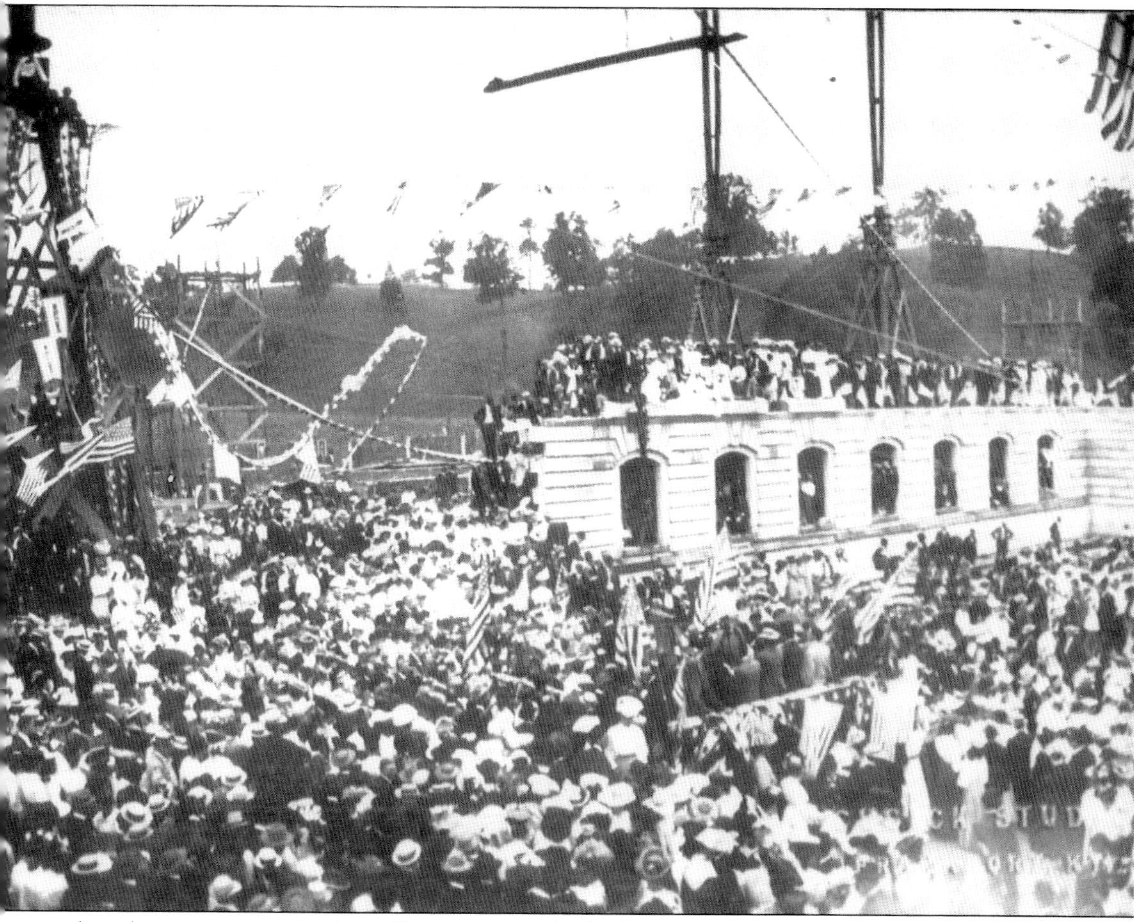

gathered at an opening in the wall, approximately the location of the main entrance portico. The crowd appears to be facing towards the south direction of the interior of the building. The specific location of the historic cornerstone is unknown; however, there is a bronze plaque on the northwest rotunda pier wall commemorating the laying of the cornerstone.

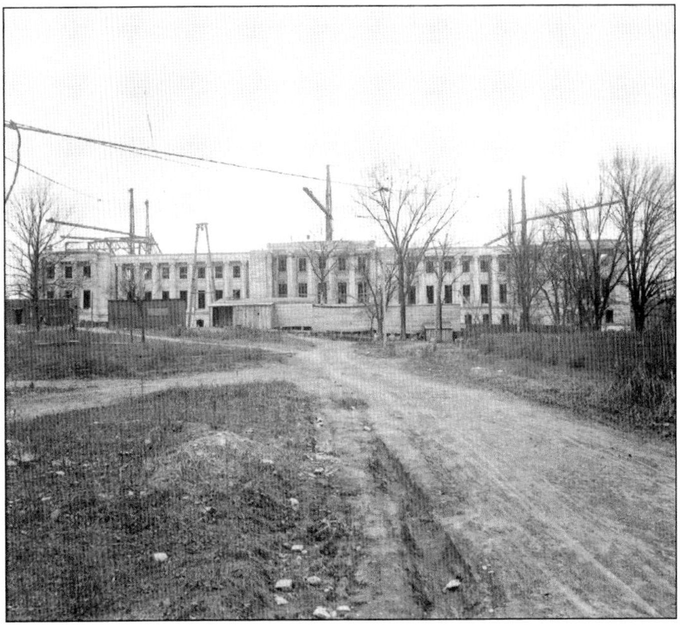

LATE 1906. As this late-season photograph shows, the capitol's early construction was swift from the ground-breaking in the summer 1905 until the structure had walls. The outer walls are already decorated with 70 Ionic columns, 32 on the front, four on either end, and 30 on the back. The interior was still almost empty at this point, and the capitol commission was getting anxious about the completion. The monolithic columns are 27 feet, 10 inches tall and weigh nearly 18 tons each.

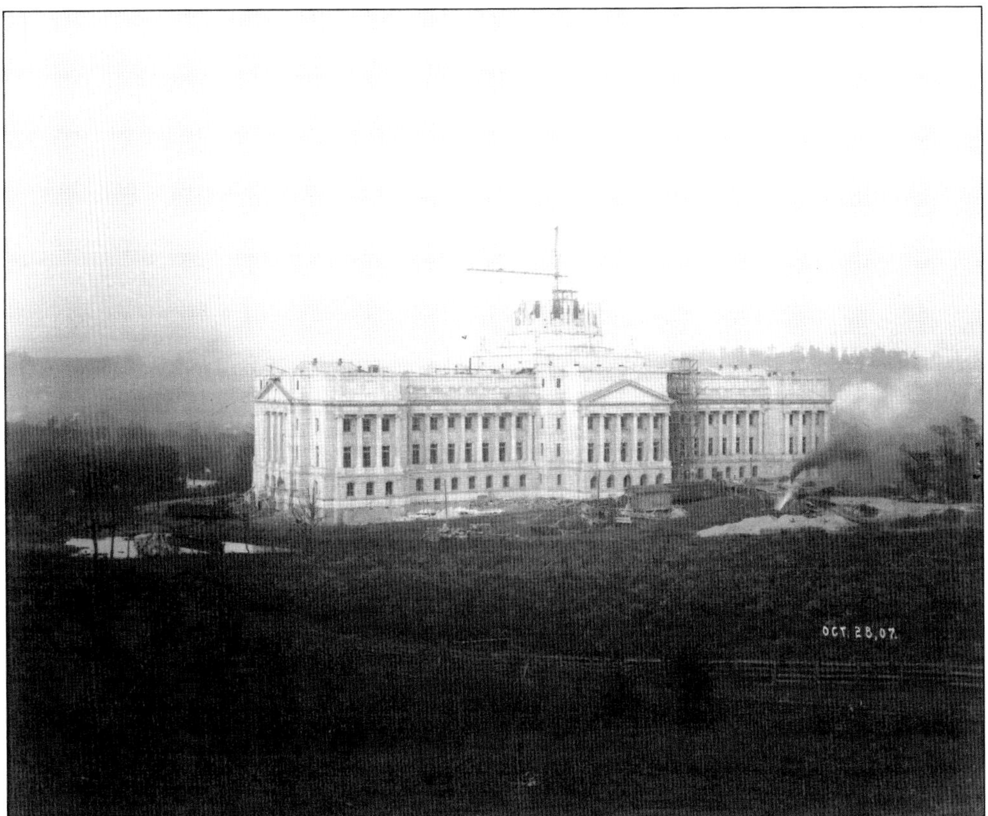

OCTOBER 28, 1907. This historic photograph is part of a series of three images that document the progress of construction from basically the same vantage point over two months. The photograph also shows the many manually operated crane and pulley systems used to build the capitol.

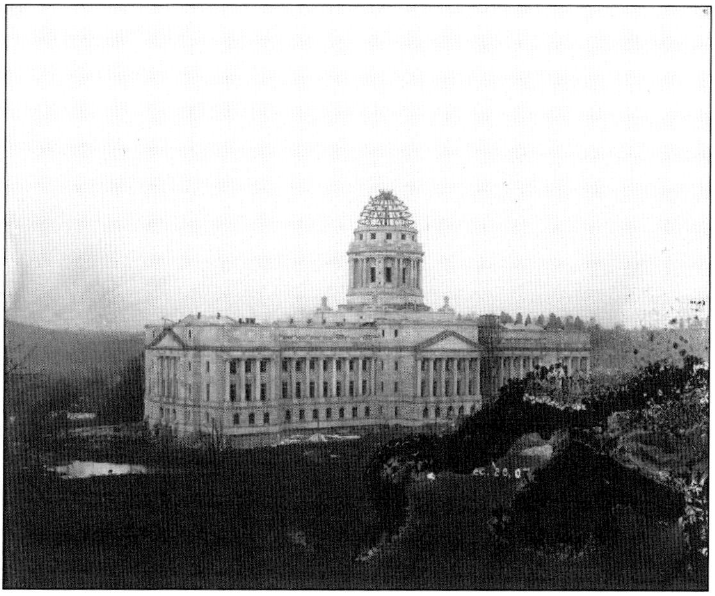

December 28, 1907. The dome begins to take shape in this image with the skeletal steel in place. If one could see the photograph much closer, it would reveal why it was alleged in 1941 that not enough steel was used in fabricating the dome's structure. The original contract called for the capitol to be completed in 1907.

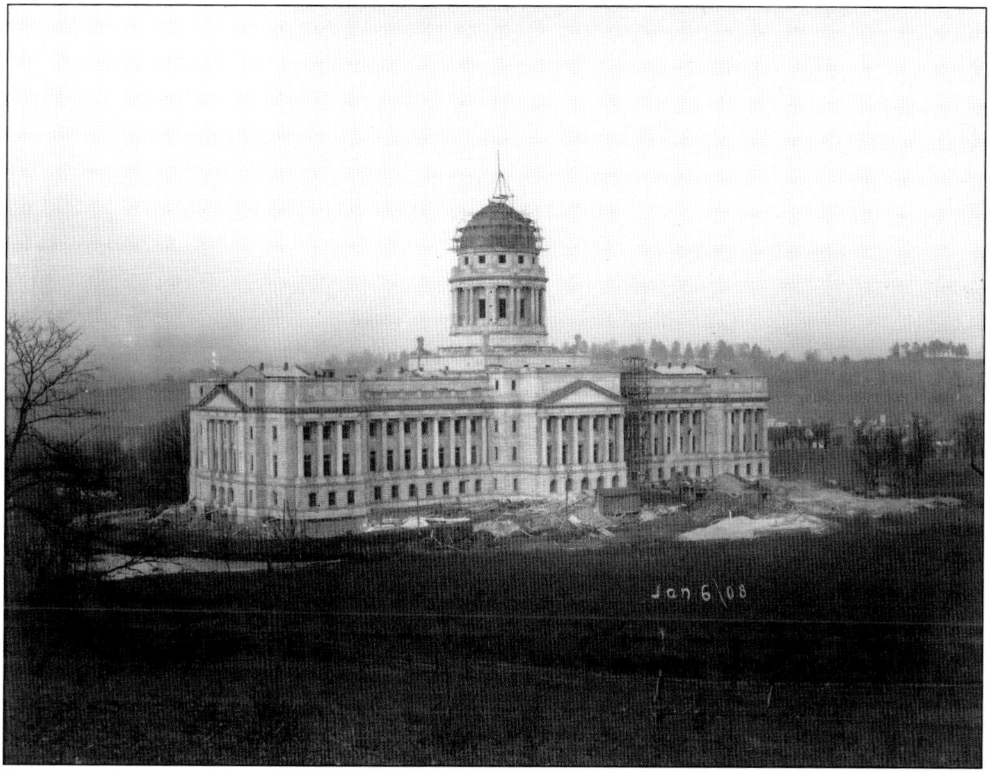

January 6, 1908. The photograph shows the progress that had been made on the capitol's construction since ground-breaking in late summer 1905, although the contract was extremely behind where it should have been. The photograph shows the exterior mostly completed and the impressive dome covered in scaffolding for installing the terra-cotta sections. Over the next year, construction would continue, with many documented delays before the first occupants entered the building in late 1909.

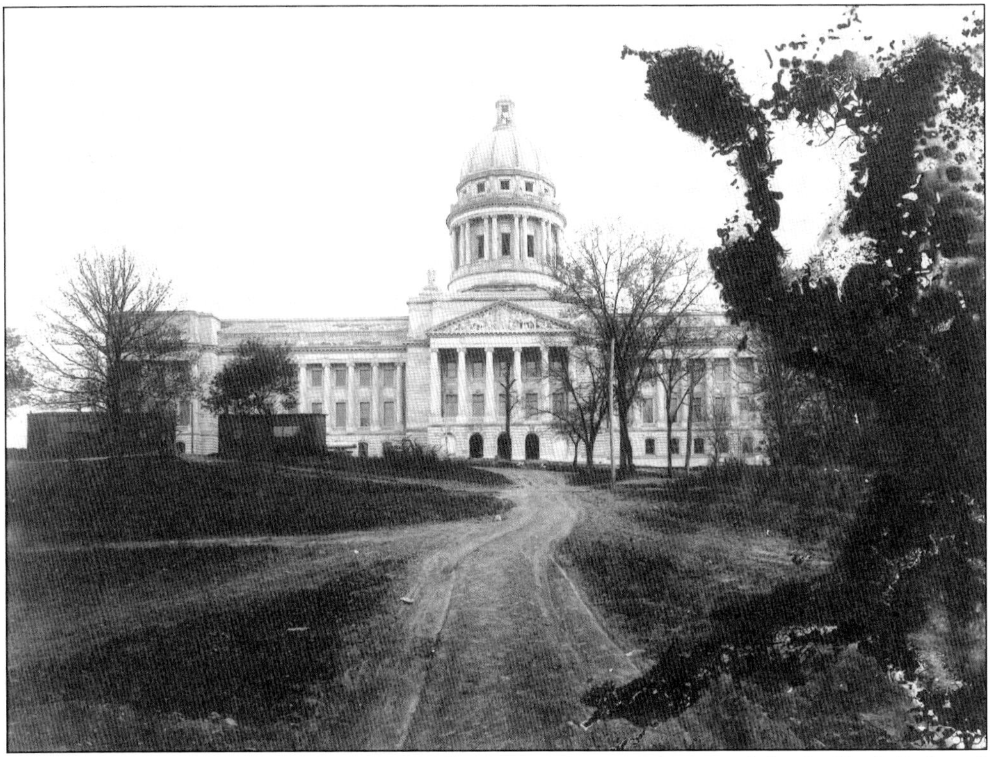

1909 PHOTOGRAPH. This photograph is effective in showing the use of the Bedford (Indiana) limestone selected as the exterior cladding for the brick-and-concrete structure. During the bidding process, alternates were requested for Bowling Green stone, Rockcastle stone, Blue Ridge marble, Kentucky freestone, Berea sandstone, and Georgia marble. Bids were opened on August 7, 1905. Bedford limestone was the lowest bid at $880,000 from the General Supply and Construction Company. The highest material bid was $1,675,000, using Tennessee marble.

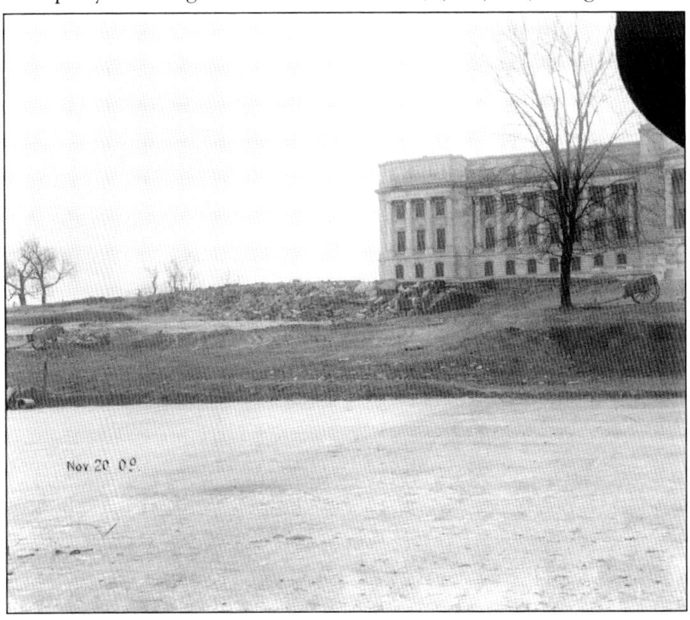

NOVEMBER 20, 1909. John Charles Olmsted of the Olmsted Brothers landscape architecture firm met with the capitol commission board on August 3, 1908. Olmsted and architect Frank Mills Andrews had not resolved differences on the design of the grounds. As a result, all bids for limited landscaping work were rejected until design issues were resolved. This photograph shows the makeshift planks leading in to the majestic building in the winter of 1909.

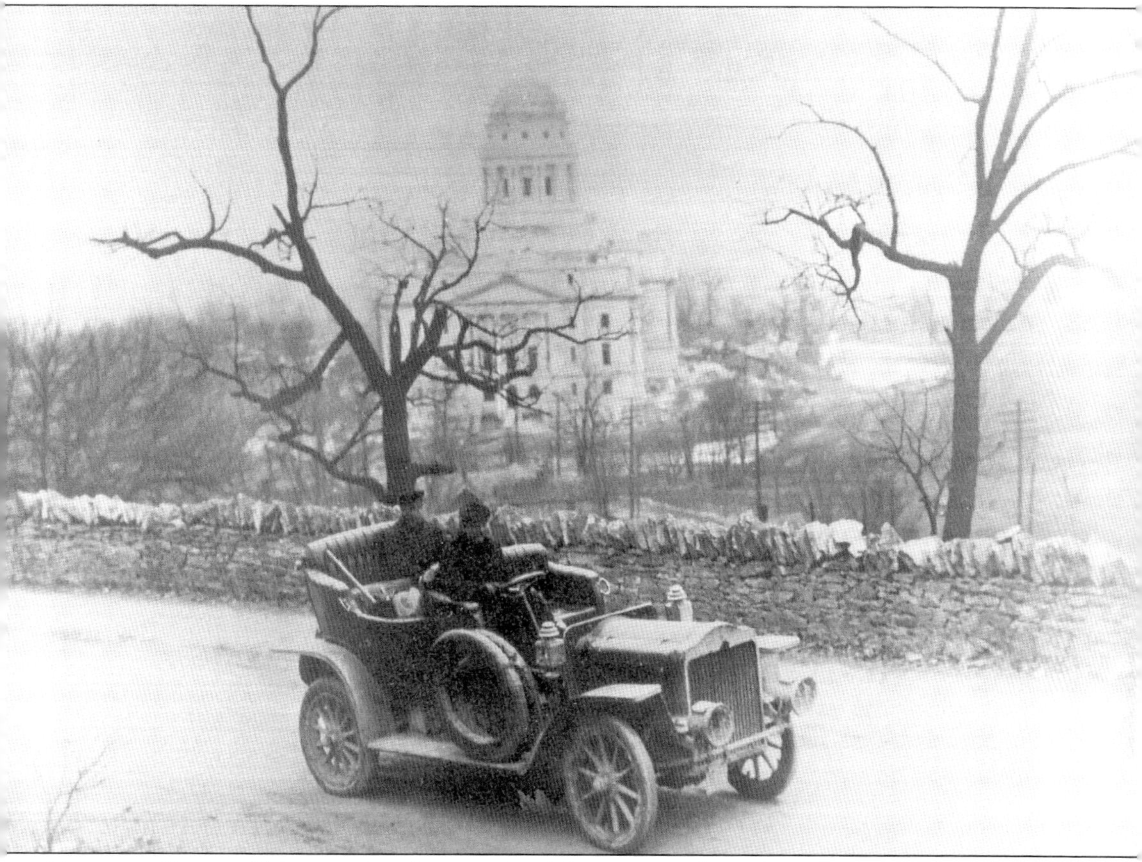

Blustery Drive. Although the photograph of the two people in the antique automobile is undated, the progress on the dome in the background, barren tree limbs, and the dress for cold weather indicate that the image is most likely from the winter of 1908. The photograph appears to be of a Frankfort resident, perhaps with a chauffeur, surveying the construction progress of the capitol building from the vantage point of Old Louisville Pike. The old pike route was higher up on the hillside then the current Louisville Road. Portions of the dry-laid stone fence that is shown bordering the road can still be found in the dense woods above Louisville Road. (Courtesy of Division of Historic Properties.)

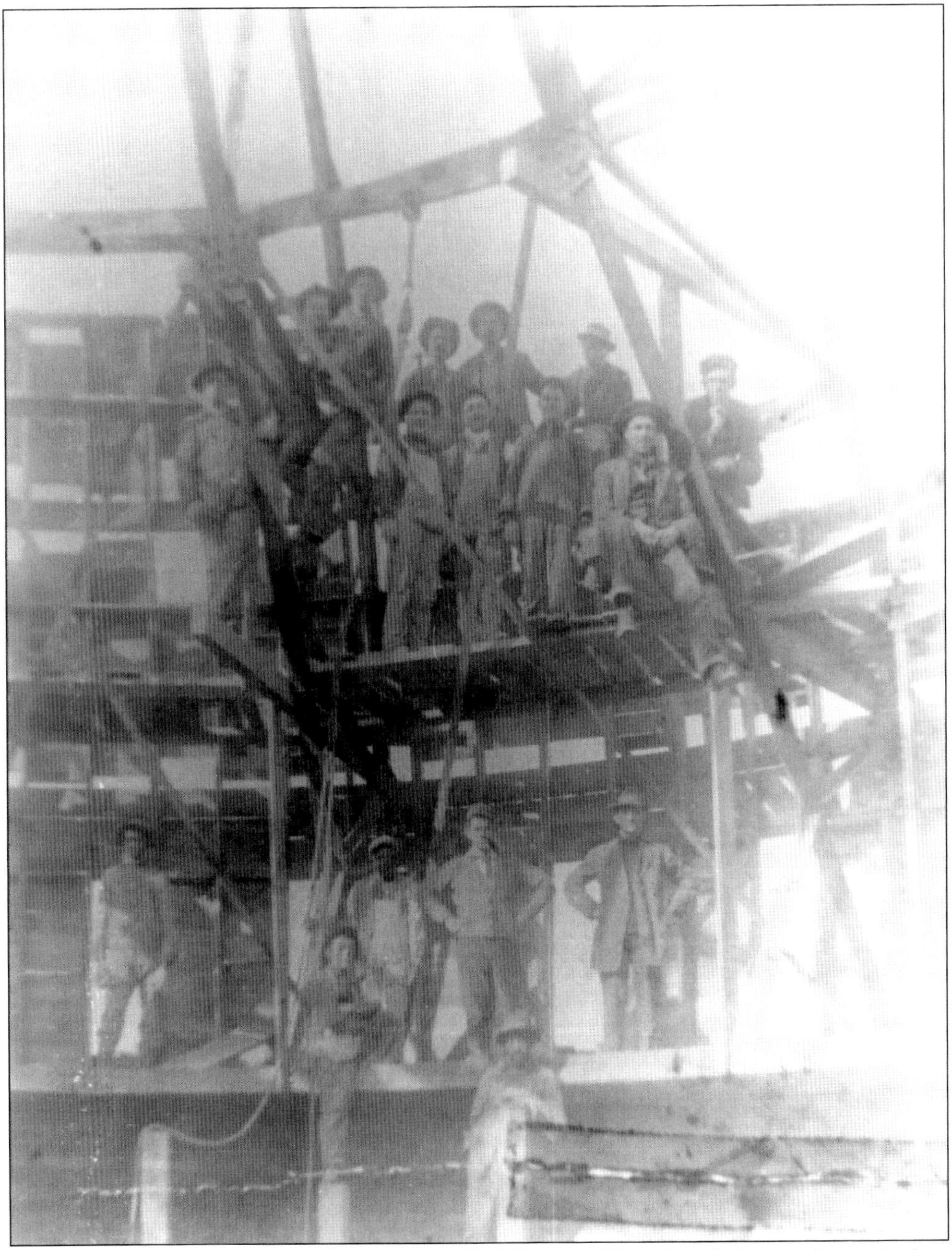

DOME SKELETON. The photograph taken around 1907 shows 17 unidentified men who worked on the capitol's dome, obviously hamming it up and posing for a brave photographer nearly 175 feet off the ground. The image also shows the steel structure of the dome, which was determined to be poorly constructed in 1941 and in danger of collapsing. Although this report was found later to be grossly exaggerated, the steel structure was partially replaced and rebuilt along with nearly three-quarters of the dome itself. The rotunda's interior plaster dome was also reproduced from original plans. (Courtesy of Division of Historic Properties.)

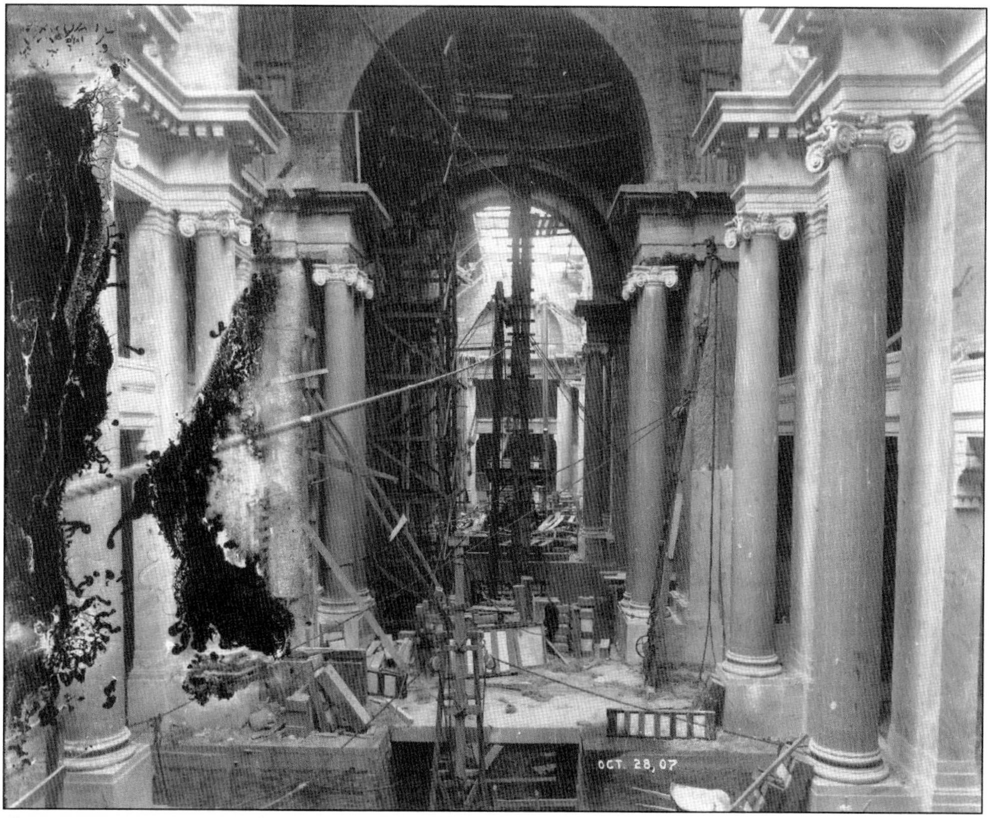

OCTOBER 28, 1907. In this damaged but important photograph, the interior is well underway in the rotunda and vast great halls. The pulleys, ropes, and other manual crane equipment are glimpses into how the 32 solid Vermont granite Ionic columns were hoisted into place.

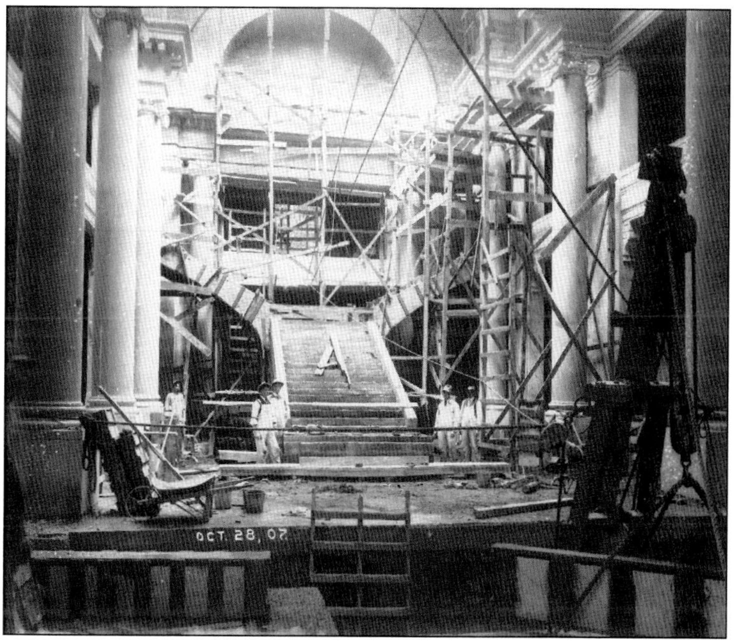

OCTOBER 28, 1907: THE GRAND STAIRS. Taken on the same day, this photograph shows five workers pausing to show pride and reflect on the monumental job they are completing. The grand stairs were just framed up in this image. In the background is the brick structure of the great arches, which will later be covered in Georgia marble.

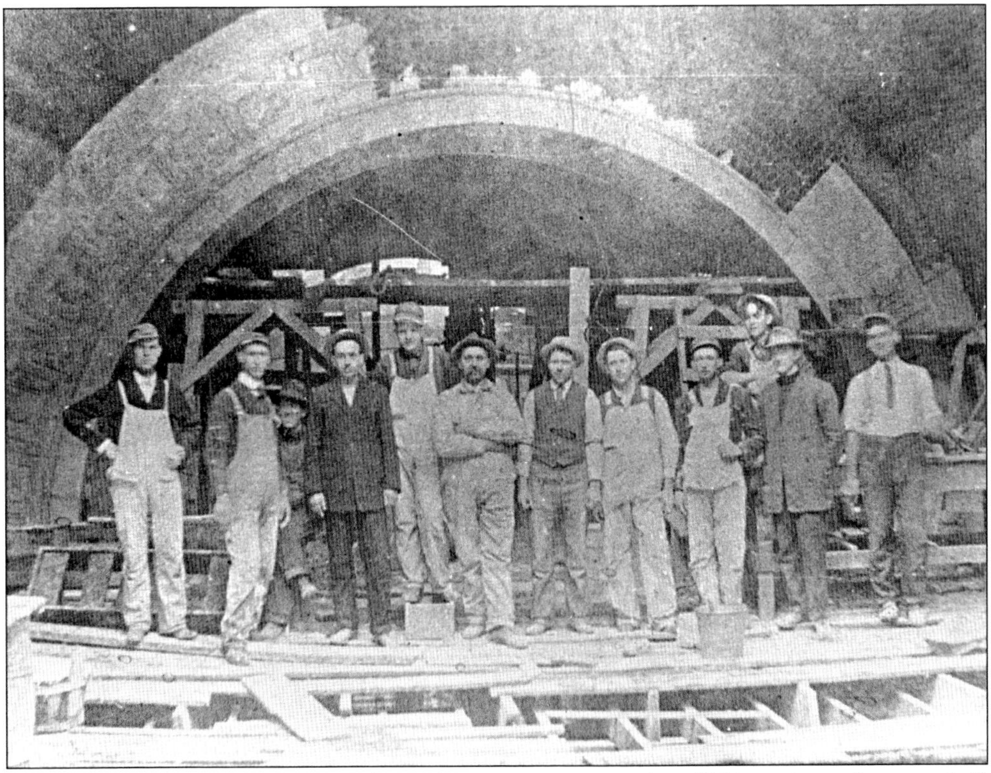

PROUD CREW. Twelve workers are shown here posing on wood scaffolding above the great hall prior to marble cladding. Hundreds of sections of Georgia marble were hoisted up to the arches and set on pins or rods that were mortared inside the masonry walls. Often visitors see all of the marble inside the capitol and assume it is solid throughout. Images like this one help to better understand the construction.

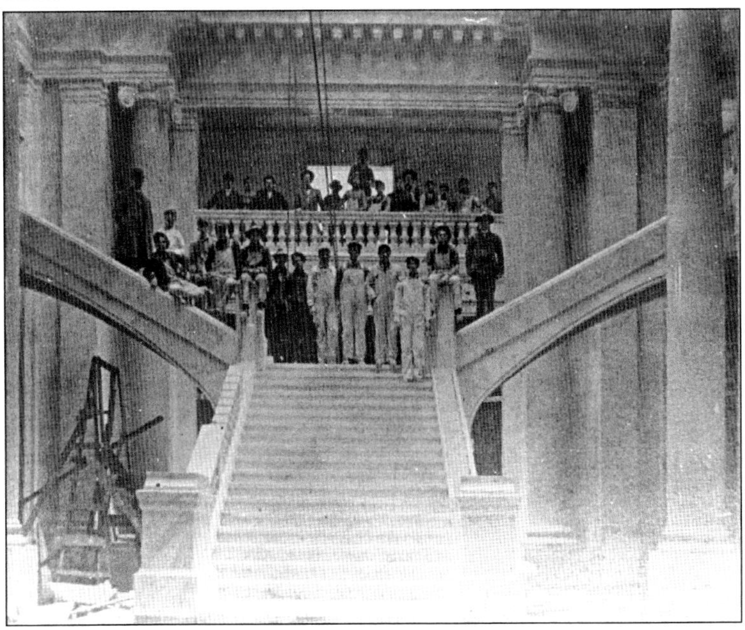

GRAND STAIRWAY. The marble staircases of the great hall, as shown in this photograph, were designed to be similar to the grand staircases in the Paris Opera House. The staircases have been a favorite for group photography and pictures with former governors and legislative leaders for many years.

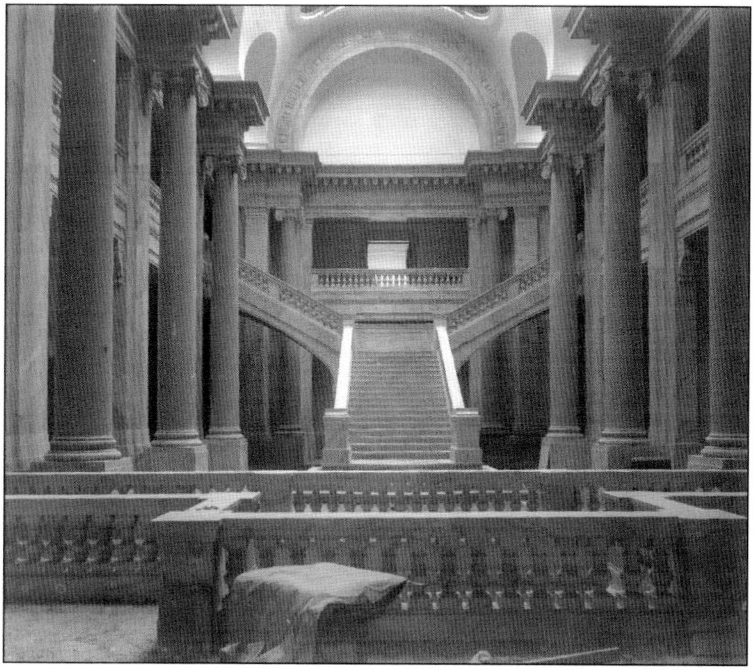

Great Hall. In this undated photograph, there are no murals in the lunette spaces on the east and west ends. The murals to be painted by T. Gilbert White were not complete, and the floors are still covered in dirt instead of the later-installed Tennessee and Georgia marble.

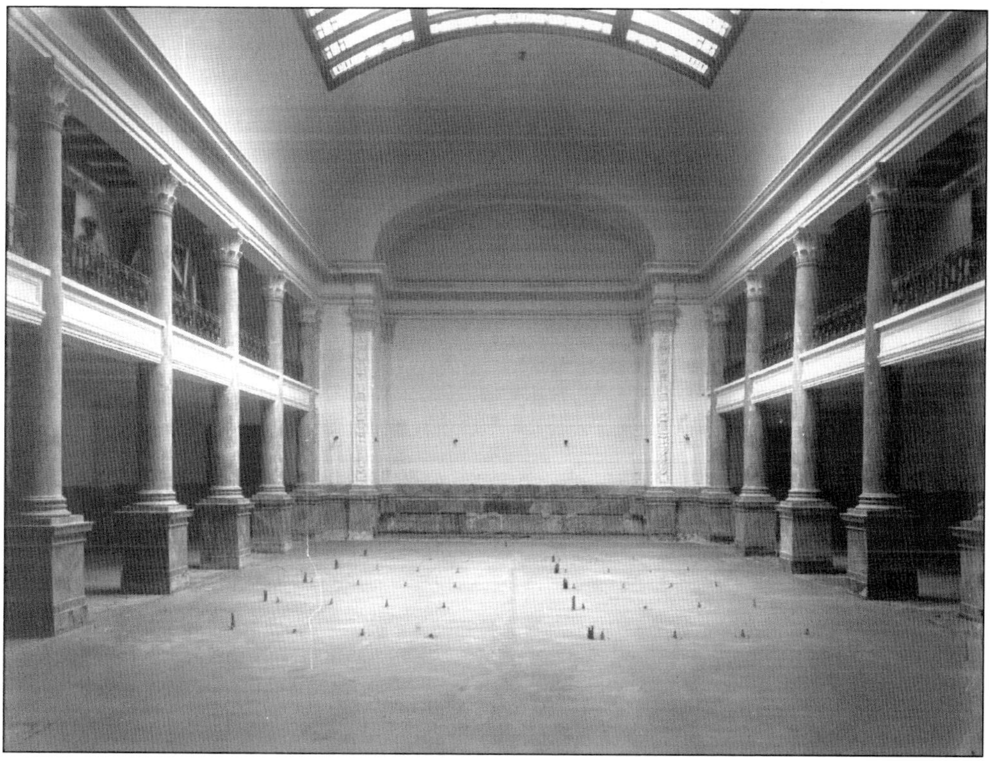

Empty Senate Chambers. The senate chambers are shown in this 1908 photograph without furnishings or carpet. The concrete floor slab is visible in the image as well as completed scagliola columns. The decorative art treatment was used extensively in the house, senate, and state reception rooms of the capitol.

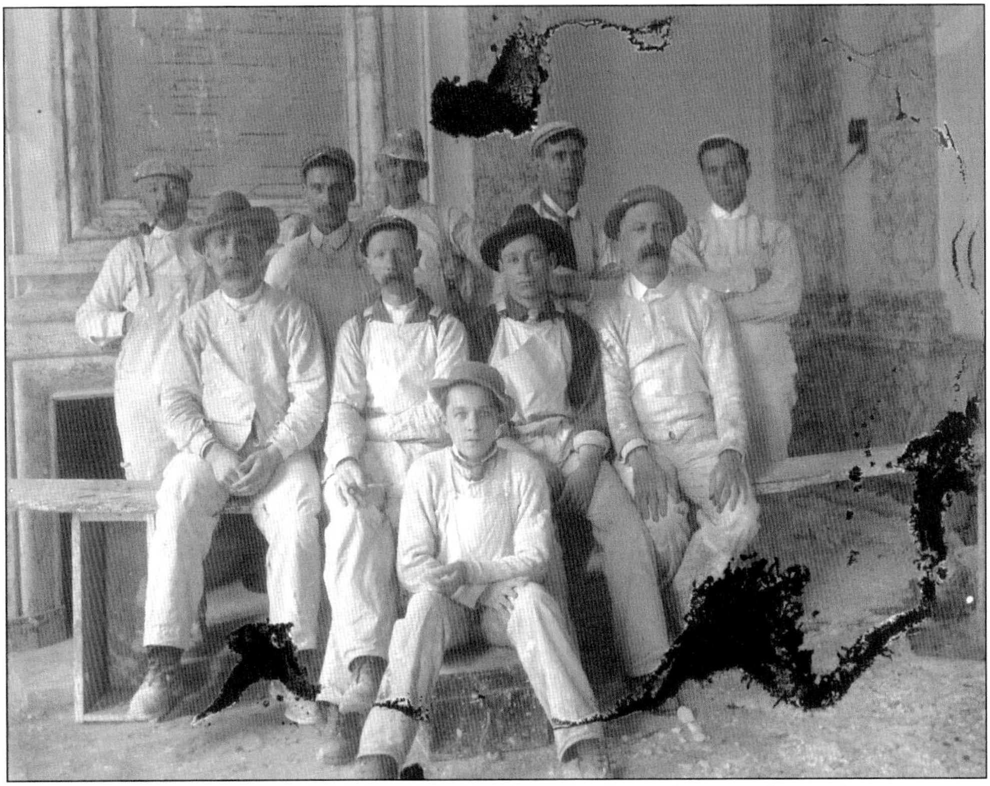

State Reception Room. No visit to the Kentucky State Capitol is complete without a visit to the opulent state reception room. When the space was completed in 1908, nearly $10,000 had been dedicated to the room for decorative arts and furnishings. In this rare photograph, 10 of the craftsmen who worked on the room pose for the photographer.

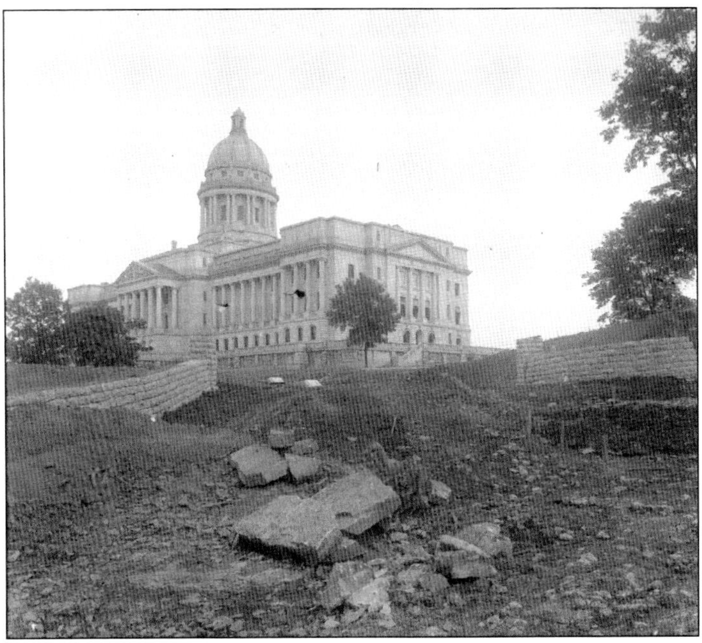

November 20, 1909. Shown here is a plank walkway that leads up to the newly completed capitol building. The photograph also clearly shows the unfinished landscape that would take nearly another year to complete. The Olmsted Brothers landscape architecture firm submitted drawings of a grounds plan for consideration in October 1908. However, those plans do not include the north entrance's grand promenade of terraces and stairs that was ultimately built.

Three

UNITED WE STAND, DIVIDED WE FALL

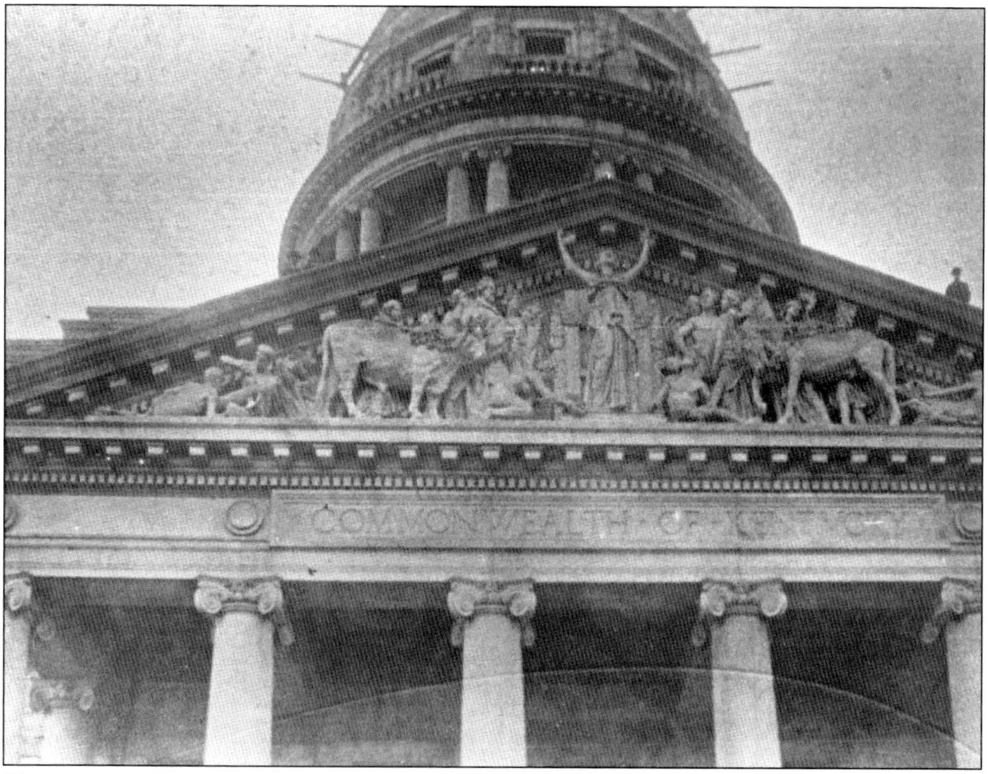

TYMPANUM OF KENTUCKY'S MOTTO. The capitol's iconic allegorical pediment sculpted by Charles Niehaus and Peter Rossack is shown here after being completed, with curious onlookers posing on both sides. With the opening of the 1906 legislative session, additional funding was sought to finish the interior of the capitol and embellish the exterior with an allegorical sculpture. The legislature appropriated $250,000, which allowed $40,000 for the installation of an allegorical sculpture group in the pediment above the main entrance. Charles Henry Niehaus was selected for the commission based on the recommendation of architect Andrews. The photograph must have been taken after 1907 but before 1909 due to the absence of the dome's top portion. The pediment's allegorical imagery will be explained through a series of important early photographs on the next three pages.

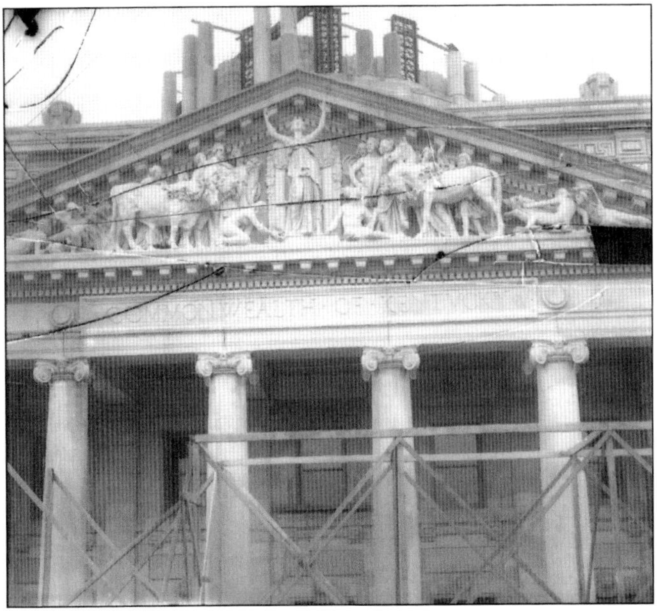

PIECES OF THE PEDIMENT. Many of the images used for work were scanned from original glass-plate negatives. Due to their fragile nature, the photographs may show cracks or distortion, or have the appearance of shattered glass. Although riddled with cracks, this photograph from September 1907 shows the rich details of the newly completed Niehaus sculpture with the center heroic allegorical female figure representative of Kentucky. She is standing with arms open and thrust out to the north in front of the chair of state.

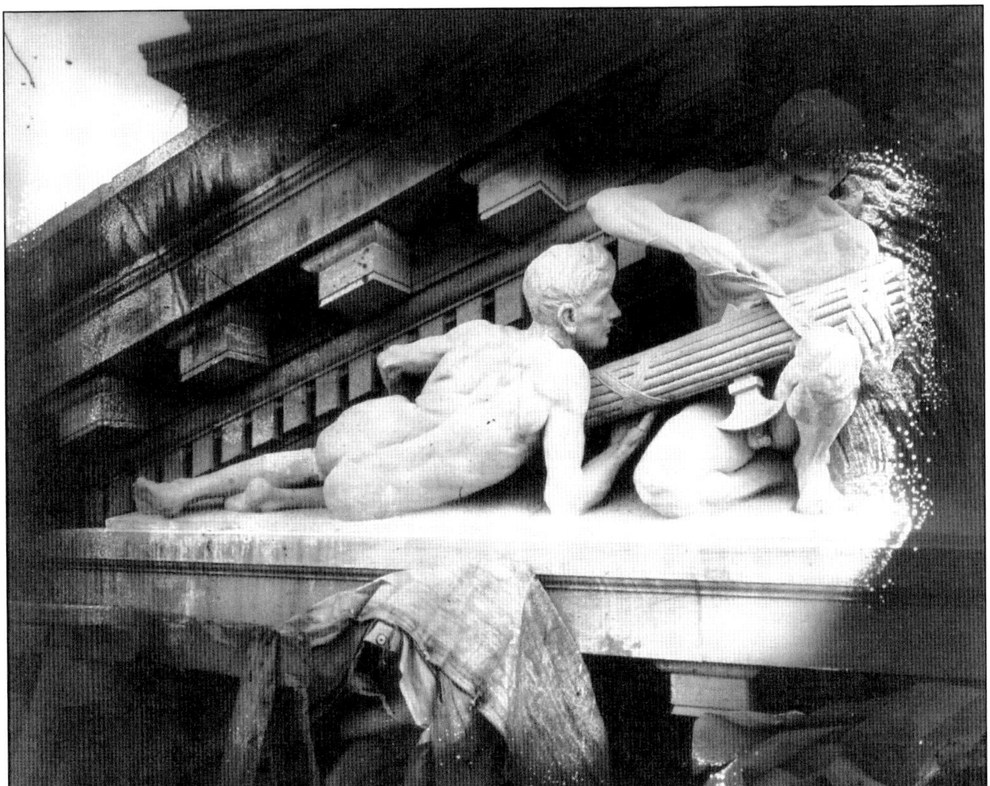

EAST SIDE OF THE PEDIMENT. The left angle of the triangular pediment symbolizes unity, as shown in this 1907 photograph with two muscular male figures—one holding a hammer and steadying a fasces while the other ties the bands symbolizing the strength of working as one or the commonwealth's motto—"United we stand, divided we fall."

LEFT MIDDLE OF THE PEDIMENT. In the 1907 photograph of middle side to the left of Lady Kentucky is a female figure offering the commonwealth winged wheels of progress and industry. The large male figure of history is representative of recording the events shaping Kentucky's rich heritage. Another female figure holds a cornucopia of plenty overflowing with fruit and grain, along with a pair of embellished cows symbolic of the agrarian progression of the state. The three other female figures represent law, which would appear to be the three branches of government.

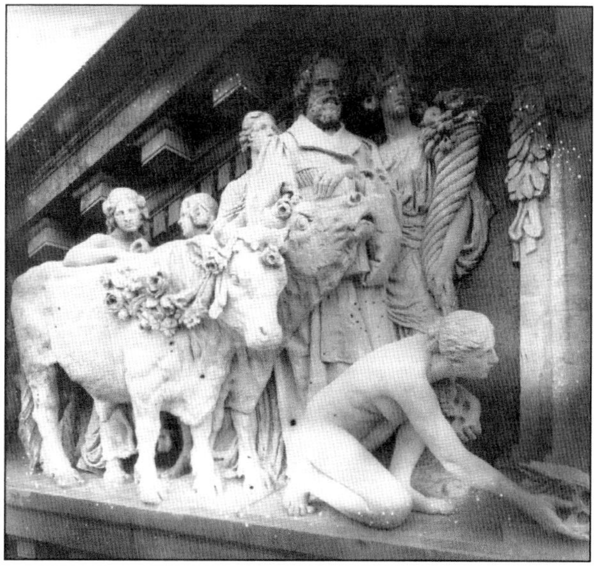

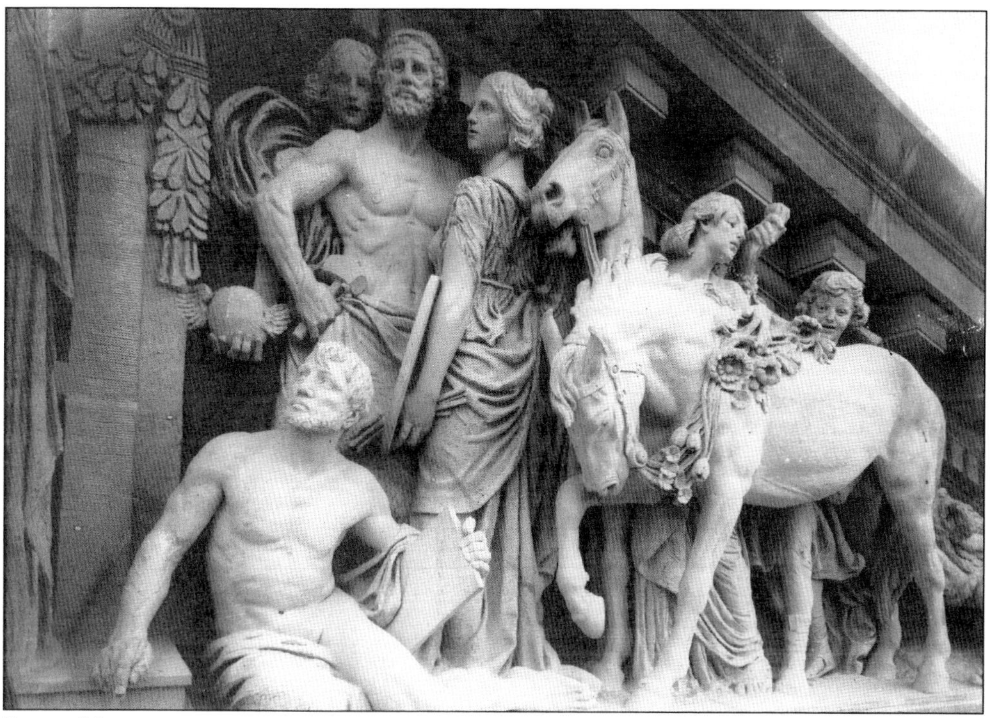

RIGHT MIDDLE OF THE PEDIMENT. In this 1907 image, the male figure of education shows a firm grip on the base of the chair of state and is draped along the pediment's edge gazing in the central female figure's direction, seemingly suggesting that education should not be pushed aside. Art is represented on the right by a robed female figure posing with a palette and brush in her hand; labor is in the background facing art, represented by a scantly clad male figure grasping a hammer, leading to a winged female holding a winged globe for possibility. The pediment would not be declarative of Kentucky without the inclusion of decorated horses. Two young girls, one older than the other, are behind the first horse and symbolize the commonwealth's growth from fertile agrarian roots.

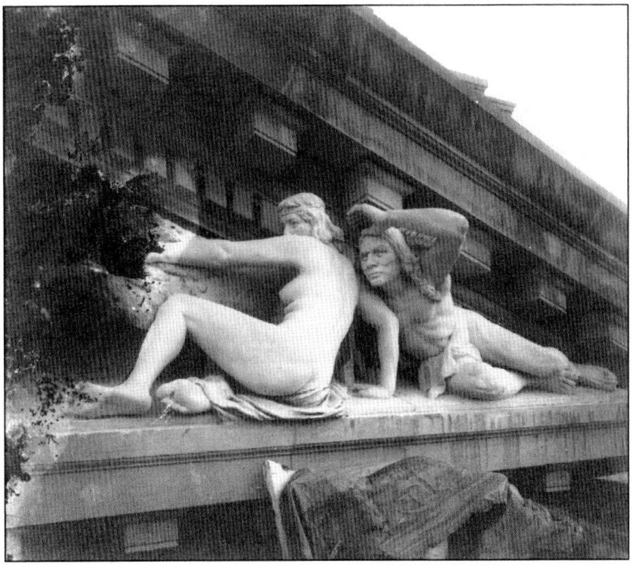

West Side of the Pediment. The final right-hand section of the pediment could be considered somewhat controversial today; however, in 1907, ideals were different. The original 1910 souvenir program noted the imagery represented Indians "crouching in fear" with the approach of civilization after conquering the wilderness or a wolf. Today it would probably be more appropriate to indicate that the Native Americans and the wolf or wilderness represent the challenges that the commonwealth faced to achieve statehood in 1792.

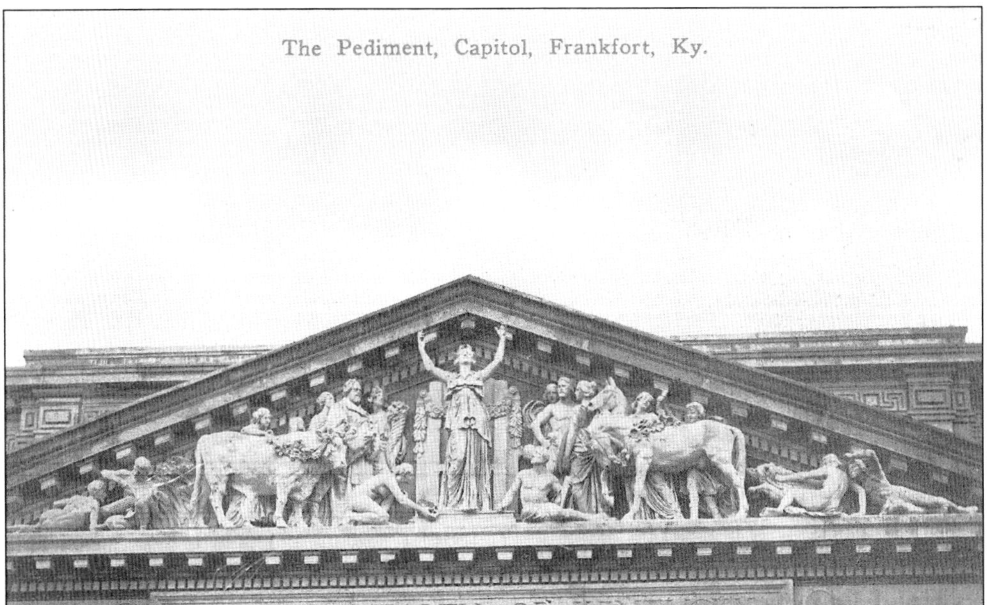

Postcard Memory. This early-1900s photograph, made into a postcard, helped visitors to the capitol to understand the allegorical imagery of the pediment. The motto of the commonwealth is clearly represented in the sculpted tympanum. Architecture postcards from this period are invaluable in historical research, because most of them were either photographs or drawings of original features. (Courtesy collection of Scot Walters.)

Four

Legacy of Many Nameless Faces

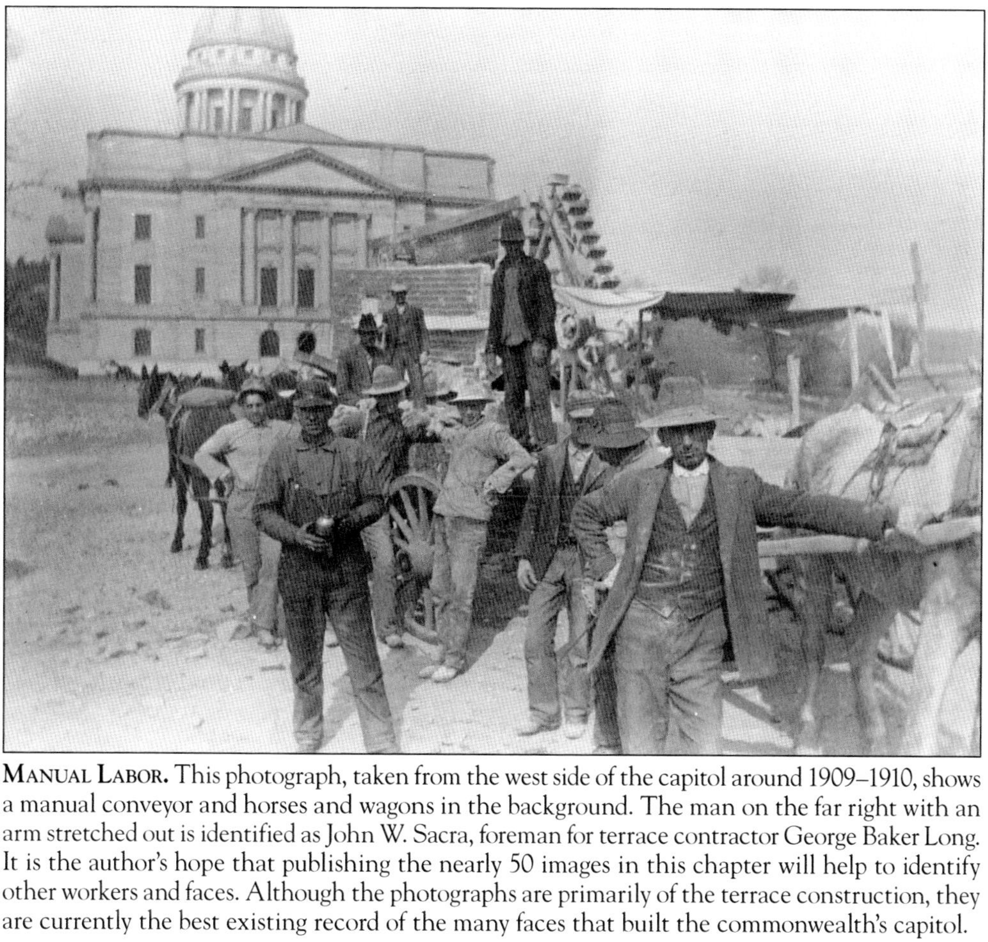

Manual Labor. This photograph, taken from the west side of the capitol around 1909–1910, shows a manual conveyor and horses and wagons in the background. The man on the far right with an arm stretched out is identified as John W. Sacra, foreman for terrace contractor George Baker Long. It is the author's hope that publishing the nearly 50 images in this chapter will help to identify other workers and faces. Although the photographs are primarily of the terrace construction, they are currently the best existing record of the many faces that built the commonwealth's capitol.

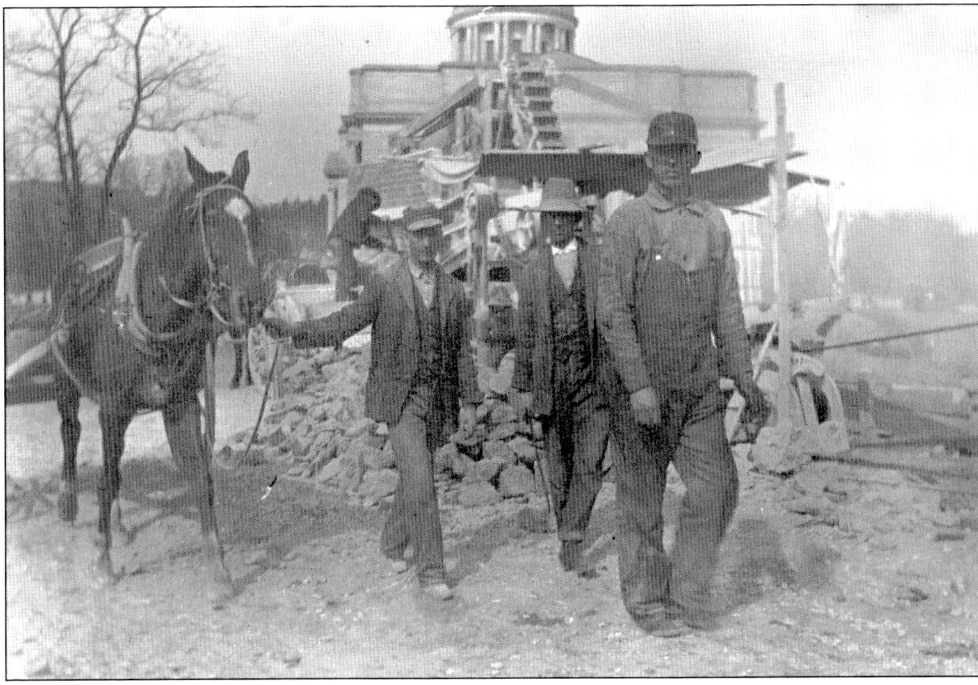

Trio of Men. The three men, including John W. Sacra, second from left, are leading a mule or horse at the construction site. The photograph also shows the construction debris on site, which was still present until early 1910.

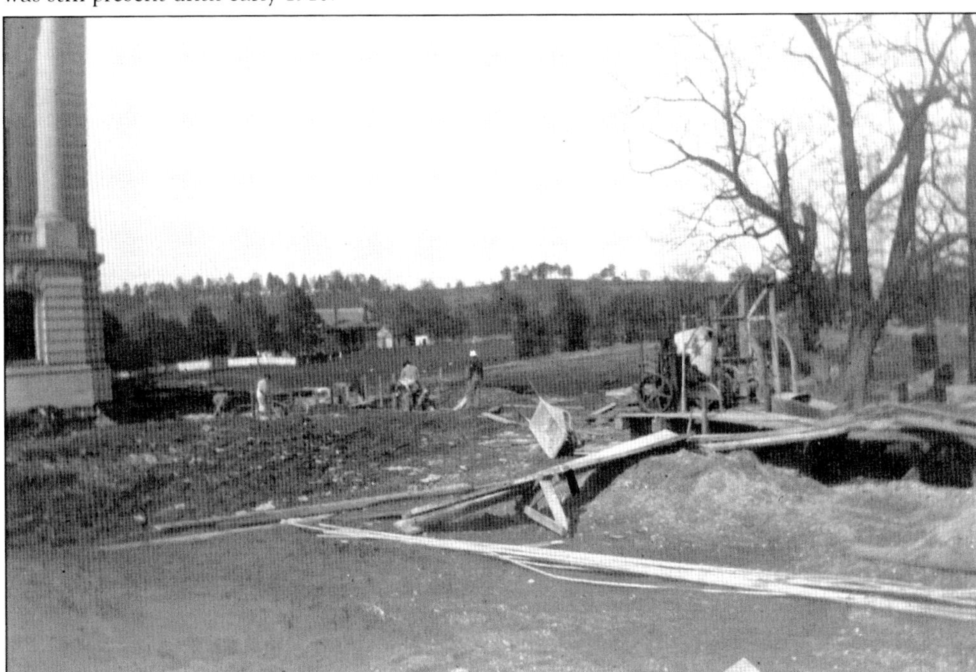

Northwest View. This photograph shows the corner of capitol terrace and at least three workers with construction equipment and wheelbarrows. The terrace was mostly constructed during late 1909 and perhaps early 1910—the recorded contractor was George Baker Long.

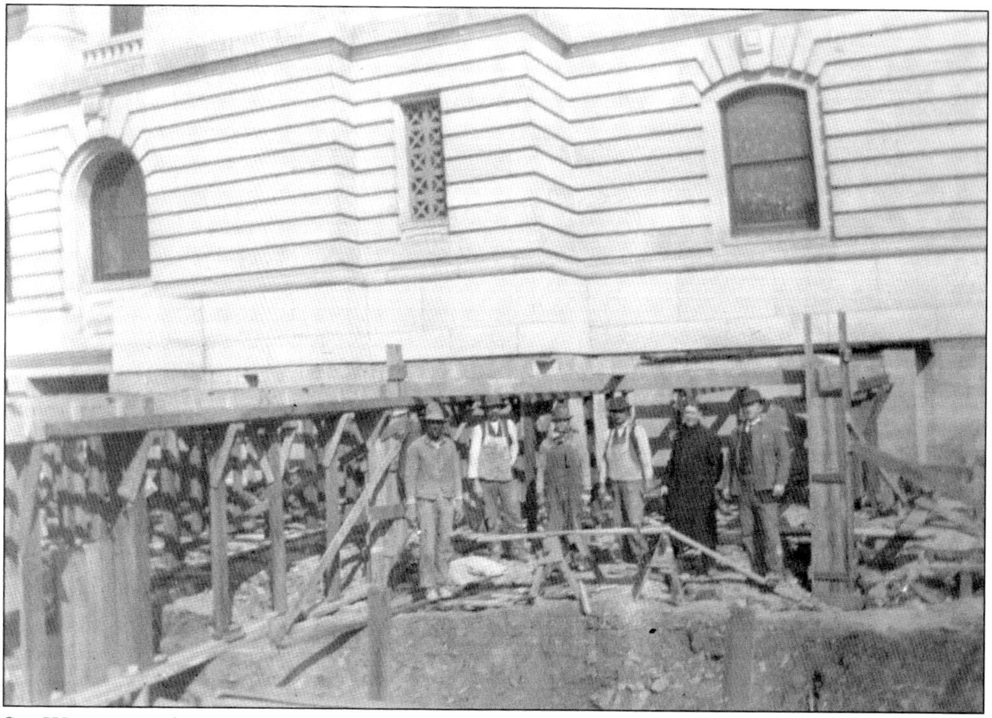

Six Workers. This 1909 photograph was taken below where the terrace level would later be. Six men are shown standing under the wooden platforms. The access was used to form the terrace for many trips of stone, sand and later concrete fill. It would likely take thousands of wheelbarrow loads to complete the entire terrace.

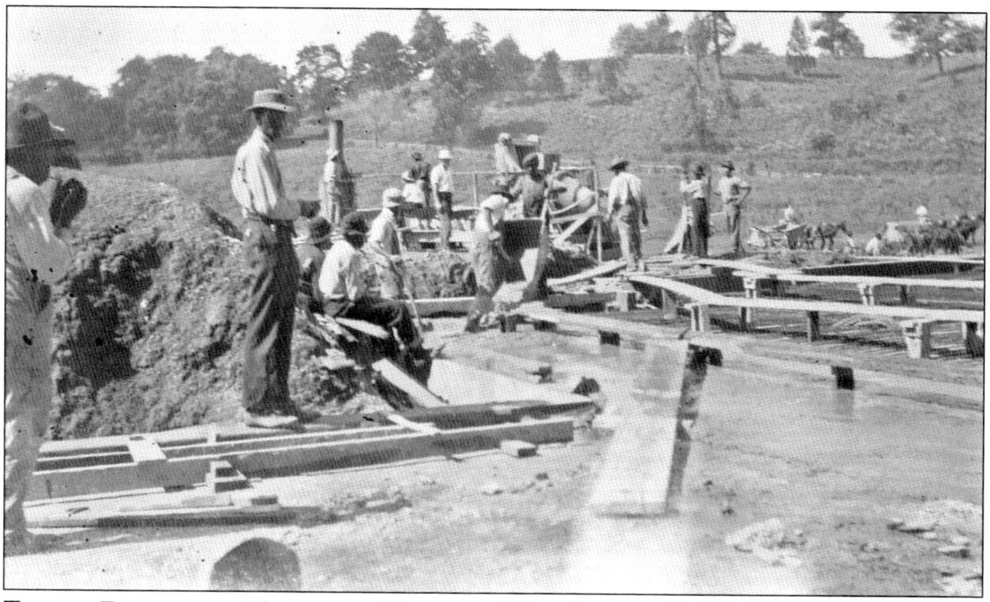

Terrace Foundation. The corner of the terrace's foundation is shown in this 1909 photograph. Seven men are seen in this photograph along with examples of the large pieces of Indiana limestone used to face the terrace and construct the decorative balustrades. With the capitol building 403 feet long without terraces, one can imagine the task that was at hand.

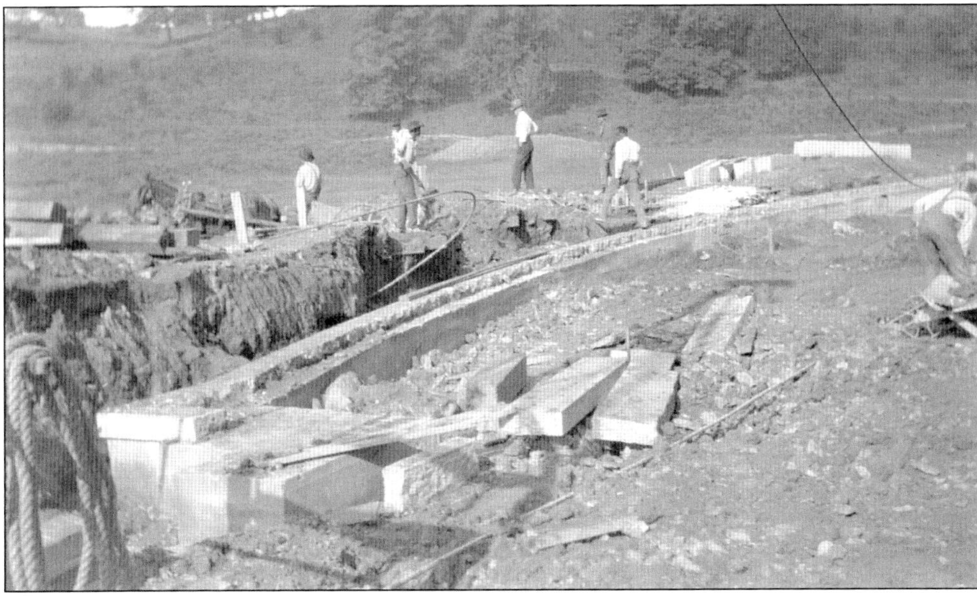

MUCH ACTIVITY. There were great stories told during the construction of Kentucky's capitol of teams of elephants, sophisticated rail systems from the river, and other methods. In reality, as shown in this 1909 photograph, the labor to build the terrace was provided by horses and men. The only machinery used for building was a steam-powered concrete mixer, which will be omnipresent in these images.

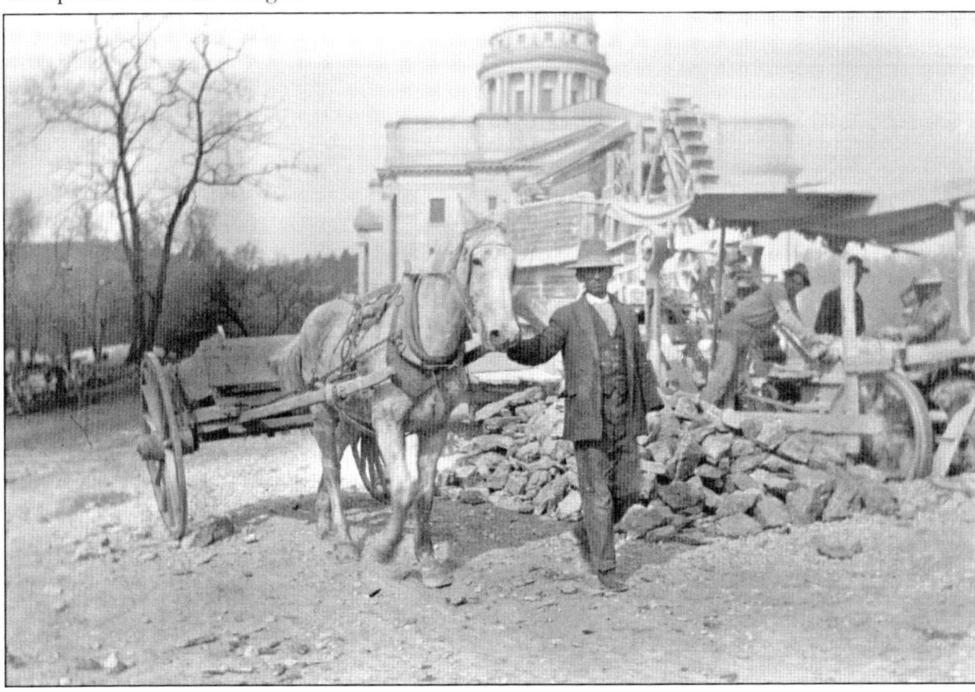

HORSE WITH WAGON. The photograph shows one man leading a horse and wagon through the construction site. The capitol's completed dome is in the background. The dome is clad in terra-cotta tiles, although original plans called for a copper-clad sheet metal cover on the dome. The terra-cotta was thought to be more striking and longer lasting.

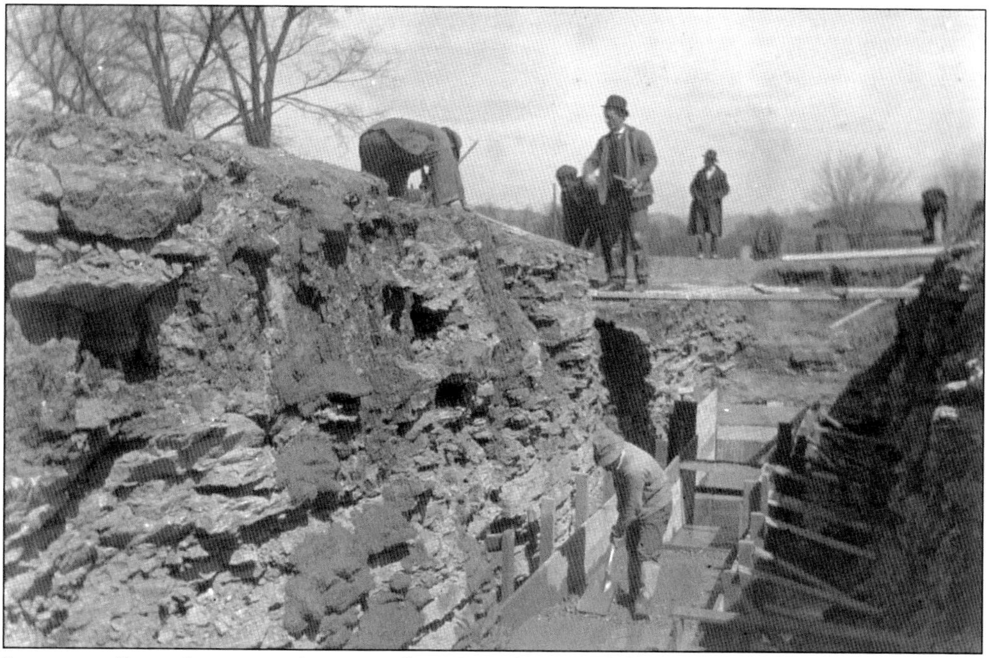

LEVELING. Several men are shown in this 1909 photograph leveling the concrete terrace with shovels. Originally the terrace had several areas with glass-block wells to provide light into basement utility areas. The terrace has been completely restored twice since it was completed in 1910—both times due to moisture and numerous freeze-thaw cycles.

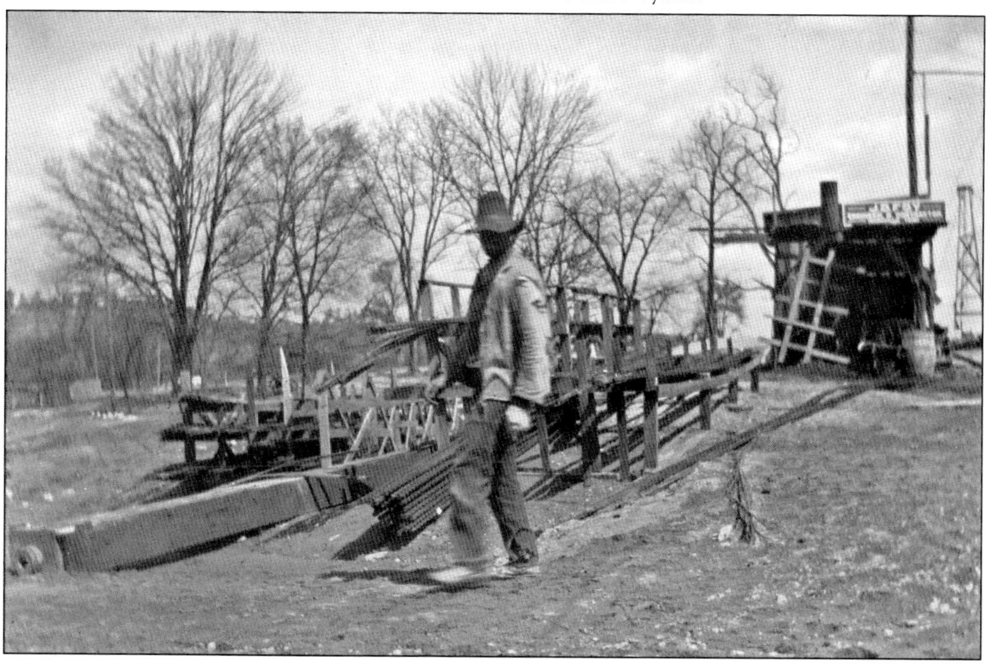

LONE MAN. Many of the early construction photographs presented in this book, such as this one, have only one or two people working. It leads one to think—why were there so few people working on such a large project? There is no way to know, and perhaps there were more in the immediate area. It appears, however, that the delay in completion could have been related to proportion of labor.

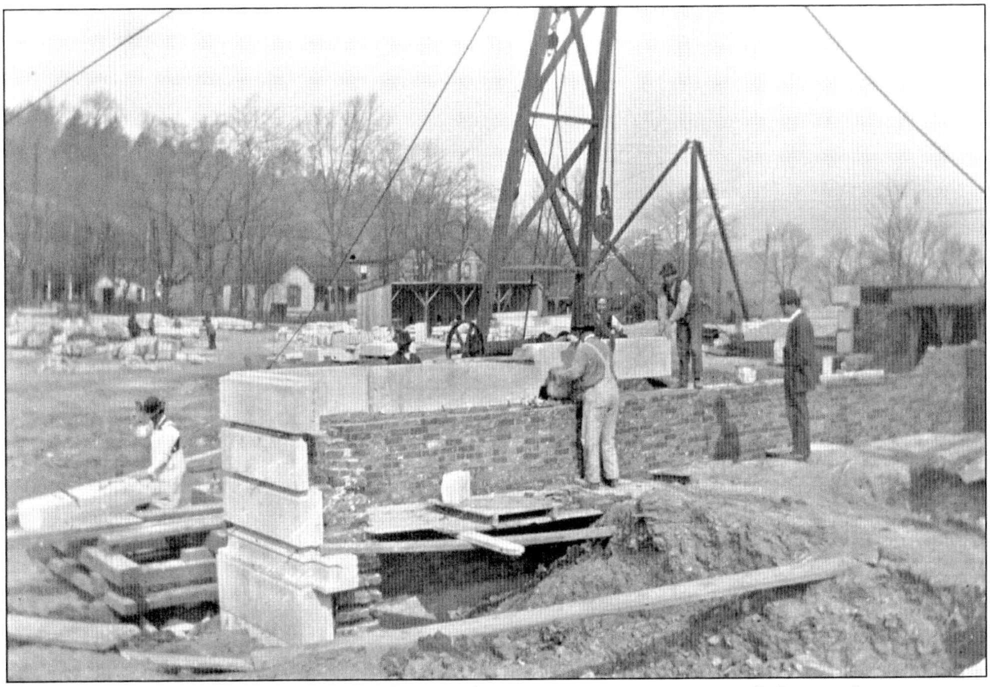

Terrace Piers. This photograph indicates the masonry construction of the northwest corner wall of the terrace. The men in the image are laying rows of brick to build support walls for the northwest corner of the terrace. This area of the terrace began to fail in the 1940s and needed to be rebuilt.

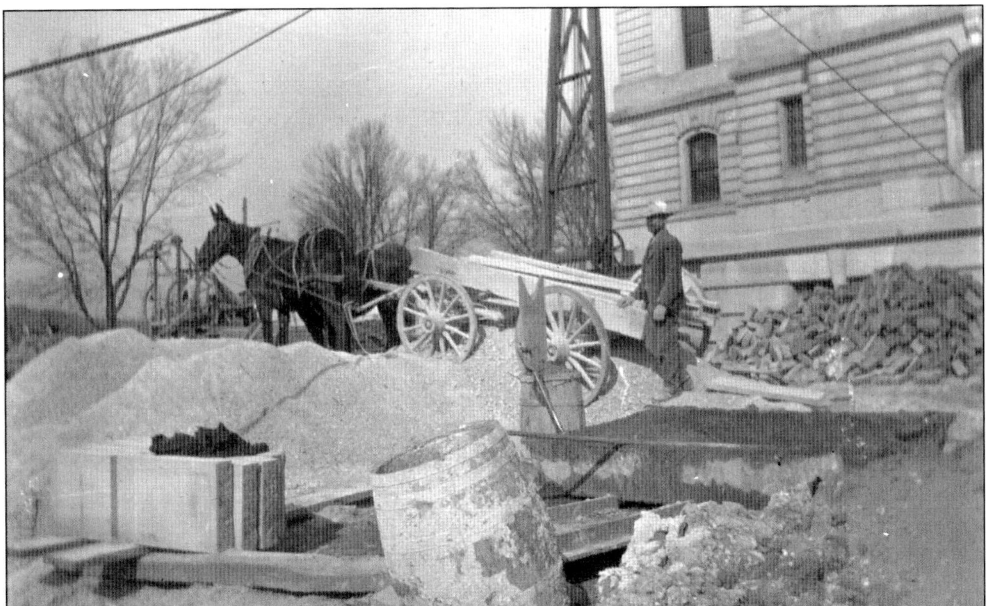

Pile of Bricks. The unidentified man and horse in this photograph were part of the 20-man wagon crew that worked on the terrace in 1909. As the Kentucky Capitol prepares for its centennial anniversary, identifying workers such as these will help to better tell the story of the capitol's construction.

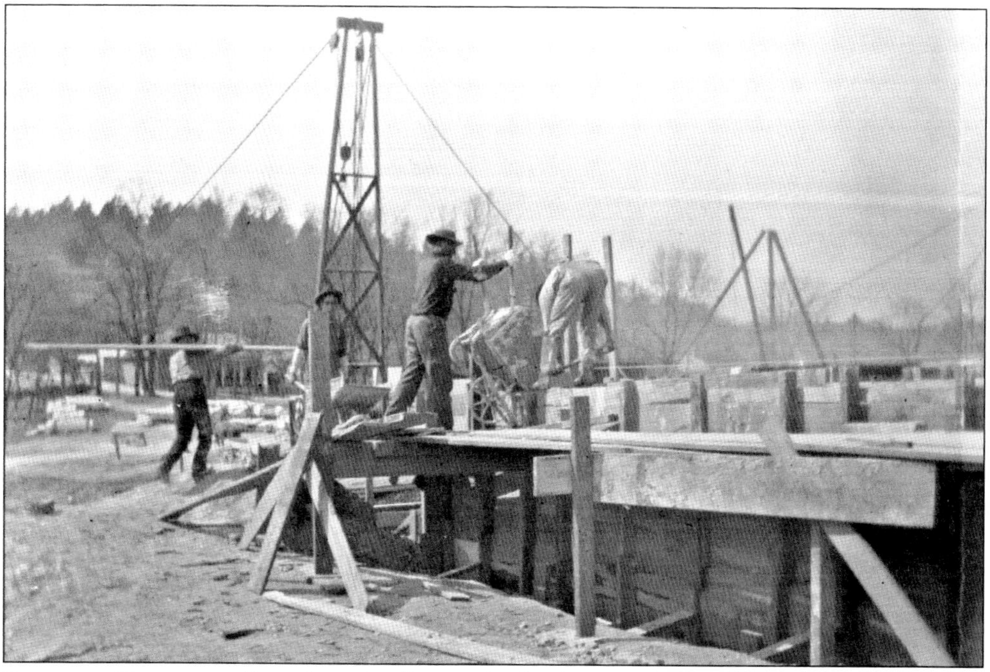

Emptying Concrete. Countless wheelbarrow-loads of concrete were dumped into the form to provide a solid floor for the terrace. Steel rebar was added in layers to increase the rigidity and strength of the floor. The three men working in the photograph from 1909 are unidentified.

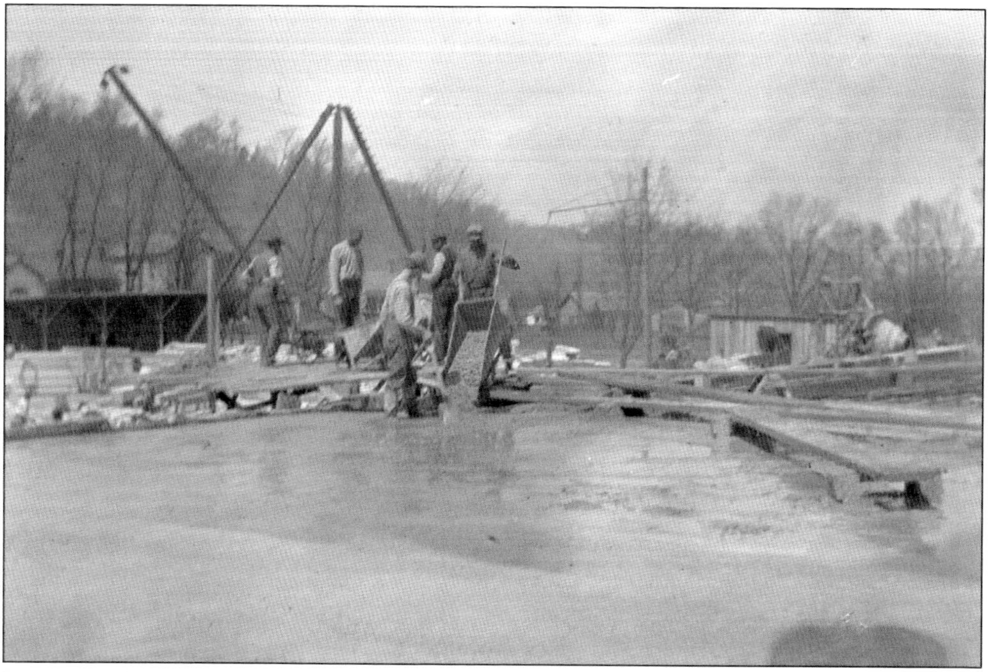

Limestone Sections. This photograph from 1909 shows the activity on the terrace construction as well as many sections of the Bedford, Indiana, limestone. The stone for the capitol was specifically from the Hoosier quarry and was used for building the balustrade that surrounds the entire terrace.

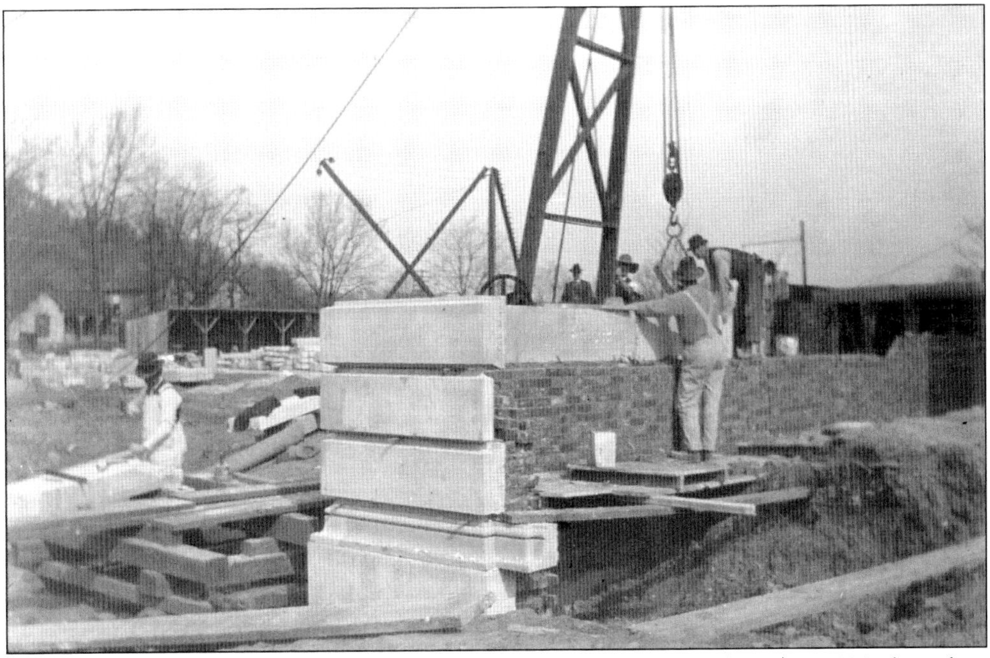

Exposed Brick. Although the bid for limestone cladding on the capitol was $880,000, there does not appear to be any information about how many tons or sections of limestone were used to complete the capitol. From examining this 1909 photograph and others, it can be theorized that the method in which the terrace was built could have contributed to its masonry failure within the next 30 years. The weight of limestone panels seems disproportionate to the number of pins used to secure the sections in place.

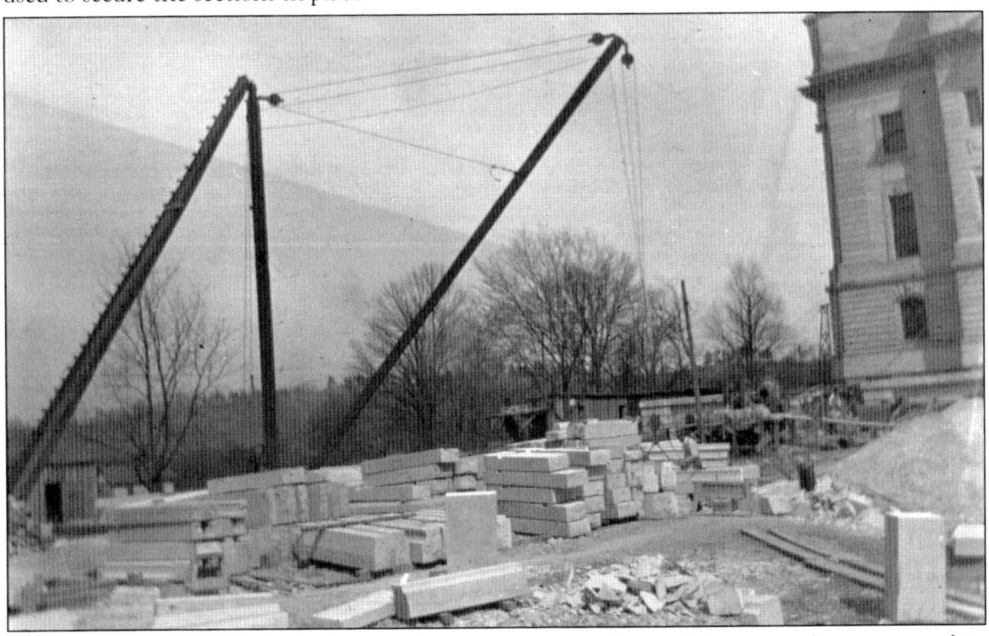

Manual Crane. This 1909 photograph shows more sections of limestone that were used in building the terrace and the hand-powered crane lifts in the background used to manipulate and set the several-hundred-pound pieces.

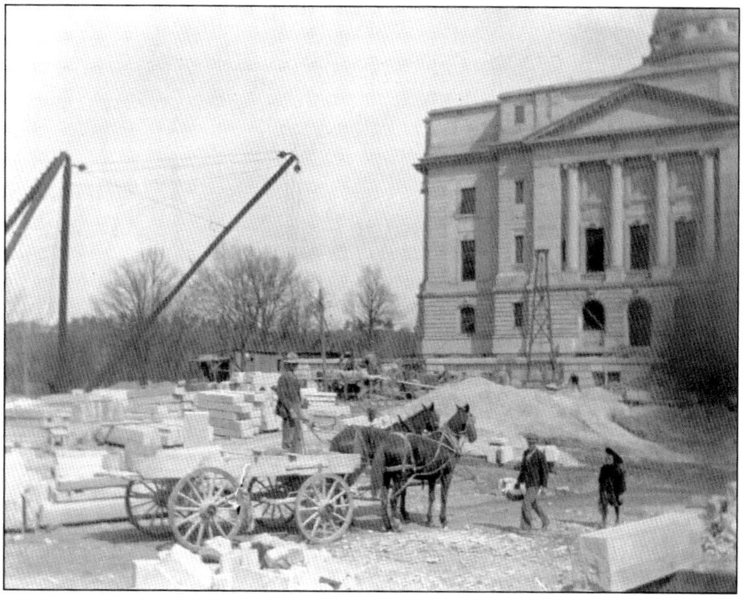

Teamwork. This 1909 photograph shows some of the 20 horses and carts managed by site foreman John W. Sacra. As mentioned earlier, his crew was responsible for delivering materials all around the capitol—no small feat considering that the capitol's footprint, including the terrace, was nearly a quarter-mile across from east to west.

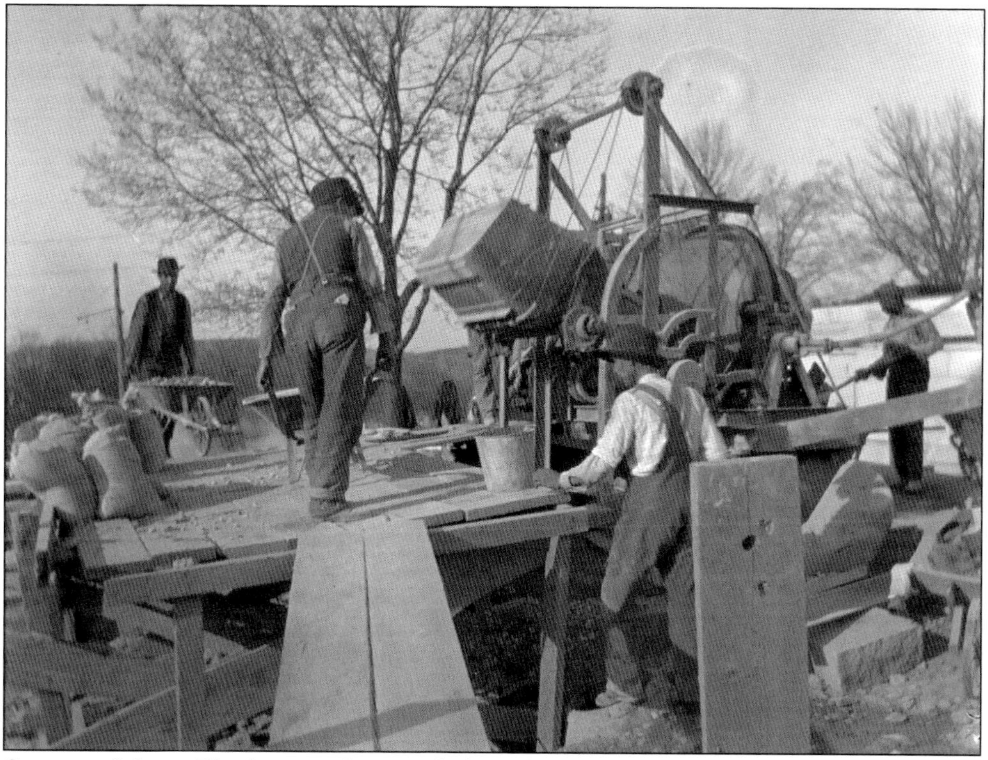

Concrete Mixer. This historic photograph shows four unidentified men working on the terrace in 1909 and provides a detailed look at the working steam-powered concrete mixer mentioned earlier as the only piece of powered machinery on site.

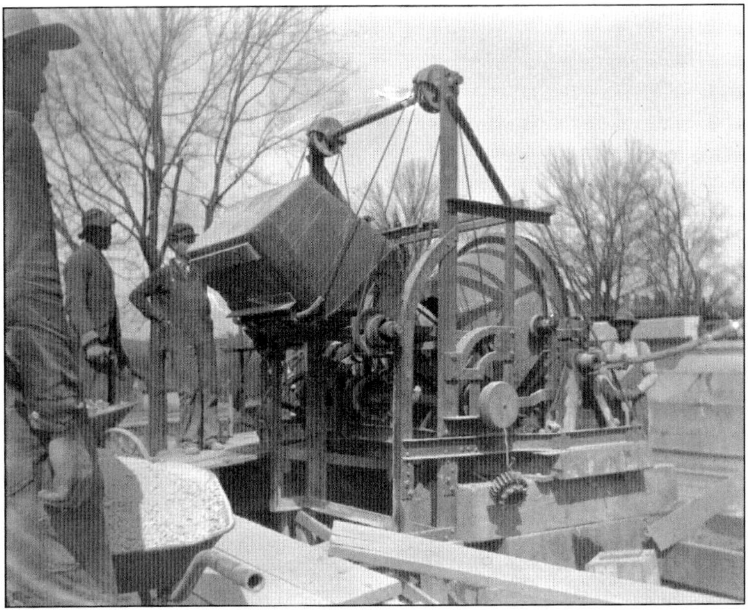

DETAIL OF MIXER. The steam-powered concrete mixer is often discussed in meetings about the capitol, because it was the only piece of powered machinery on the building site. This rarely seen 1909 image is another somewhat closer view of the mixer with three unidentified workers.

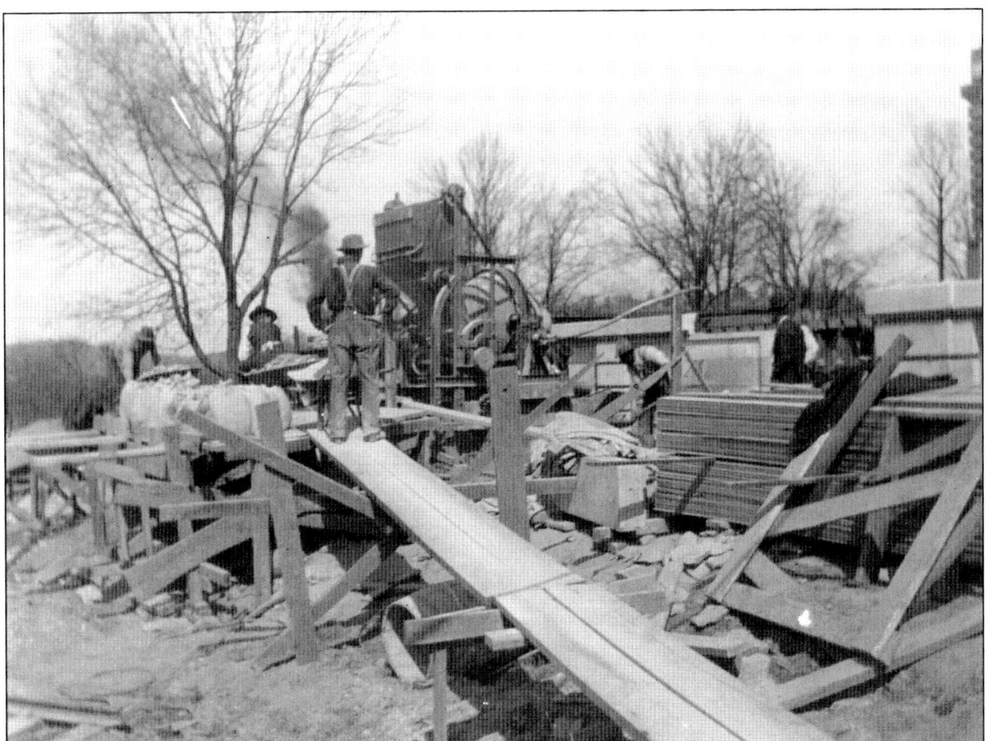

WALKING THE PLANK. As this photograph from 1909 shows, the workers picked up their loads of concrete in wheelbarrows and walked the heavy loads up inclined wooden ramps to the terrace level. Steam from the mixer is visible in this image taken from the southwest corner of the terrace.

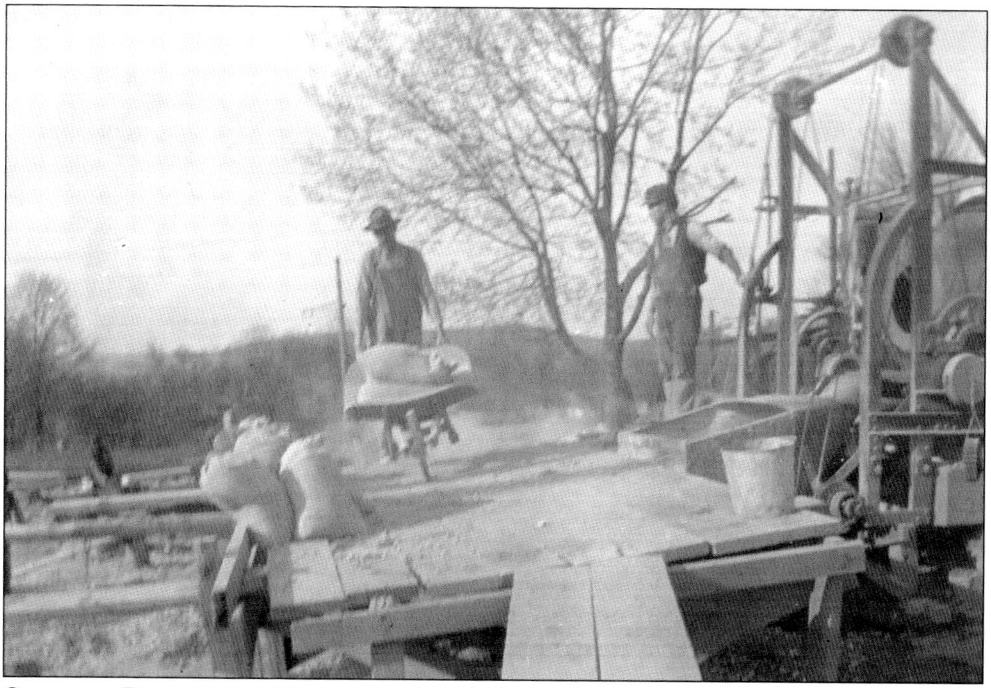

Concrete Production. The two unidentified men shown in this undated photograph are heading towards the elevated concrete mixer with loads of sand to fill the hopper, which will churn wheelbarrow-loads of concrete to be delivered to the terrace.

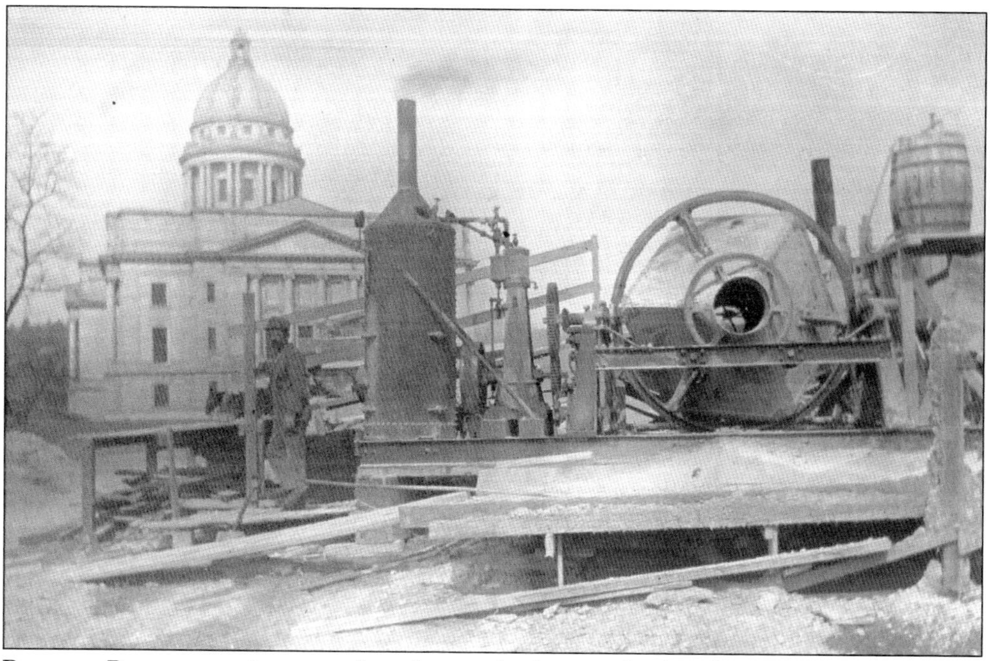

Portable Production. It appears from these early photographs that the steam-powered concrete mixer was somewhat portable and could be pulled by a few horses or mules around to the various areas of work. It is also probable that a single mixer was used on the site for the entire project, which could be another reason the capitol was completed over two years behind schedule.

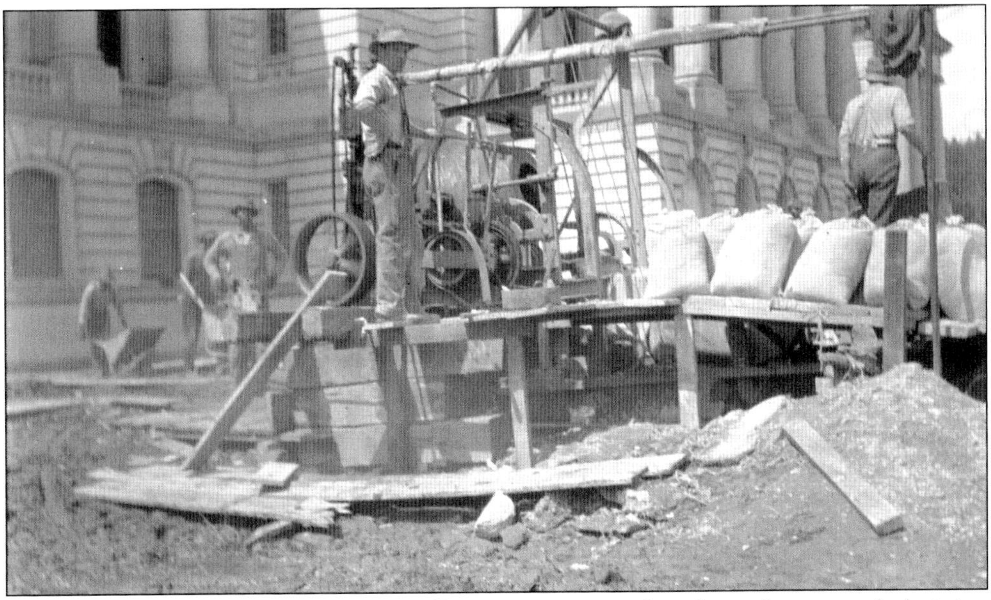

Bags of Sand. Shown here in 1909 is a pulley system on a wooden, elevated structure for hoisting the bags of sand used in making concrete. The sand for the Kentucky State Capitol's construction likely was from the Kentucky River.

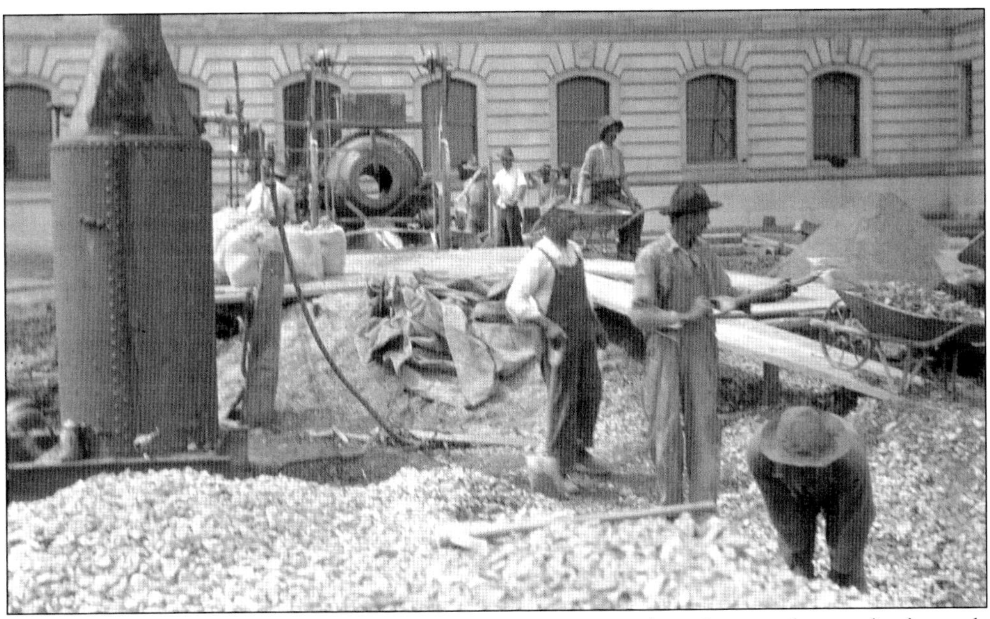

Hard Work. Building the capitol in 1910 was very strenuous work, with many thousands of pounds of sand and rock needing to be moved where it could be used for fill or concrete production. This very detailed photograph of piles of rock and sand along with a man emptying his shovel into a wheelbarrow gives some perspective on how arduous the work must have been.

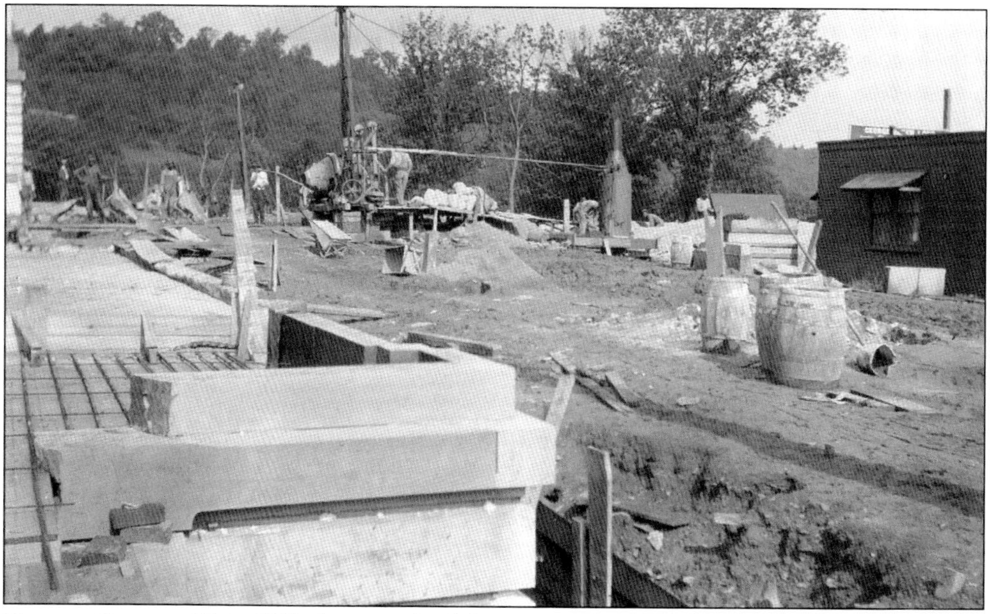

Offices On-site. This 1909 photograph of the on-site George Baker Long office is similar to today's construction trailers except that this was built on the job site. George Baker Long was the subcontractor for the terrace construction. This image also shows the rebar set in the terrace before concrete is formed around it.

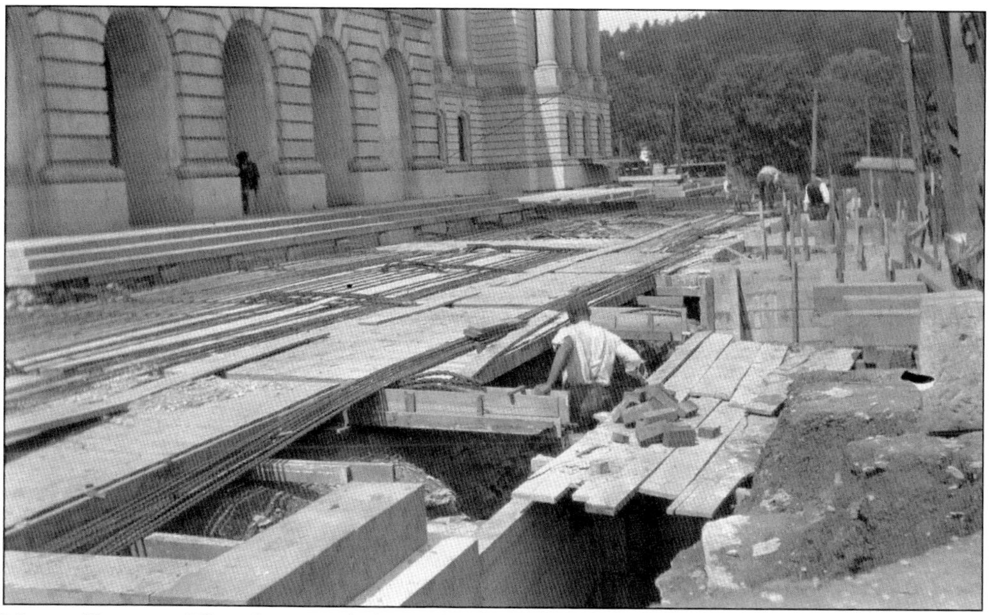

North Terrace. This photograph shows the concrete in-fill on the terrace as well as steel rebar set for reinforcement. As early as 1930, problems were reported with the durability of the terrace, and minor repairs were conducted. During the 1940s, the brick retaining walls covered with limestone veneers had failed. Reinforced concrete replaced the brick, and limestone cladding was reinstalled by 1942.

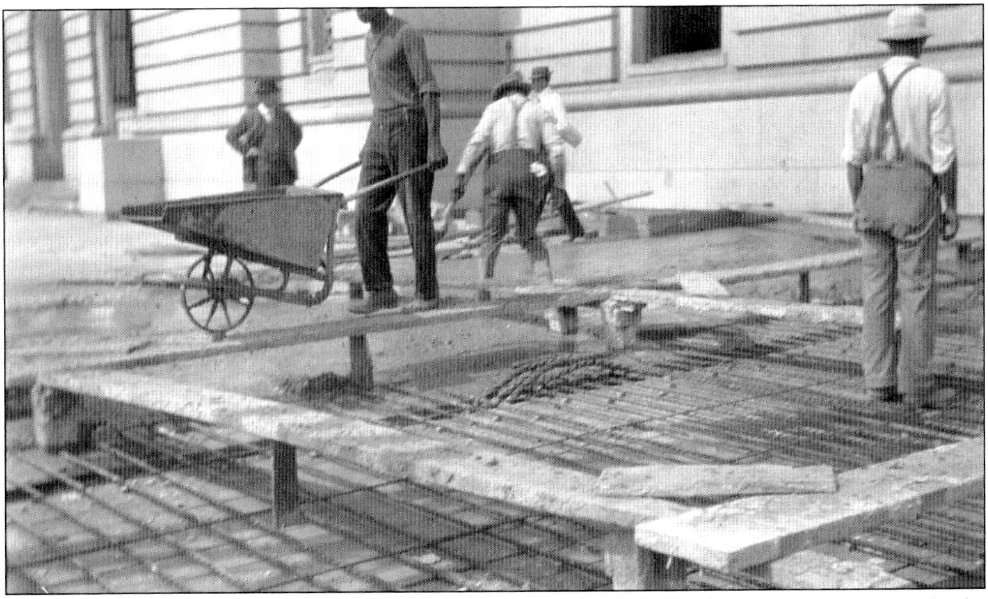

SUPERVISOR WATCHES. In this 1909 image, a man with a loaded wheelbarrow is traversing planks that are placed across steel rebar as he works to fill the terrace concrete floor. An unidentified supervisor surveys the progress in the background.

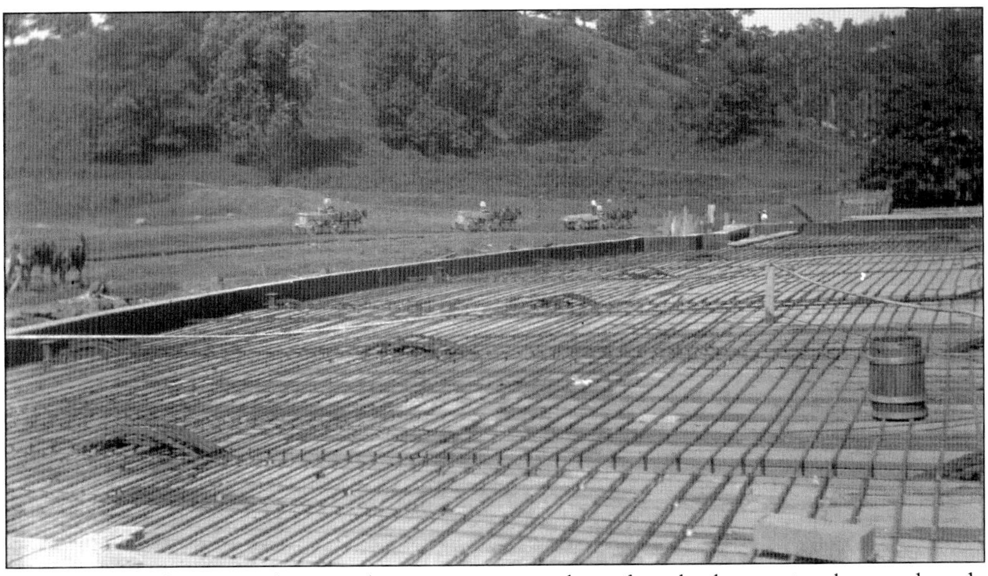

REBAR GRID. This 1909 photograph is an expansive shot of steel rebar set in place and ready for concrete to be poured on the north entrance terrace. Four teams of horses with carts are in the background.

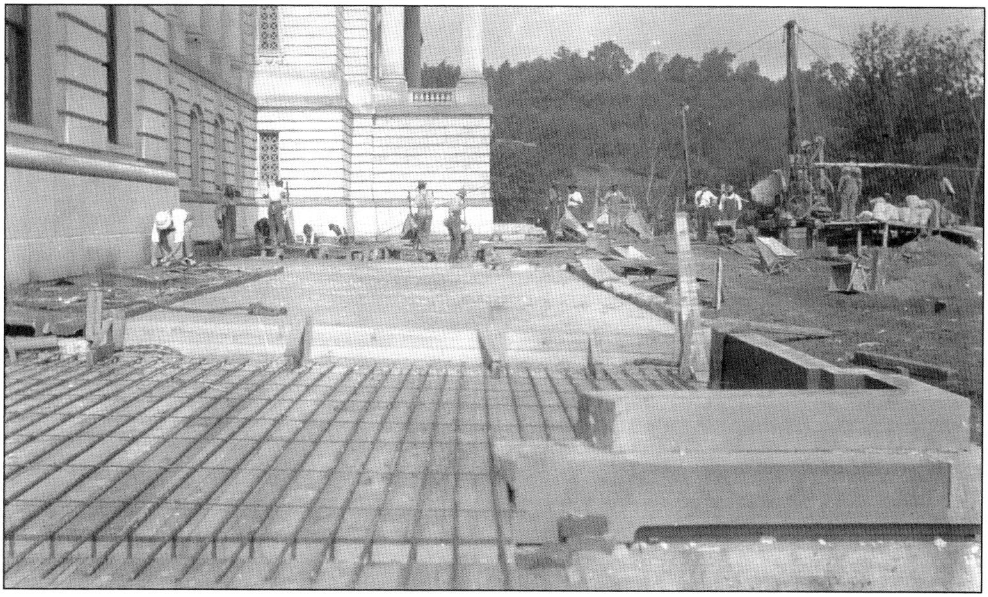

CONCRETE FLOOR. Although one cannot see it without knowing where to look, concrete was used extensively in the construction of the Kentucky State Capitol building. A good example is the floor of the brick-paved terrace, shown here in 1909 being completed with concrete and leveled.

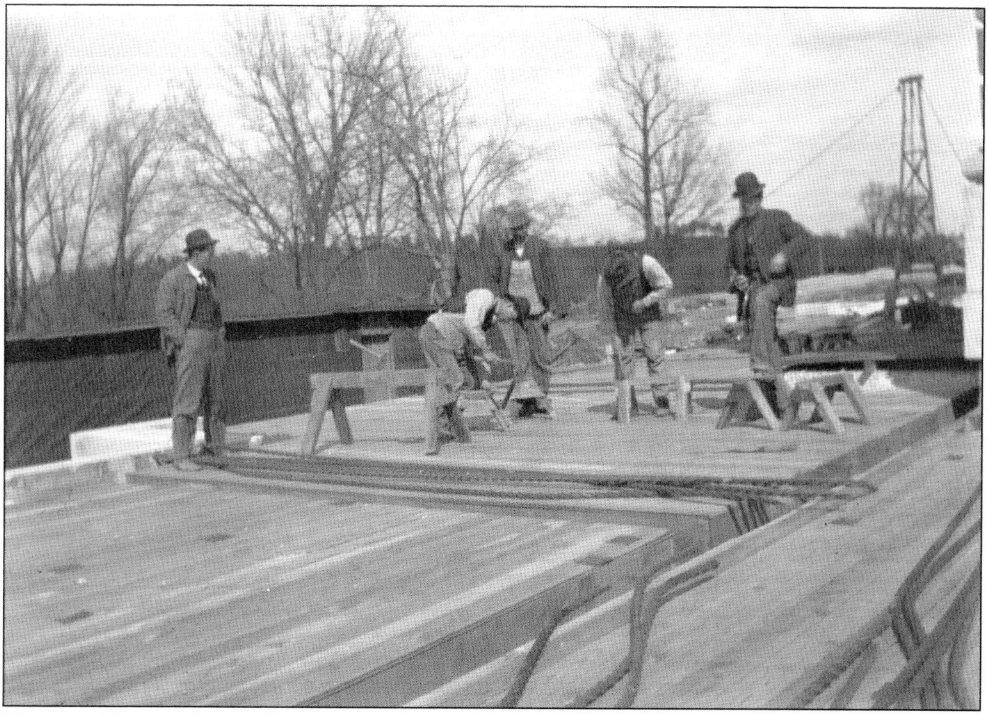

TERRACE TAKING SHAPE. Five men are seen in this 1909 photograph working on placing rebar to complete the north terrace. It appears from the bare trees in these photographs that the season was getting late for outdoor construction.

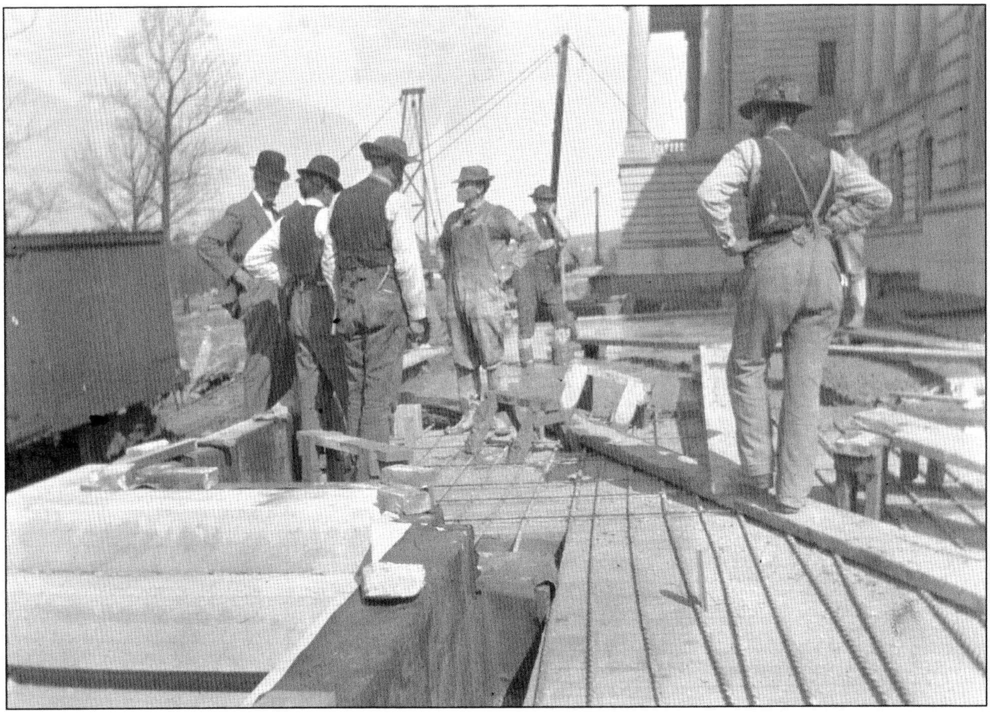

INSPECTION TIME. Several men, most probably supervisors or foremen, are shown in this photograph. It could be inferred that they are inspecting the placement of steel rebar and fill material to determine if more work is needed before pouring concrete.

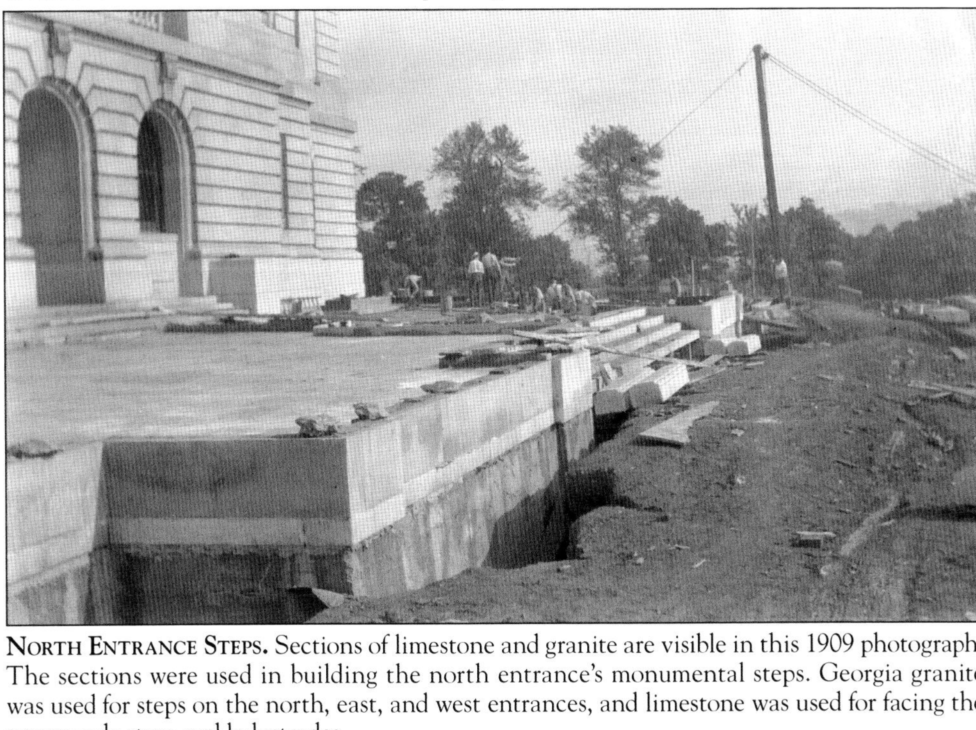

NORTH ENTRANCE STEPS. Sections of limestone and granite are visible in this 1909 photograph. The sections were used in building the north entrance's monumental steps. Georgia granite was used for steps on the north, east, and west entrances, and limestone was used for facing the promenade steps and balustrades.

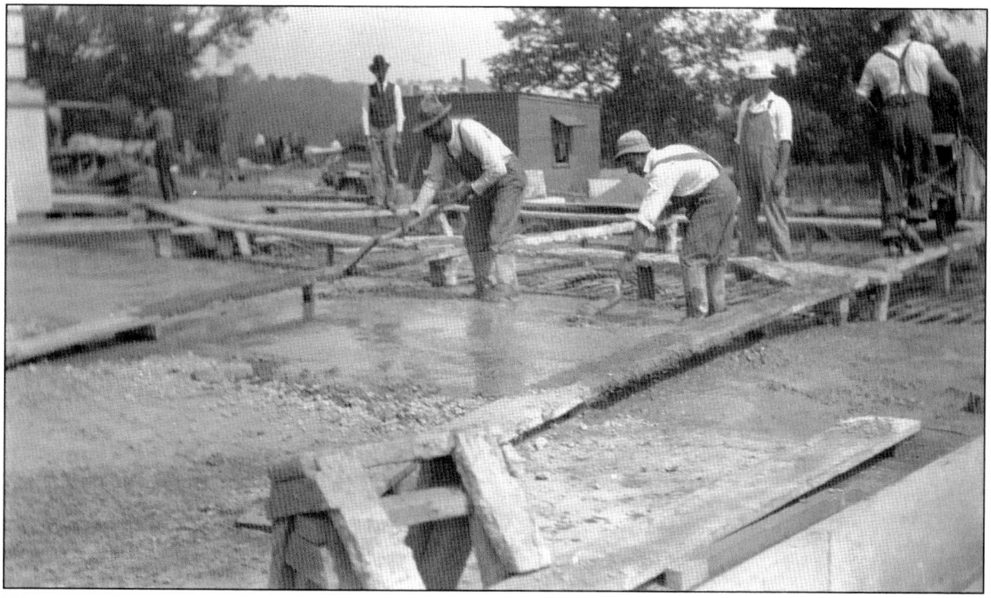

WETTING CONCRETE. Six to eight men are shown in this 1909 photograph wetting freshly poured concrete with a hose, attempting to level the terrace. Without a perfectly level surface, the vitreous brick pavers would have been a trip hazard for pedestrians, a problem the capitol terrace still faces today.

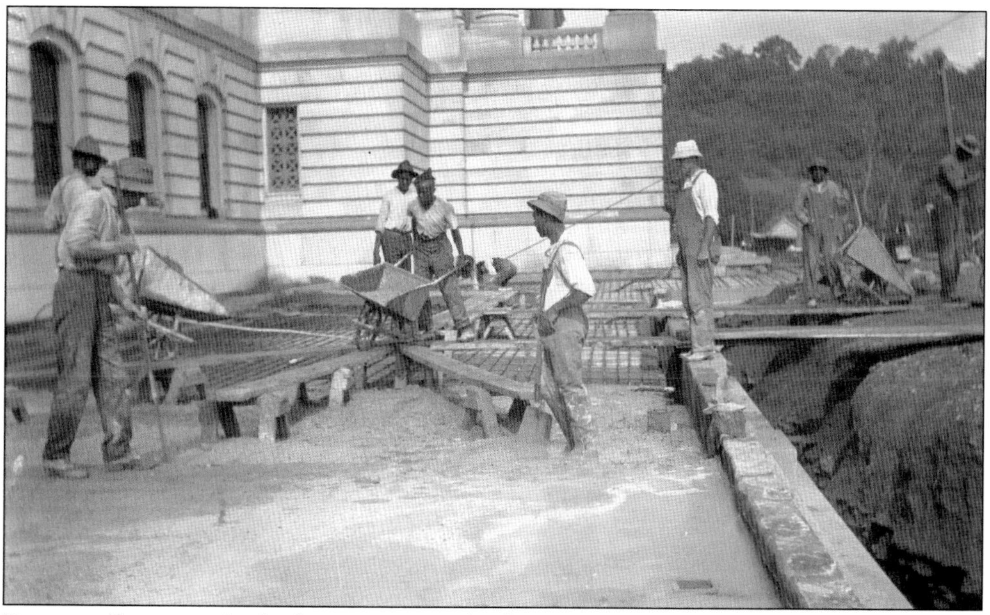

DUMPING CONCRETE. In this historic image, wheelbarrows of concrete mix are being dumped over steel rebar grids into forms below. A foreman standing on the ledge of the terrace above keeps a watchful eye on workers. The terrace was nearing completion in these late 1909 images.

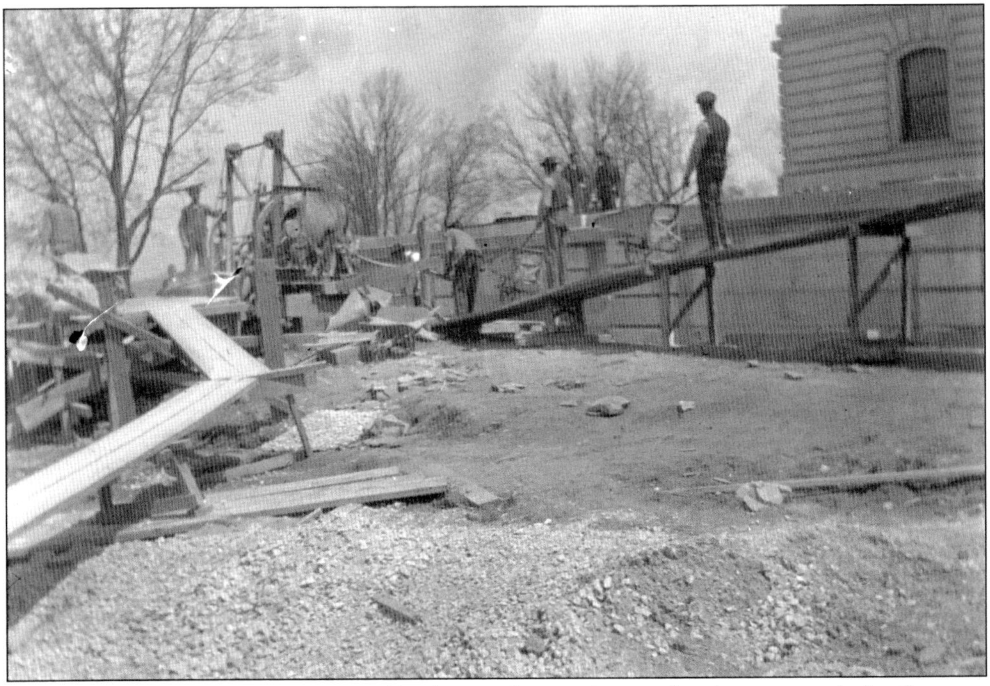

READY FOR BRICKS. A ramp is pictured leading to the mostly completed terrace, and wheelbarrows are loaded with vitreous brick to begin filling the terrace with pavers. The vitreous brick was selected for better traction during ice and snow, and it did not reflect light and heat in the summer.

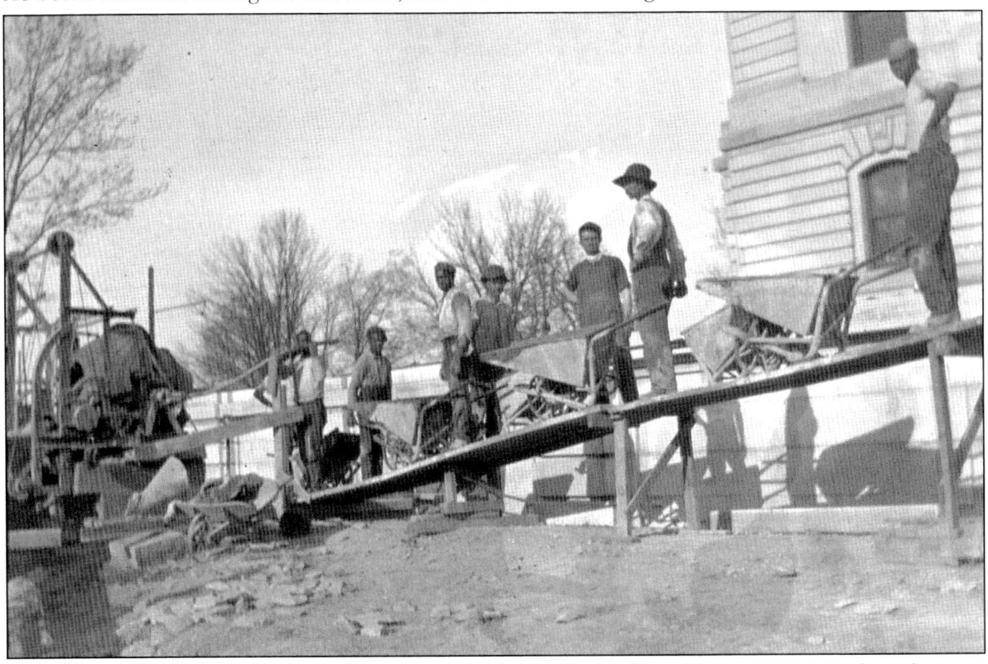

EIGHT MEN ON. This photograph is a view of the ramp leading to the terrace with eight men bringing loads of bricks in wheelbarrows for installation on the terrace. It appears from these 1909–1910 photographs that the labor for installing the pavers on the terrace was primarily young African American men.

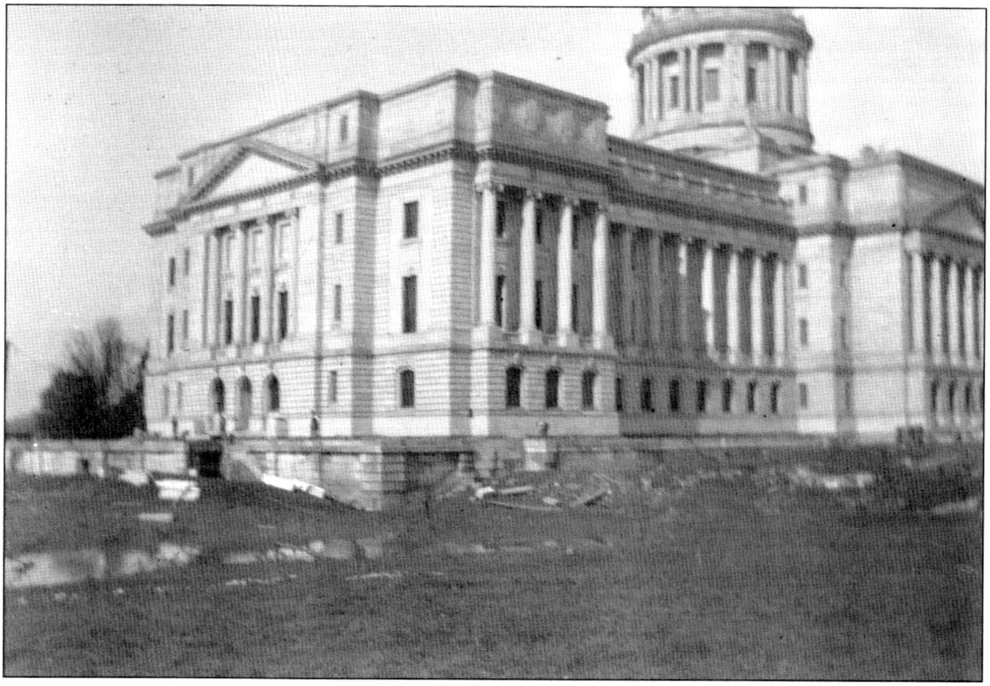

NEARING COMPLETION. This southwest corner view of the capitol from 1910 shows all the construction equipment removed, and terrace bricks are being laid in background. With the terrace complete, the west entrance's two flights of 21 granite steps are evident in the photograph.

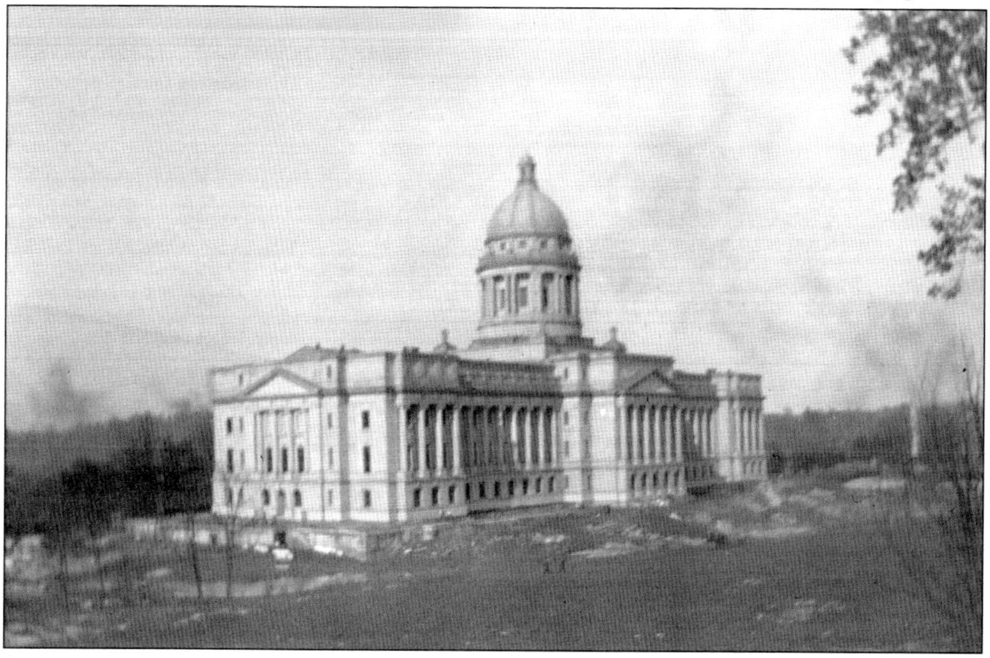

SOUTHWEST VIEW. The capitol building itself is over 95 percent complete in this 1910 photograph. This image was taken from same vantage point as the iconic series of dome construction images earlier. The landscaping would still be delayed several months and was not really complete at dedication ceremonies in June.

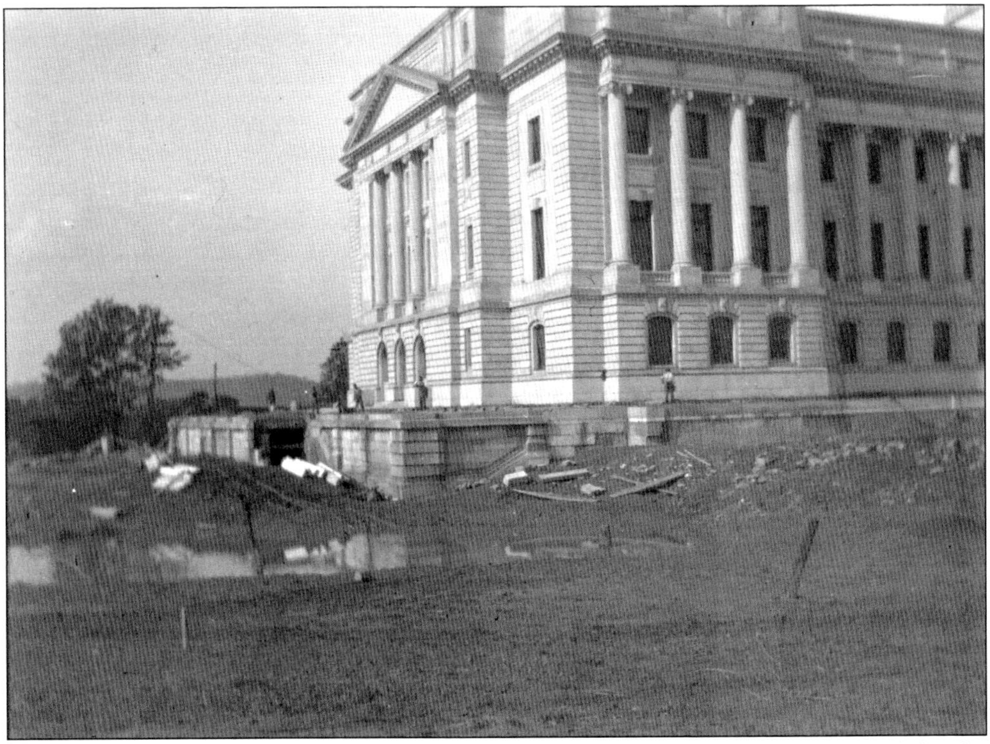

Terrace Work. Workers are shown in this late 1909–1910 photograph laying brick for the terrace, which was complete by early 1910. It is unknown whether the labor forces for the capitol were local or brought in, but it would be wonderful to determine the identity of any of the faces presented in these pages.

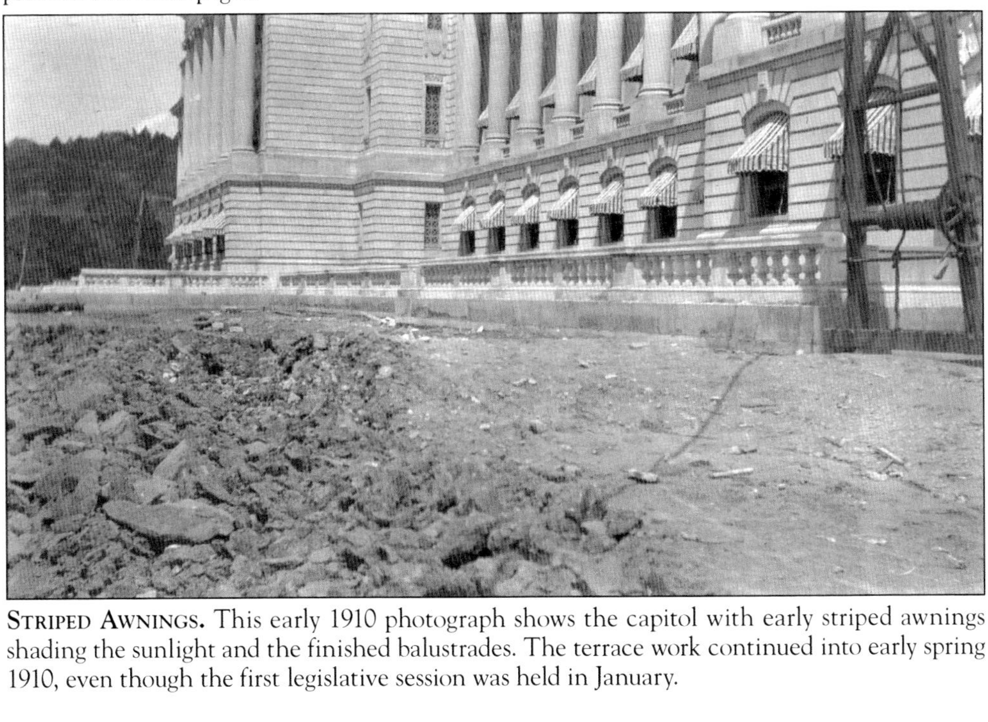

Striped Awnings. This early 1910 photograph shows the capitol with early striped awnings shading the sunlight and the finished balustrades. The terrace work continued into early spring 1910, even though the first legislative session was held in January.

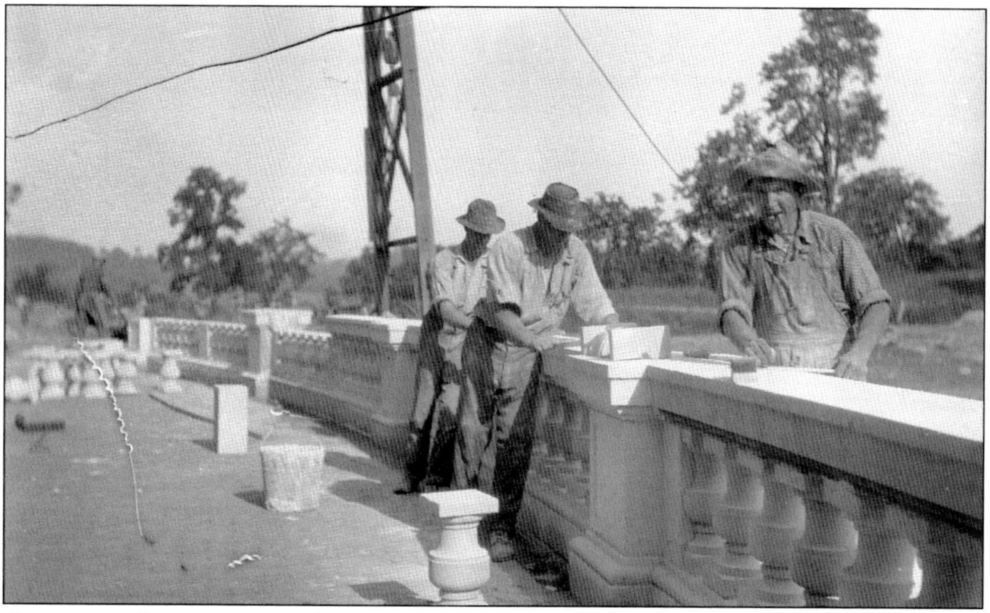

Balustrade Construction. Three men are pictured in this late 1909–early 1910 photograph. One man is shown smoking a pipe while working to install the balustrade that surrounds the capitol. Any of these three men could have installed one of the balustrade columns on the northwest stairs upside down, a curiosity on the terrace that still is evident today.

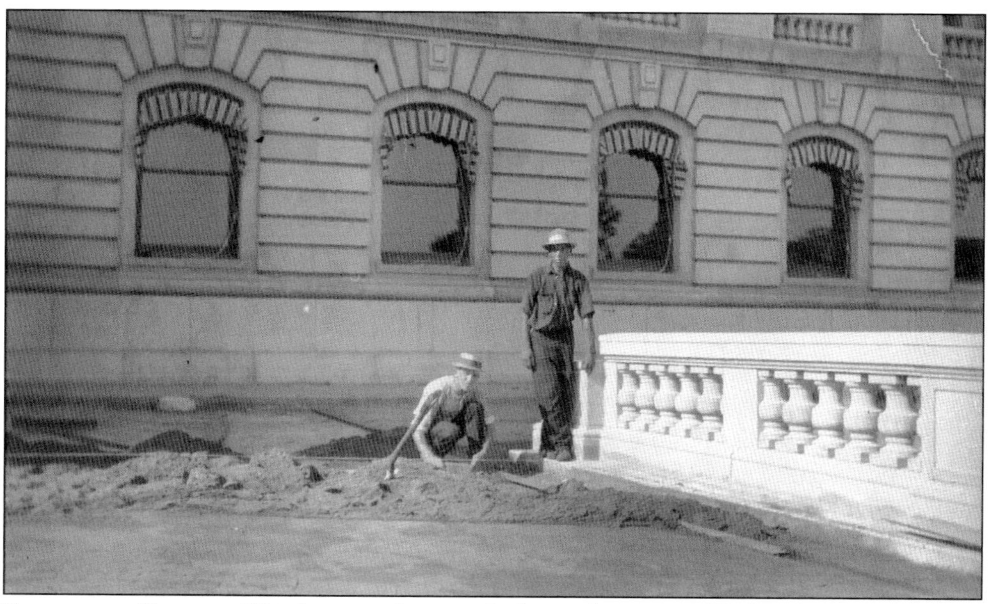

Filling the Terrace. This historic photograph shows the terrace filled with concrete, which provided a floor for decorative pavers. The balustrades were also installed in this image taken from the northwest side of the capitol building.

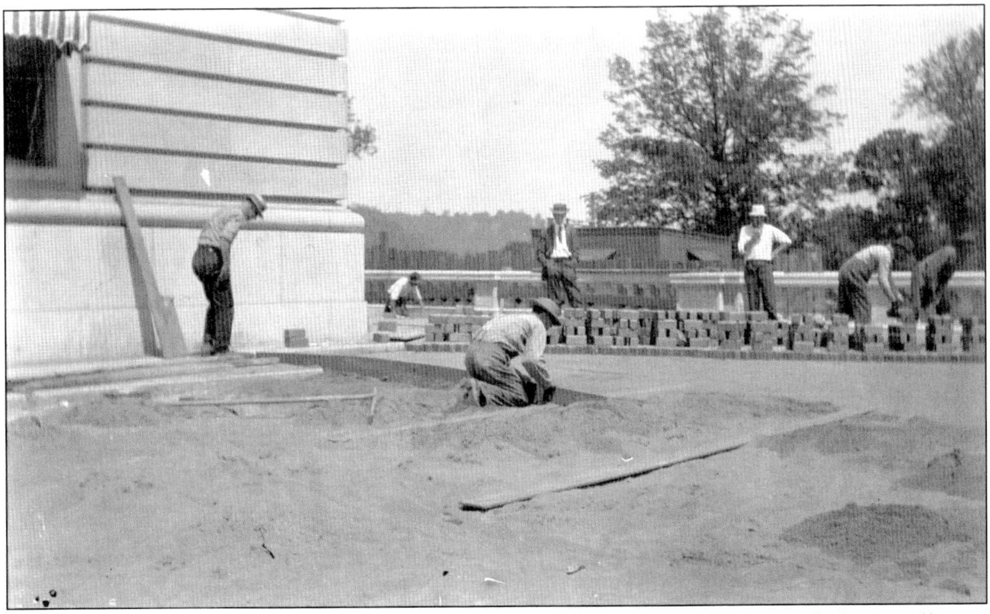

STACKS OF PAVERS. In this 1909–1910 photograph, many stacks of bricks are ready for installation on the terrace. Because the Kentucky State Capitol was so far behind in construction, scenes are often shown in varying stages of progression. This image is no exception, as workers are also continuing to fill and level the terrace while some of the terrace is already complete.

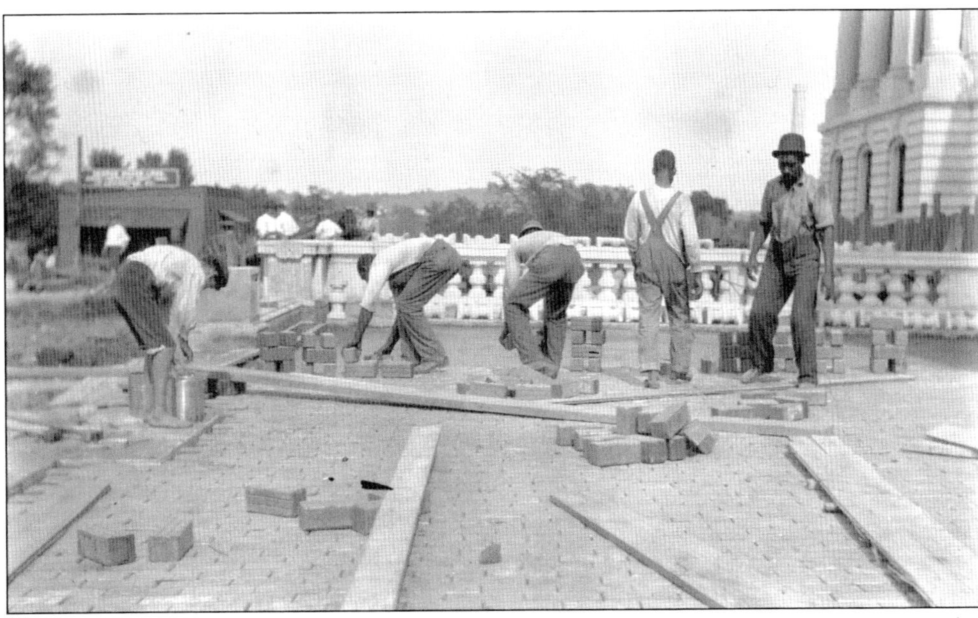

GEORGE BAKER LONG. With the construction of the capitol severely delayed, the George Baker Long Company was hired to complete the terrace. The firm worked part of 1909 into 1910 to finish the job. The only documented name involved with the terrace project is John W. Sacra, who was mentioned earlier.

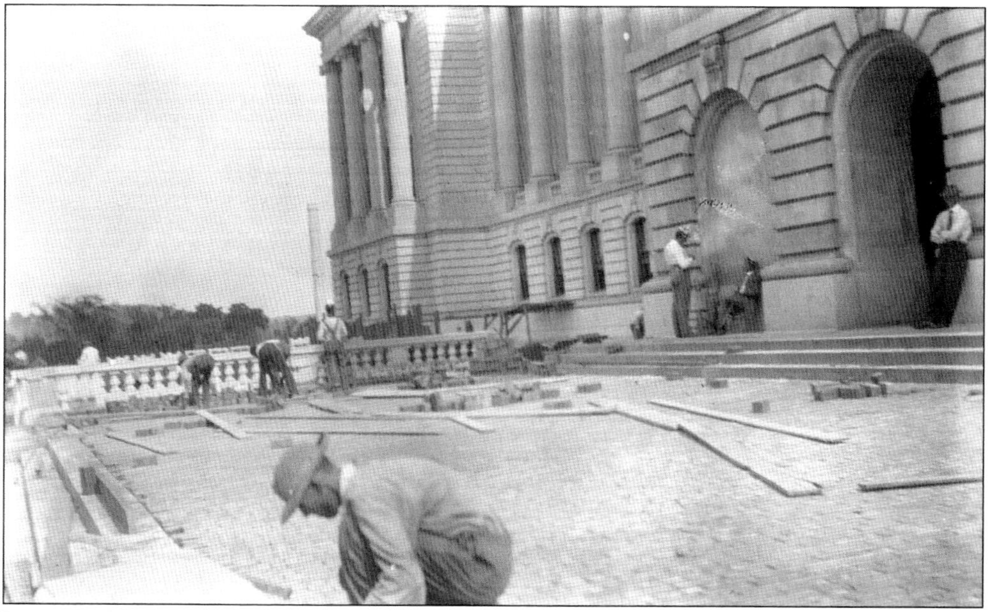

LEVELING BRICKS. The vitreous brick pavers were placed by hand on the terrace, and long wood planks were used to level them, as shown in this 1909 photograph. One man in the scene has obviously made himself comfortable in the north entrance vestibule, leaning back in a chair.

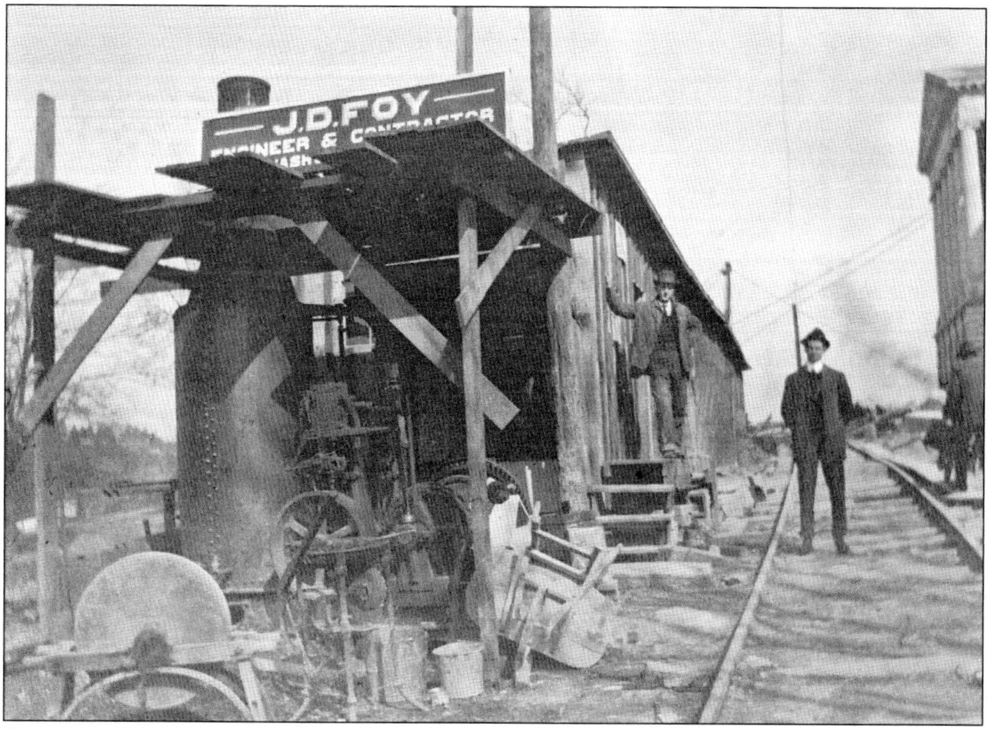

GRINDING WHEEL. The construction office of J. D. Foy, one of the last subcontractors to work on the capitol building, is seen in this 1909 photograph. Two unidentified men are also pictured with a grinding wheel in the foreground for sharpening tools such as saws, chisels, and other implements used for making on-site modifications to limestone, marble, and granite.

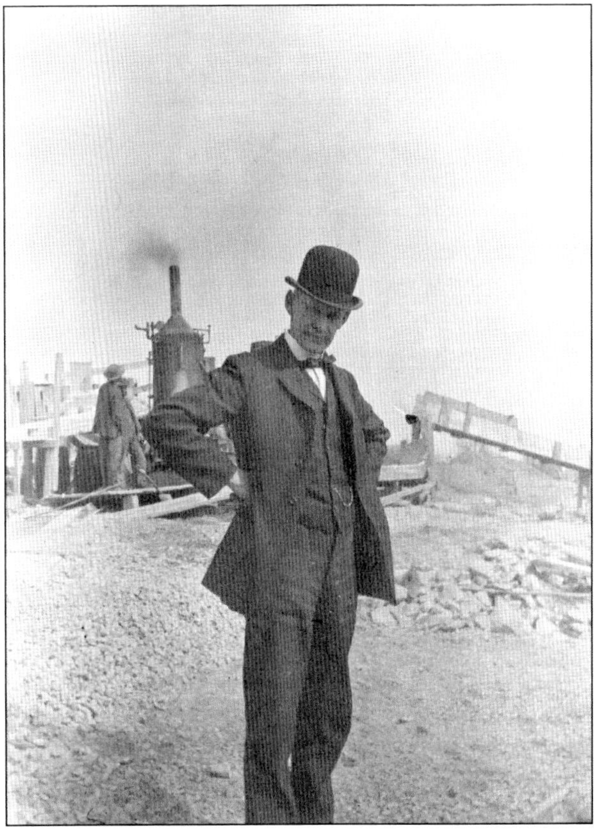

Mr. Johnson. Architect Frank Mills Andrews had several projects ongoing along with the Kentucky State Capitol and was rarely seen on site other than for meetings with the capitol commission. Mr. Johnson, seen in this 1909 photograph, was Andrew's chief inspector and superintendent for the project.

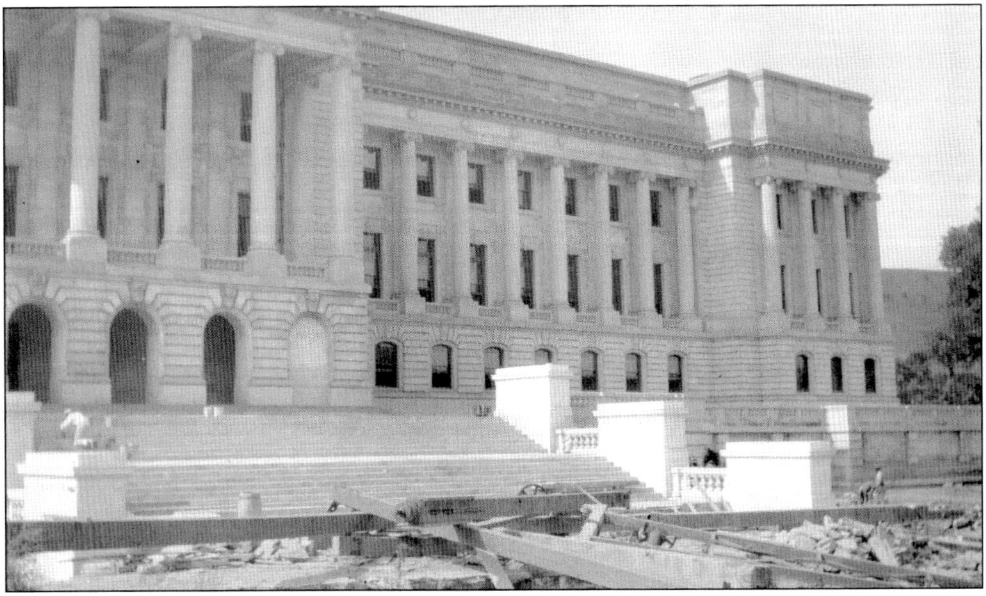

Promenade Taking shape. This photograph shows four of the six large, decorative architectural boxes that flank the stairs on the promenade leading to the north entrance of the capitol. Ionic columns, which are visible on the front of the capitol, are somewhat unique in that the architect specified monolithic columns.

Five

The New Kentucky Home Unveiled

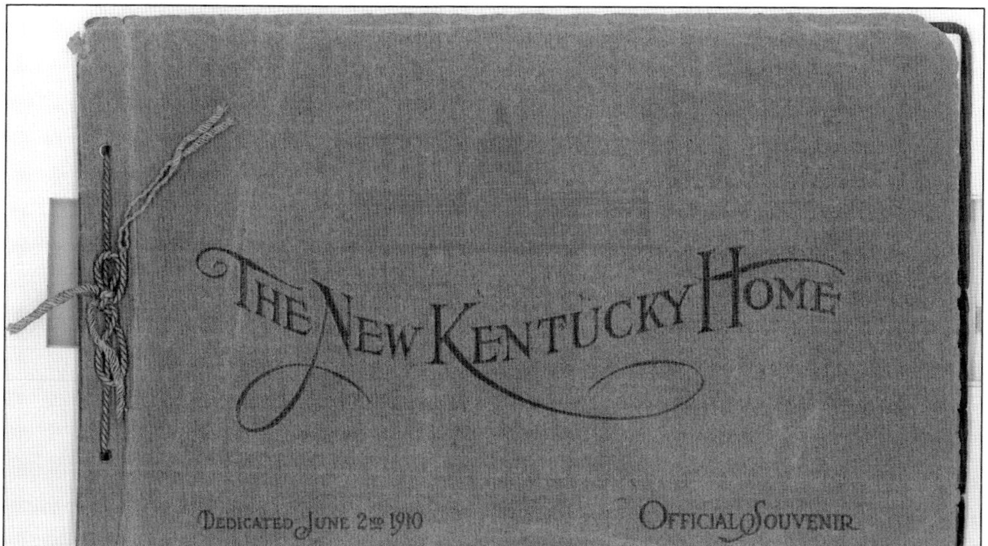

Souvenir Program from 1910. At 12:00 p.m. on June 2, 1910, the formal dedication ceremony began at the new capitol building. This photograph is of the original programs of that day. The capitol building was decorated with flags on the exterior and adorned with plants and flowers in its interior spaces. Dignitaries on the speaker's stand included Gov. August and Mary Elizabeth Willson, Senator William O. and Margaret Bradley, former governors of Kentucky, judges, generals, and congressmen. Senator Bradley, who had been the commonwealth's governor in the 1890s, delivered the keynote address. (Courtesy of Division of Historic Properties.)

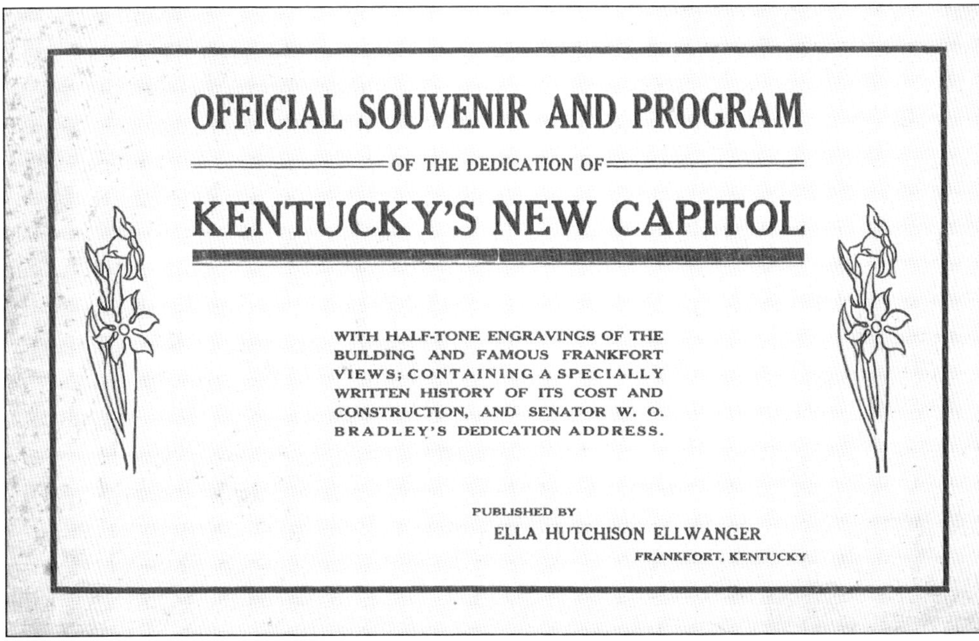

OFFICIAL SOUVENIR AND PROGRAM

OF THE DEDICATION OF

KENTUCKY'S NEW CAPITOL

WITH HALF-TONE ENGRAVINGS OF THE BUILDING AND FAMOUS FRANKFORT VIEWS; CONTAINING A SPECIALLY WRITTEN HISTORY OF ITS COST AND CONSTRUCTION, AND SENATOR W. O. BRADLEY'S DEDICATION ADDRESS.

PUBLISHED BY
ELLA HUTCHISON ELLWANGER
FRANKFORT, KENTUCKY

DEDICATION PROGRAM. The final official costs of the new capitol included $1,180,434.80 for the building; $63,793 for the grounds; $141,881 for furnishings, special finishes, and mural paintings; $45,188 for file cabinets and other office storage equipment; $90,000 for the power plant; $108,703.20 for heating, lighting, and electrical fixtures; and $190,000 for terraces and landscaping. The architect's final fees ($82,730) were counted in each of these items. (Courtesy of Division of Historic Properties.)

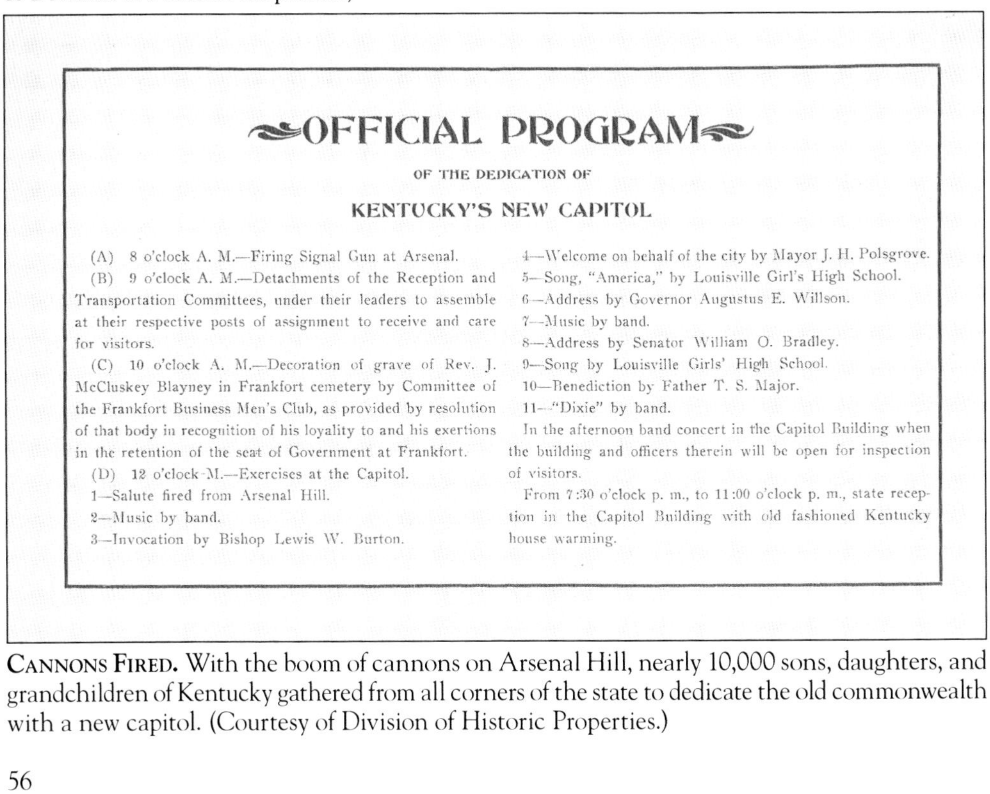

OFFICIAL PROGRAM

OF THE DEDICATION OF

KENTUCKY'S NEW CAPITOL

(A) 8 o'clock A. M.—Firing Signal Gun at Arsenal.

(B) 9 o'clock A. M.—Detachments of the Reception and Transportation Committees, under their leaders to assemble at their respective posts of assignment to receive and care for visitors.

(C) 10 o'clock A. M.—Decoration of grave of Rev. J. McCluskey Blayney in Frankfort cemetery by Committee of the Frankfort Business Men's Club, as provided by resolution of that body in recognition of his loyality to and his exertions in the retention of the seat of Government at Frankfort.

(D) 12 o'clock M.—Exercises at the Capitol.

1—Salute fired from Arsenal Hill.

2—Music by band.

3—Invocation by Bishop Lewis W. Burton.

4—Welcome on behalf of the city by Mayor J. H. Polsgrove.

5—Song, "America," by Louisville Girl's High School.

6—Address by Governor Augustus E. Willson.

7—Music by band.

8—Address by Senator William O. Bradley.

9—Song by Louisville Girls' High School.

10—Benediction by Father T. S. Major.

11—"Dixie" by band.

In the afternoon band concert in the Capitol Building when the building and officers therein will be open for inspection of visitors.

From 7:30 o'clock p. m., to 11:00 o'clock p. m., state reception in the Capitol Building with old fashioned Kentucky house warming.

CANNONS FIRED. With the boom of cannons on Arsenal Hill, nearly 10,000 sons, daughters, and grandchildren of Kentucky gathered from all corners of the state to dedicate the old commonwealth with a new capitol. (Courtesy of Division of Historic Properties.)

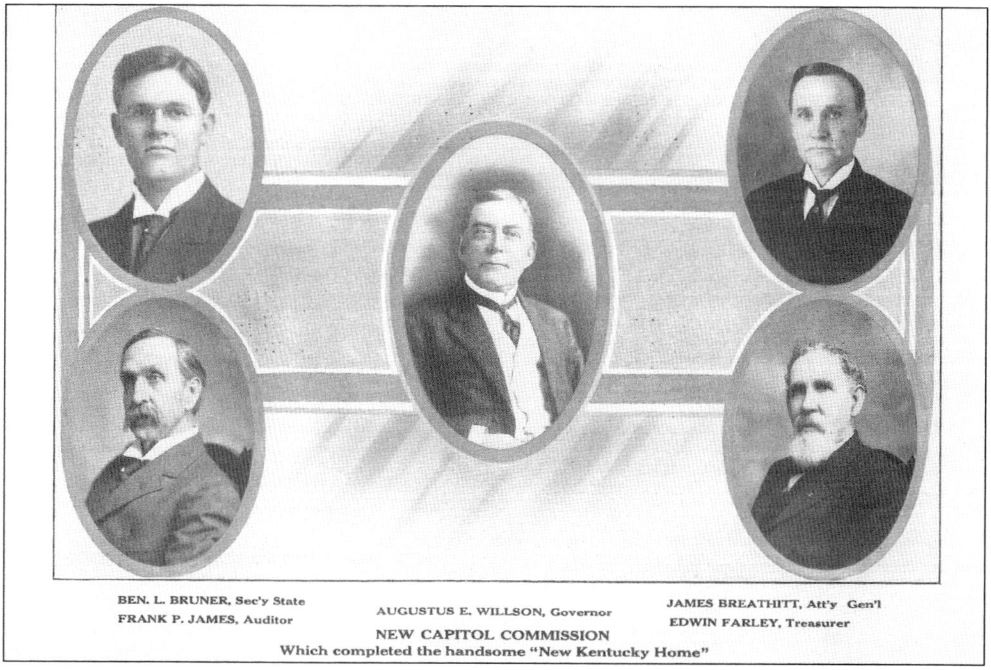

NEW CAPITOL COMMISSION. There are bronze tablets on either side of the north entrance to the capitol rotunda, the one on the west wall bearing the names of the commission under Governor Beckham's administration who oversaw the early stages of the erection of the building, including laying the cornerstone. The tablet on the east wall bears names of the commission who completed it with Governor Willson. (Courtesy of Division of Historic Properties.)

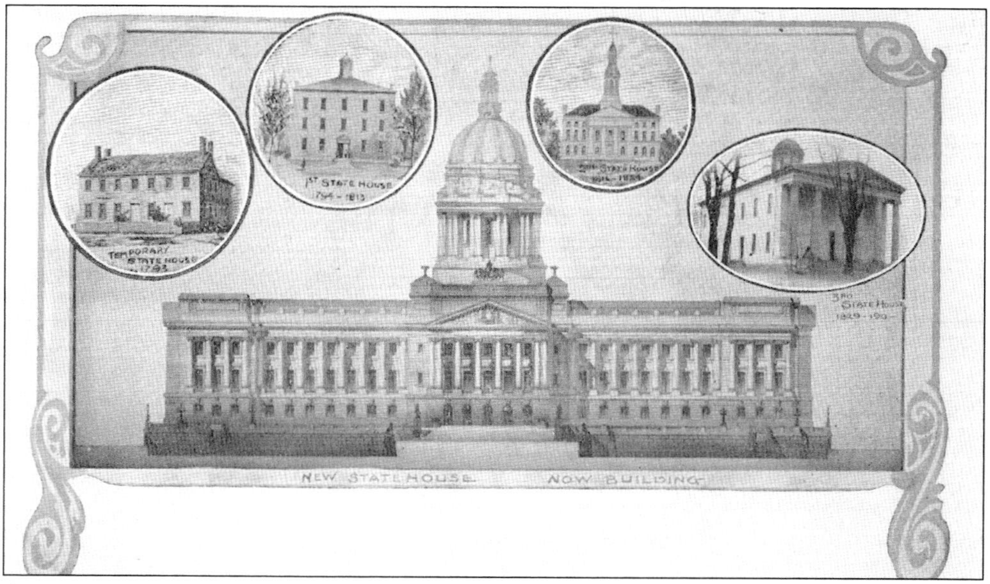

COMMONWEALTH STATEHOUSES. The five statehouses of the commonwealth are represented in this historic postcard from around 1900–1905. In 1869, the state determined that the 1827 capitol was inadequate to meet its needs. The legislature appropriated $100,000 to begin the construction of a new building, which later substantially increased to nearly $2 million with the U.S. government contribution discussed earlier. (Courtesy collection of Scot Walters.)

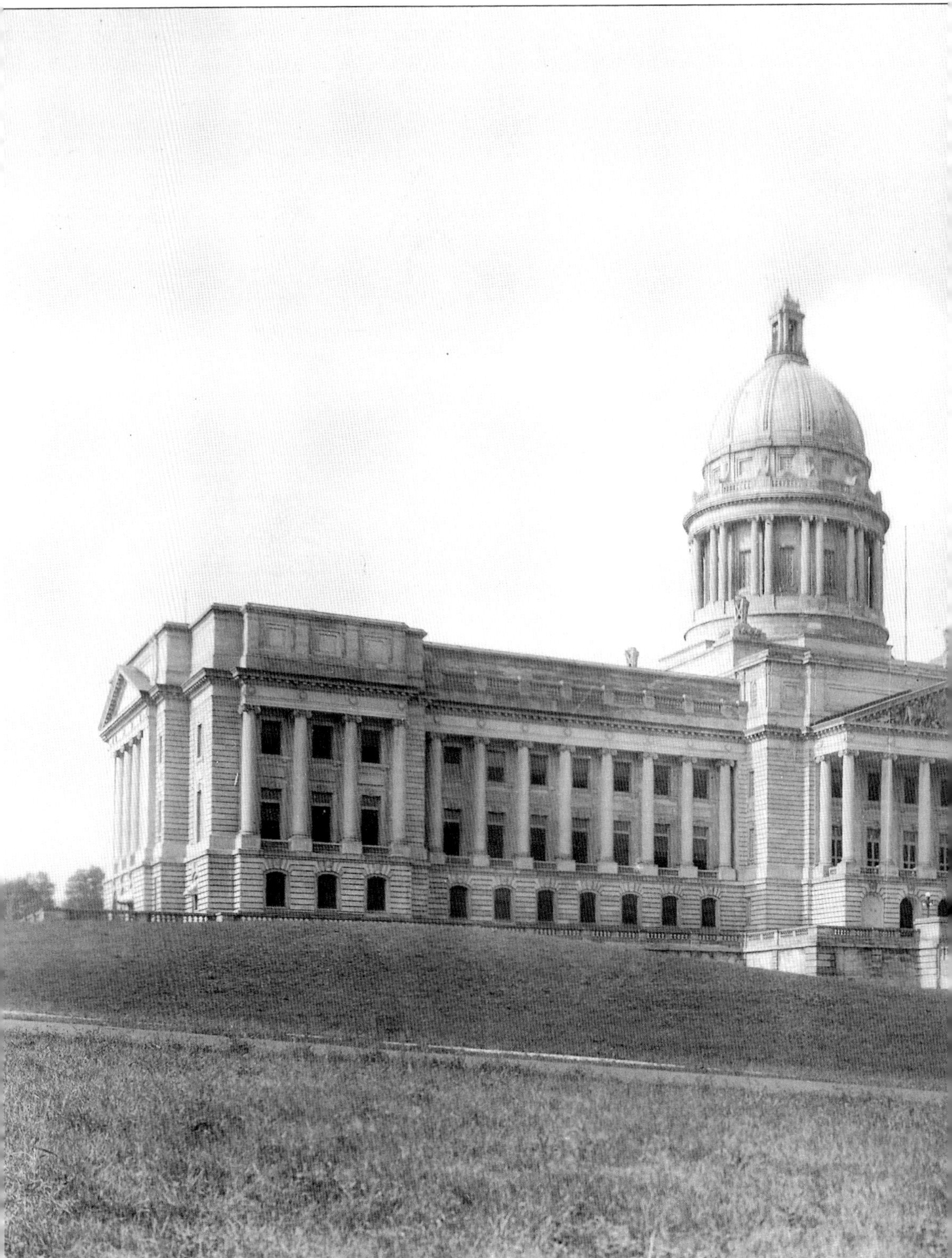

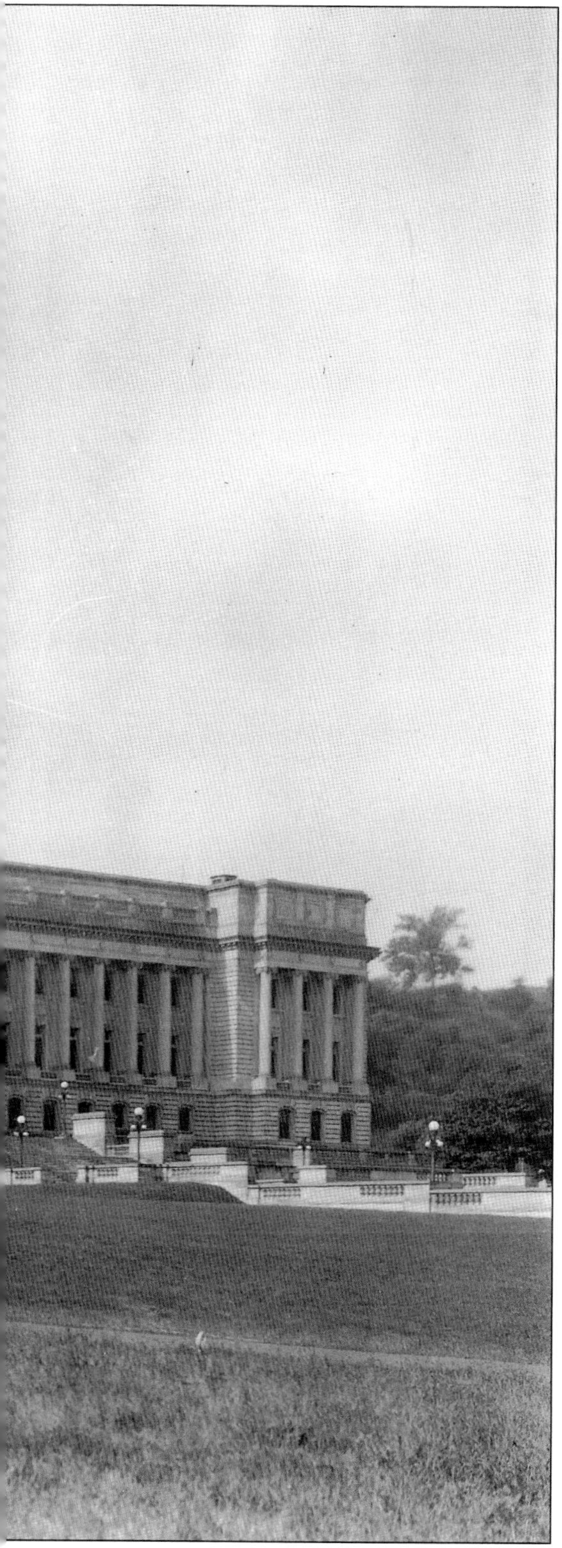

New Capitol, 1912. This photograph, taken around 1912–1915, showcases the formality of the Kentucky State Capitol's architectural lines from the northeast side. The architect, Frank Mills Andrews, was born in Des Moines, Iowa, in 1867. He graduated from Iowa State University and studied architecture at Cornell University. After his graduation in 1888, he worked first in Ithaca, New York, for William H. Miller, later moving to New York City to draft for George B. Post, and he spent some time working in Chicago. Andrews traveled extensively in Europe and wrote a paper published in the *British Journal of the Royal Society of Arts* in 1911 discussing the development of American architecture. He stressed the influence of the beaux-arts classical style. (Courtesy of Caufield and Shook Studio Collection, Ekstrom Library Special Collections, University of Louisville.)

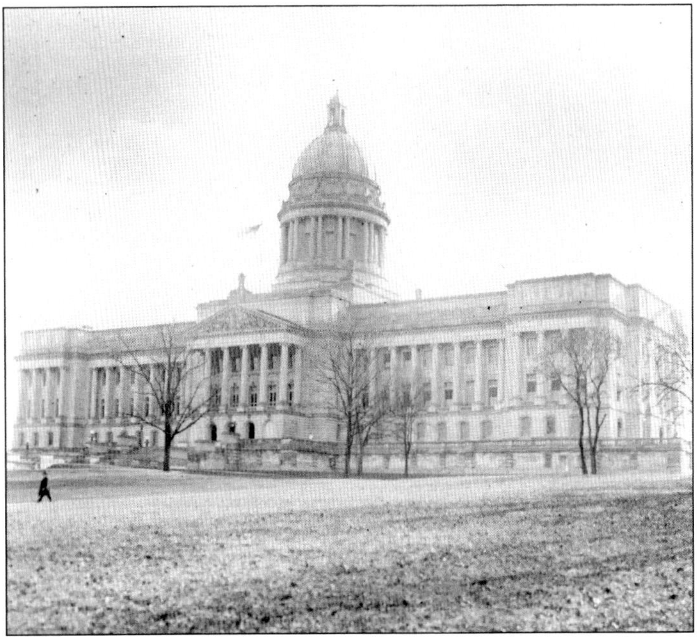

WINTER, 1915. This photograph, shot from the west side on a blustery winter day, shows the capitol from a different angle. Frank Mills Andrews credited the 1893 Chicago Exposition as establishing architecture as a profession with distinct public and social standing. Andrews was a proponent of beaux-arts architecture typified by the work of architects such as McKim, Mead, and White and Richard Morris Hunt. (Courtesy of Division of Historic Properties.)

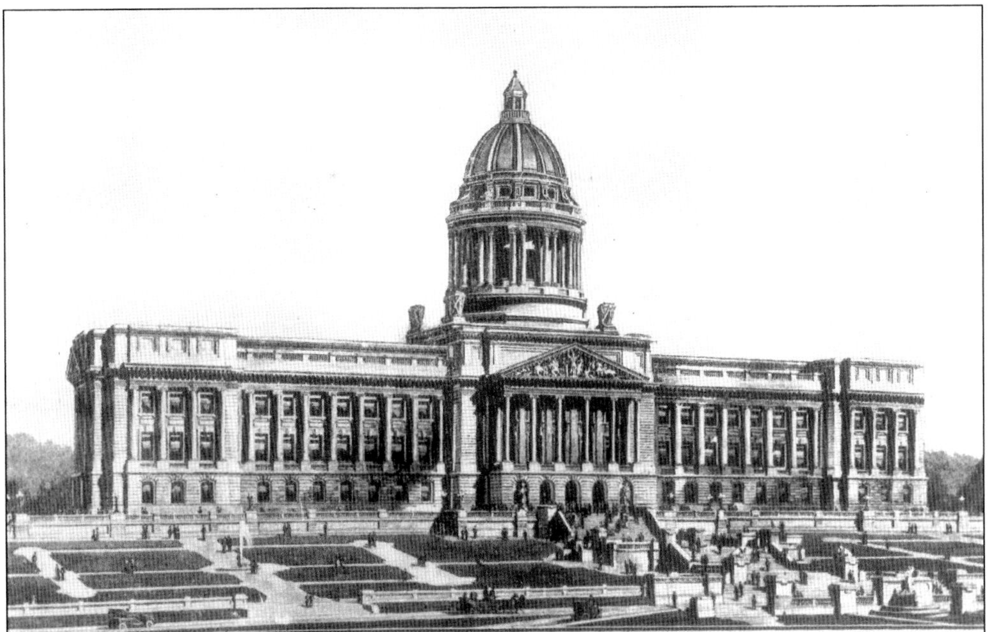

THE NEW STATE CAPITOL BUILDING.

CAPITOL POSTCARD. This postcard, taken from a hand-drawn rendering, may be one of the first designs that Frank Mills Andrews submitted of the Kentucky State Capitol. The formal grounds, fountains, and some architectural features of the finished building turned out much differently than this representation from 1905–1907. (Courtesy of Division of Historic Properties.)

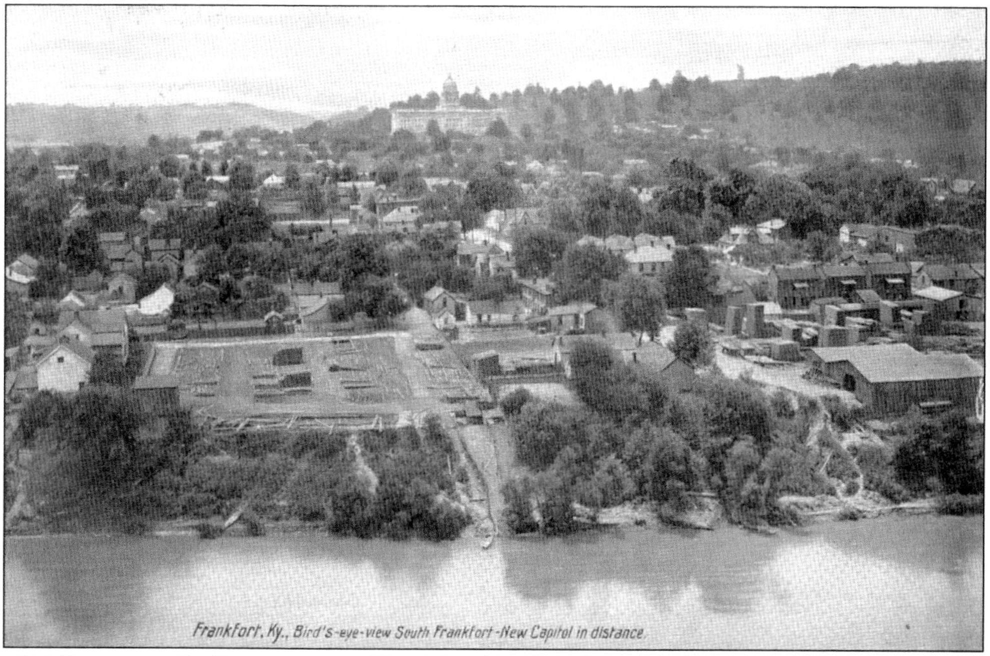

1910 POSTCARD. Bird's-eye images of Frankfort, like that shown in this 1910 postcard, were almost always photographed from the Frankfort Cemetery. The vantage point near the Daniel Boone gravesite has always been popular with photographers and artists. This photograph shows some of the bygone river lumber industry. (Courtesy collection of Scot Walters.)

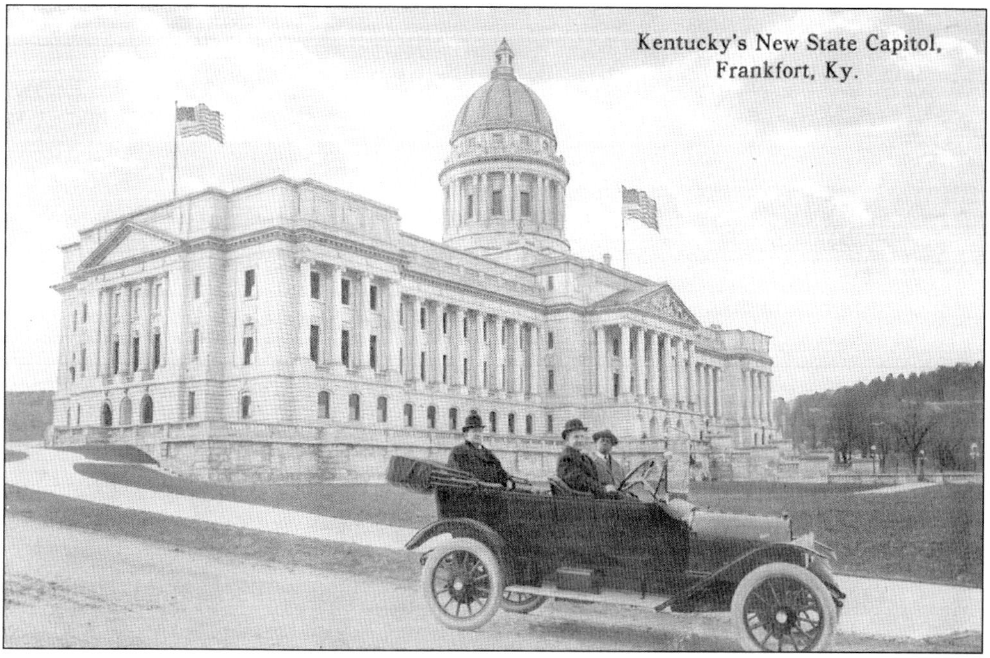

KENTUCKY'S NEW STATE CAPITOL. Governor Willson is chauffeured around the completed new state capitol in this 1910–1912 postcard picturing the north elevation. When Governor Willson took office in 1908, he found the capitol severely behind schedule. Willson made it a priority in his administration to have the great building completed and open by 1910. (Courtesy collection of Scot Walters.)

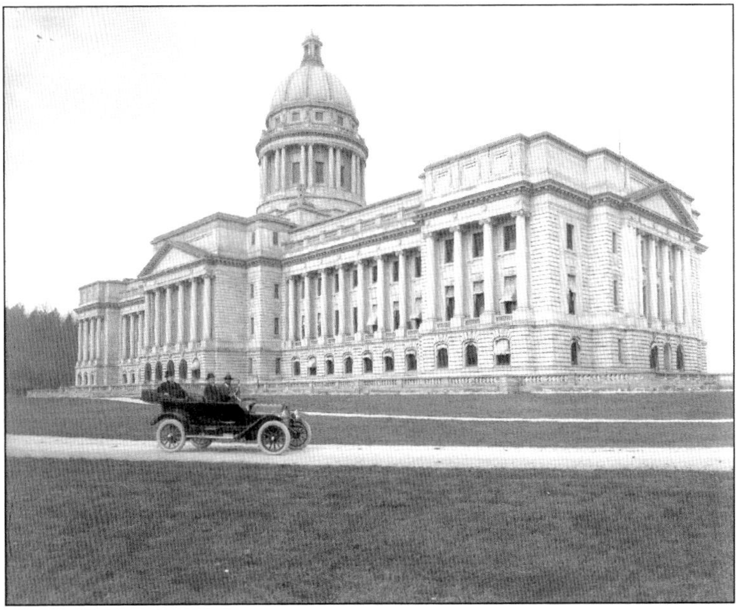

Governor Willson. This image of Governor Willson from the south side of the capitol appears to have been taken the same day as the previous image, which was used for a postcard. (Courtesy of Division of Historic Properties.)

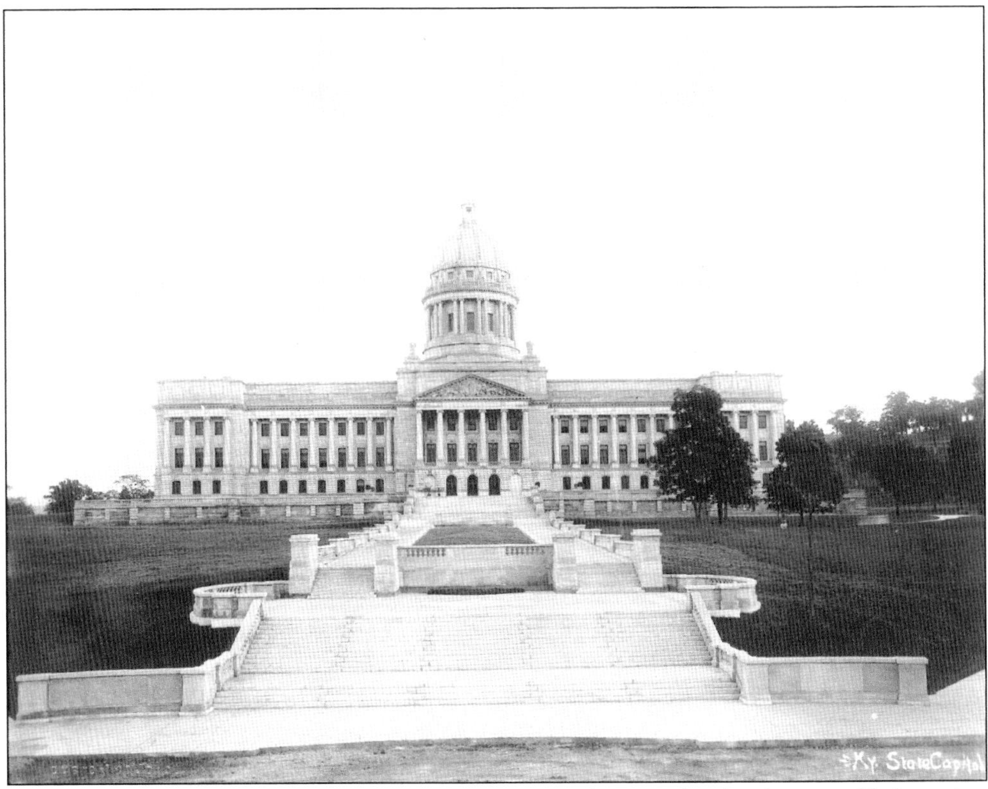

No Exterior lights. This image can be dated to just after 1910 by the absence of lights other than some rudimentary temporary streetlights on the exterior of the capitol. The bronze light standards that would later grace the promenade were not yet installed. This photograph notes on the back that more than 50,000 tourists visited the previous year. Today nearly 100,000 people visit the Kentucky State Capitol annually.

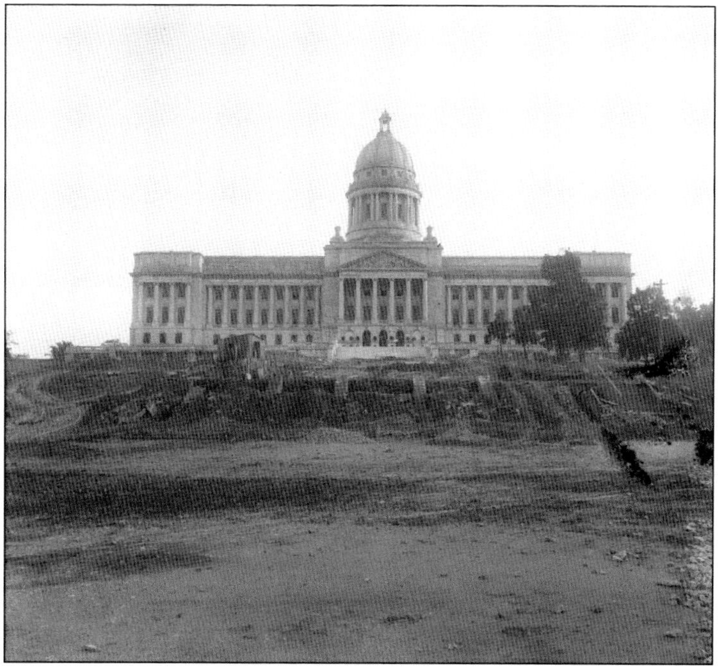

FRONT VIEW OF THE CAPITOL. This historic photograph shows the bareness of the capitol grounds after the building and terrace were completed. The image, from approximately 1909, shows potted plants on the terrace, promenade, and grounds, which are still incomplete. It appears from the new capitol commission's minutes in 1908 that discussions with Olmsted Brothers after initial plans for the grounds were submitted did not move forward.

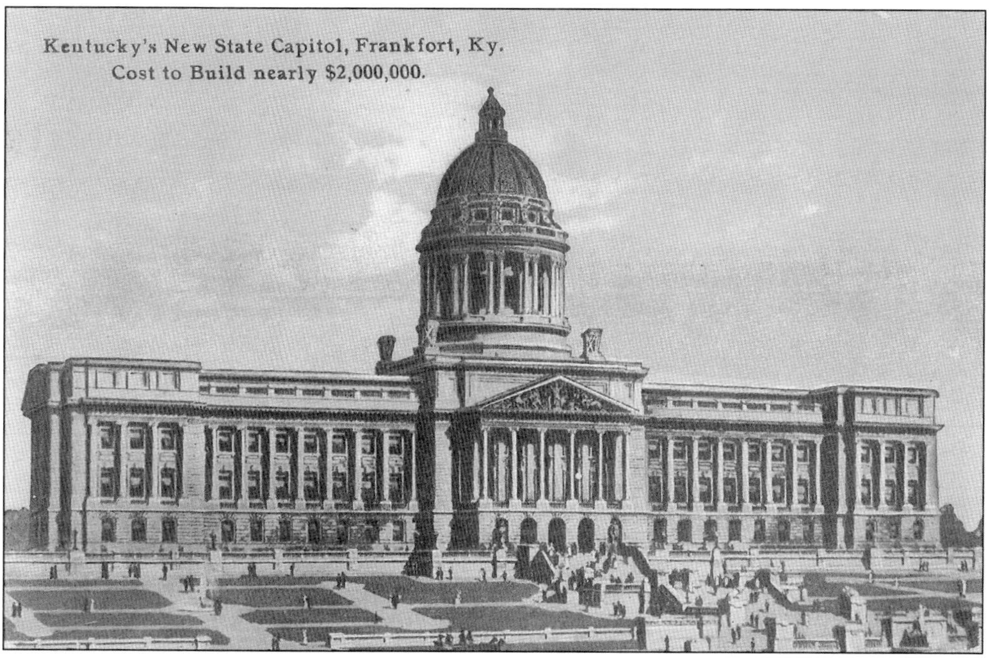

COST TO BUILD NEARLY $2 MILLION. This 1910 postcard boasts the final official costs reported for the new capitol, including $1,180,434.80 for the building; $63,793 for the grounds; $141,881 for furnishings, special decorative finishes, and mural paintings; $45,188 for office equipment; $90,000 for the power plant; $108,703.20 for heating, lighting, and electrical fixtures; and $190,000 for terraces and landscaping. The grand total was just over $1.8 million. (Courtesy collection of Scot Walters.)

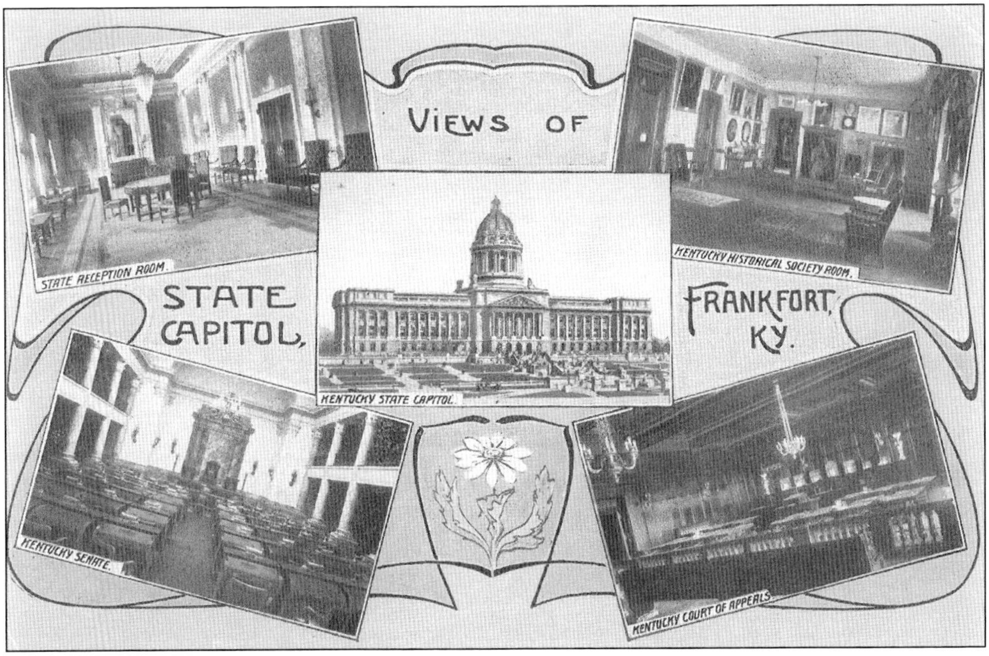

VIEWS OF THE STATE CAPITOL IN FRANKFORT, KENTUCKY. This early-1900s postcard showcases four of the impressive spaces in the interior of the Kentucky State Capitol. The views are of the state reception room, Kentucky Historical Society's hall of fame rooms, senate chambers, and the court of appeals chamber. (Courtesy collection of Scot Walters.)

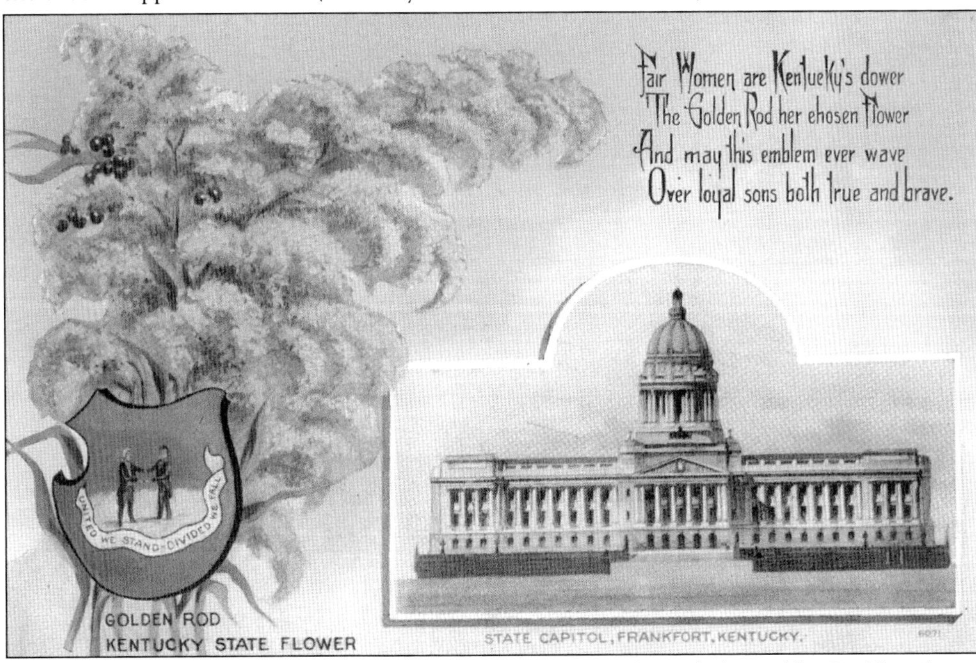

GOLDENROD: THE STATE FLOWER. "Fair women are Kentucky's dower / The Golden Rod her chosen flower / And may this emblem ever wave / Over loyal sons both true and brave." A beautifully illustrated early 1900s postcard is represented in this image with the original commonwealth seal and motto. (Courtesy collection of Scot Walters.)

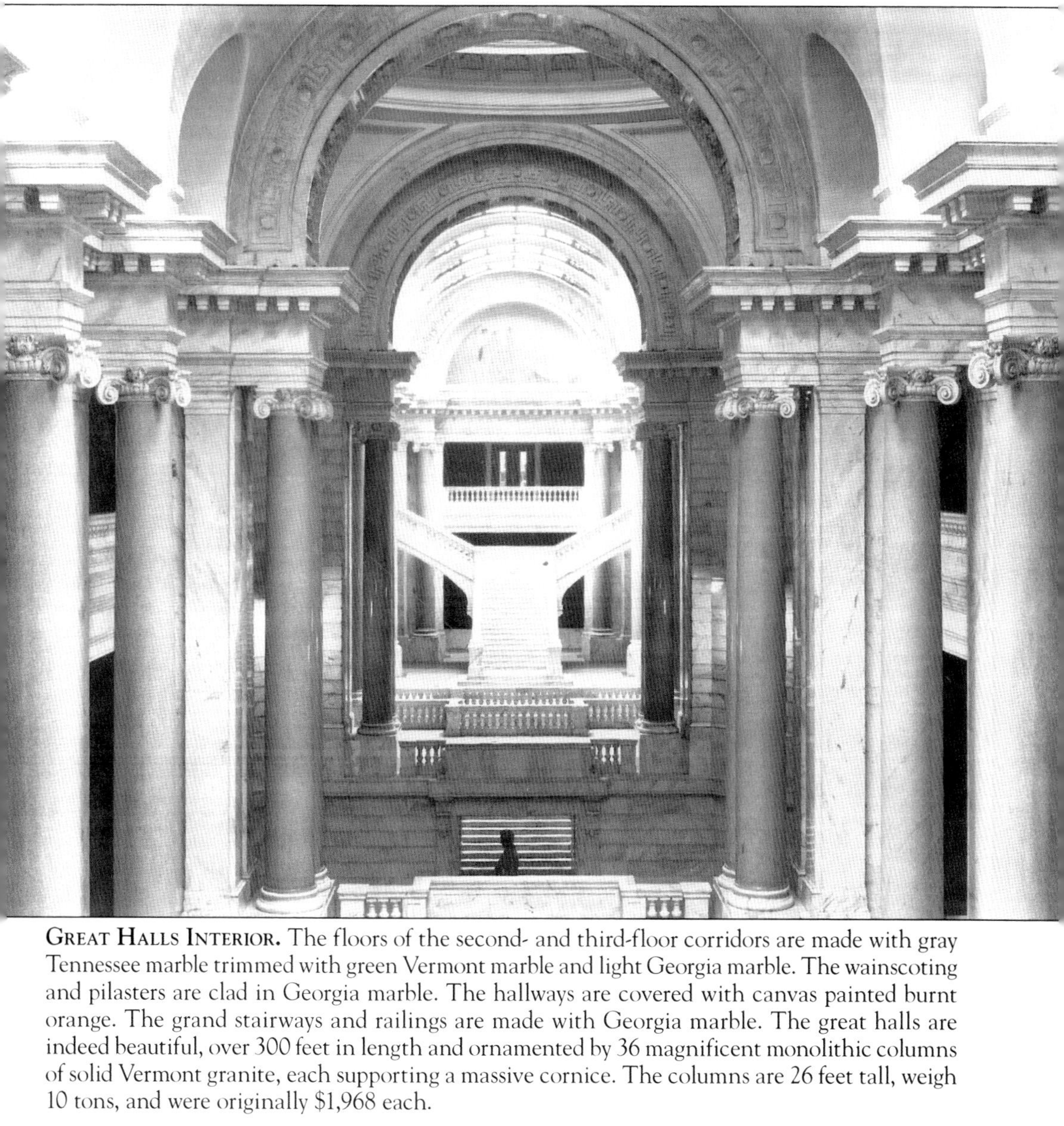

GREAT HALLS INTERIOR. The floors of the second- and third-floor corridors are made with gray Tennessee marble trimmed with green Vermont marble and light Georgia marble. The wainscoting and pilasters are clad in Georgia marble. The hallways are covered with canvas painted burnt orange. The grand stairways and railings are made with Georgia marble. The great halls are indeed beautiful, over 300 feet in length and ornamented by 36 magnificent monolithic columns of solid Vermont granite, each supporting a massive cornice. The columns are 26 feet tall, weigh 10 tons, and were originally $1,968 each.

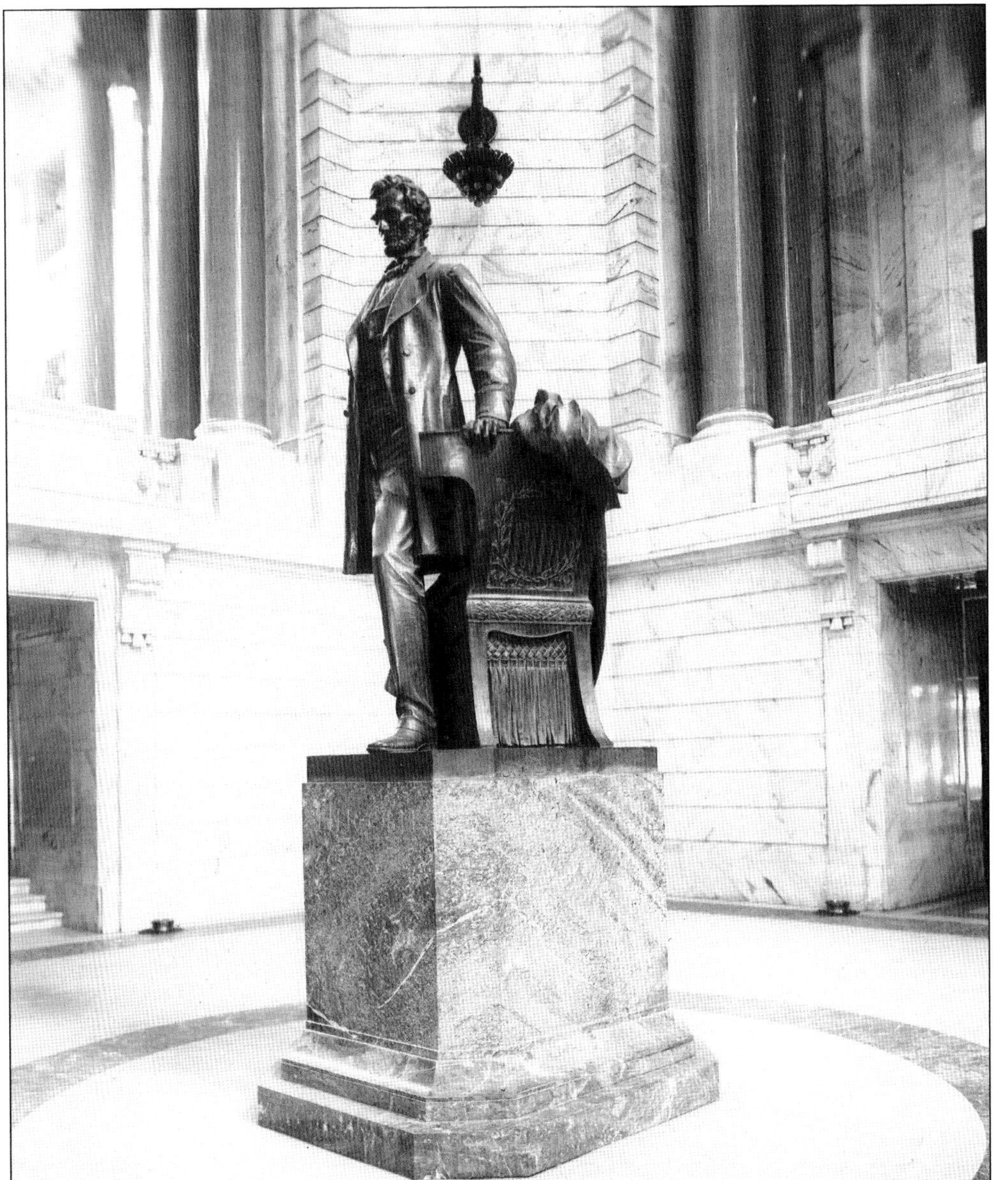

ABRAHAM LINCOLN STATUE. In May 1910, Governor Willson wrote a letter to J. B. Speed of Louisville and suggested that it would be appropriate for Speed to provide the funding for commissioning an imposing statue of Lincoln for the capitol's rotunda. The commonwealth was still seeking an ornament for the newly completed capitol, and Willson wrote that a temporarily placed bust of Abraham Lincoln in the rotunda was not appropriate for the scale of the grand building. Speed agreed to the challenge, and Adolph Alexander Weinman, who was also the sculptor of the Hodgenville Lincoln statue, was commissioned for the statue. The impressive bronze statue was cast in New York City and placed on a striking green serpentine marble base quarried in Pennsylvania, bringing it to a height of nearly 15 feet. Pres. William H. Taft was present for the unveiling on November 9, 1911.

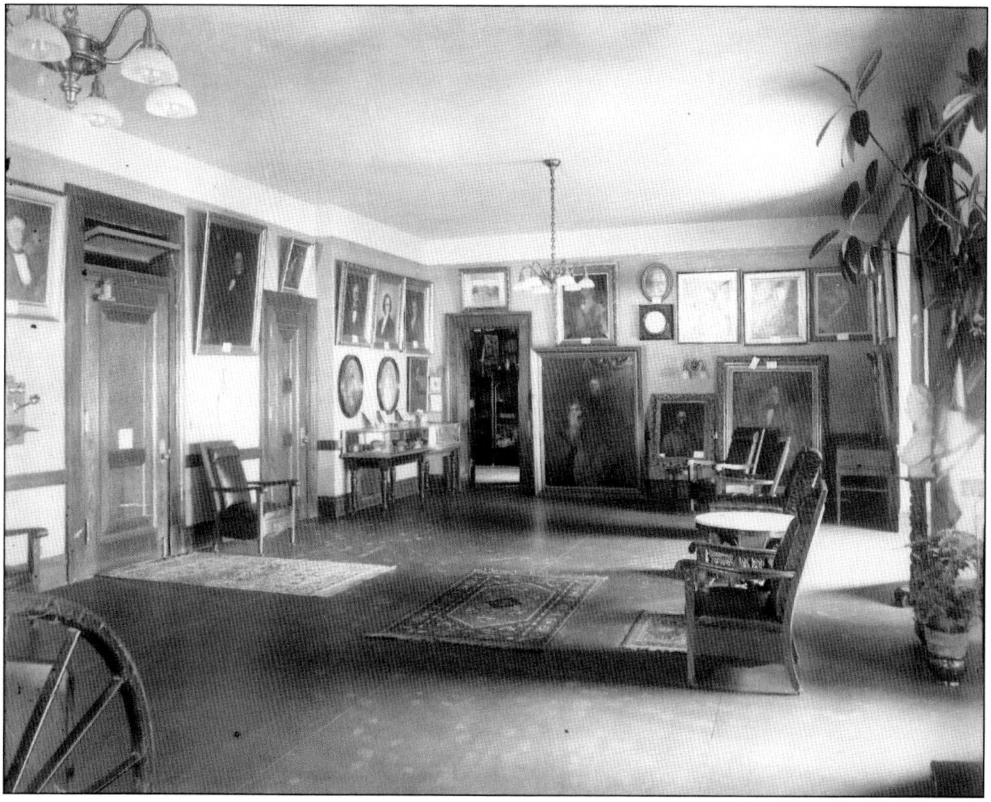

Hall of Fame. The Kentucky Historical Society moved into two rooms in the new capitol, which were called the hall of fame rooms. This photograph, taken around 1910–1912, pictures the main room from the east side. The image shows a curious feature as well as portraits of former governors and artifacts—footprints are visible on the painted concrete floors.

Commonwealth Artifacts. This second image of the hall of fame or historical society room from around 1910–1912 shows more governors' portraits, a cannon or type of gun, paintings by Kentucky artists, and busts of prominent Kentuckians. These spaces are now the governor's office, which was moved from the second floor during Gov. Lawrence Wetherby's 1955 term.

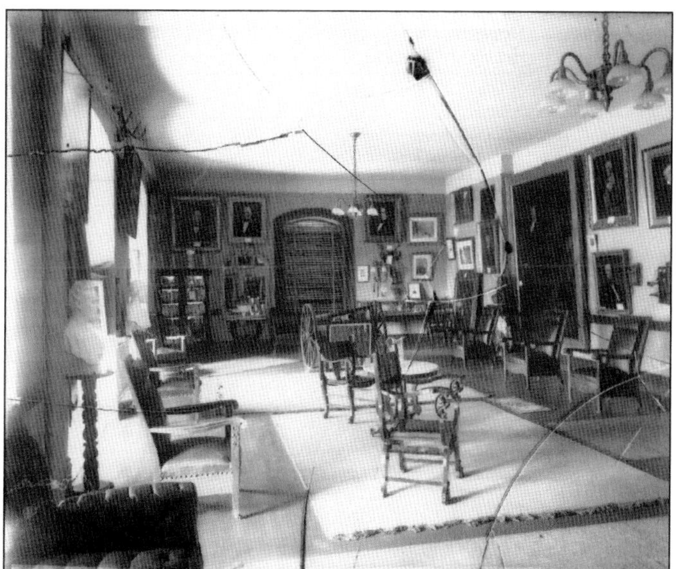

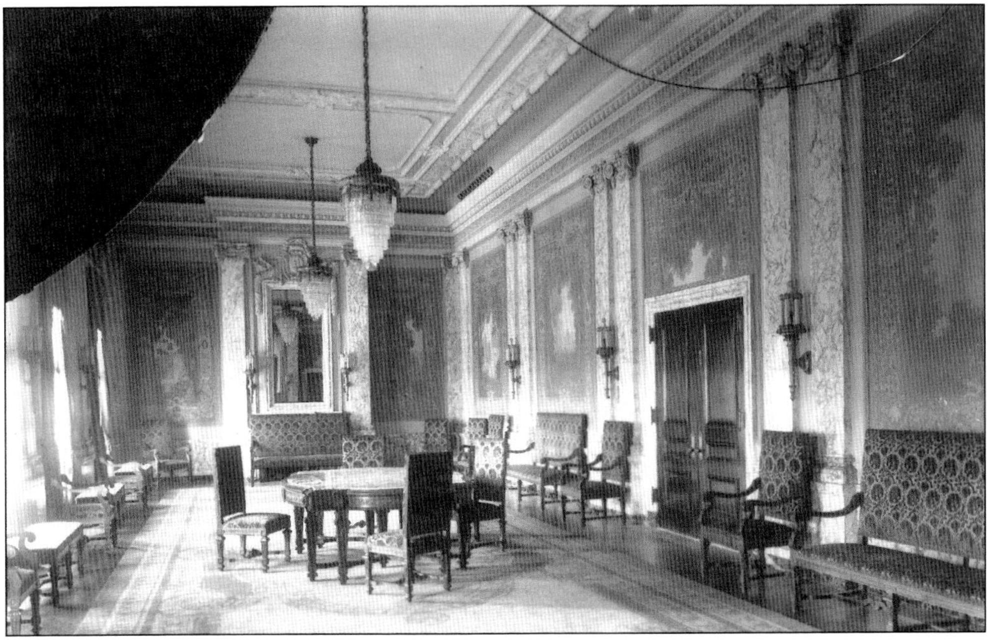

STATE RECEPTION ROOM IN 1910. Even though the corner of this original glass negative was damaged at some point, the image is very valuable. The photograph is a record that documents the original furnishings and decorative finishes for this room. Records indicate that $10,000 was spent to decorate and furnish this room in 1908—far more than any other room. The state reception room remains one of the most important spaces in the capitol today.

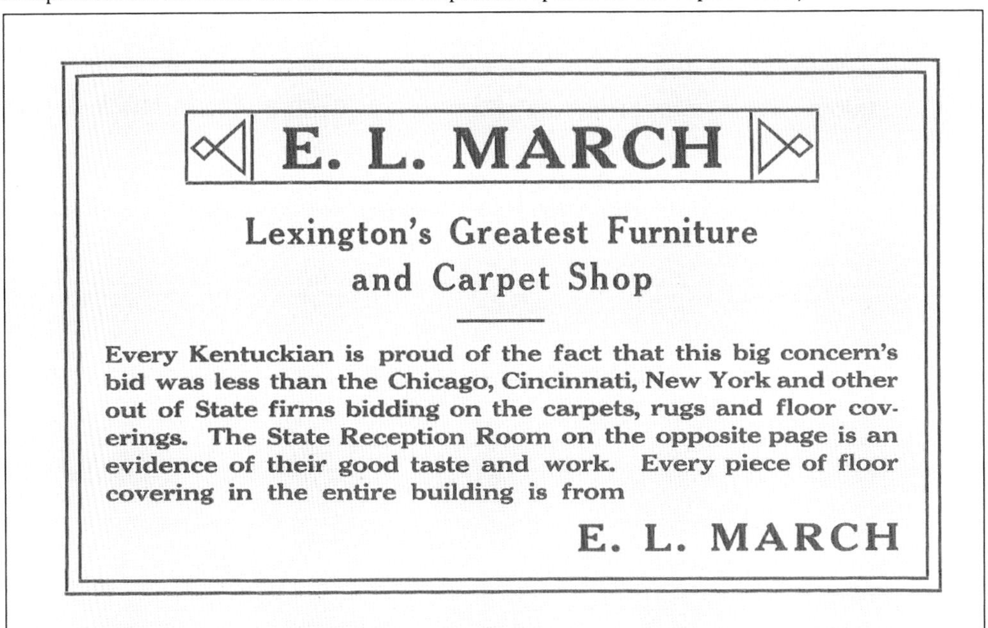

E. L. MARCH ADVERTISEMENT IN 1910. The rug mentioned in this advertisement for the state reception room required four months to make. The story is that the loom broke three times while making it. The rug is 54 feet by 16 feet and weighs nearly 1,200 pounds. The rug is currently in proper storage for future conservation considerations. (Courtesy of Division of Historic Properties.)

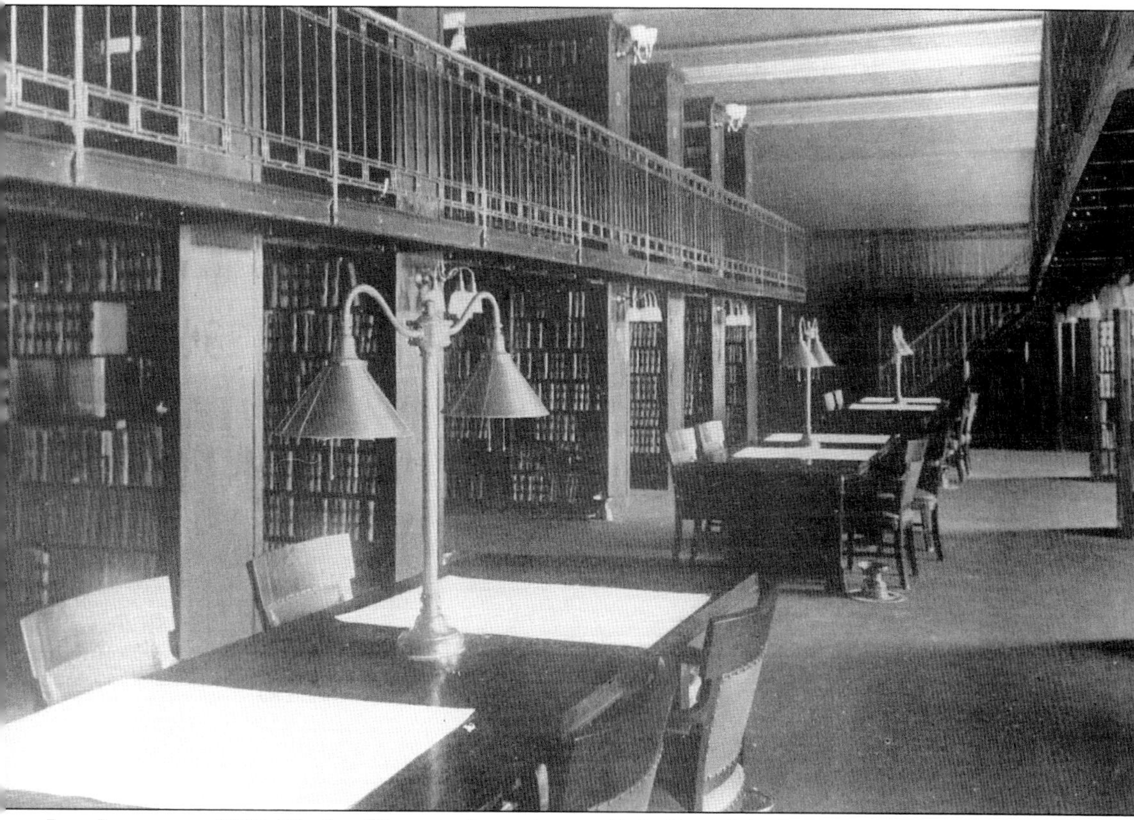

LAW LIBRARY IN 1910. The law library is shown here in 1910. One of the most interesting features of the library is the built-in bookshelves and catwalk system. The bookshelves were designed to be fireproof and are enameled to appear like fine mahogany. The photograph shows all of the original furnishings and fixtures, most of which were replicated in 2005.

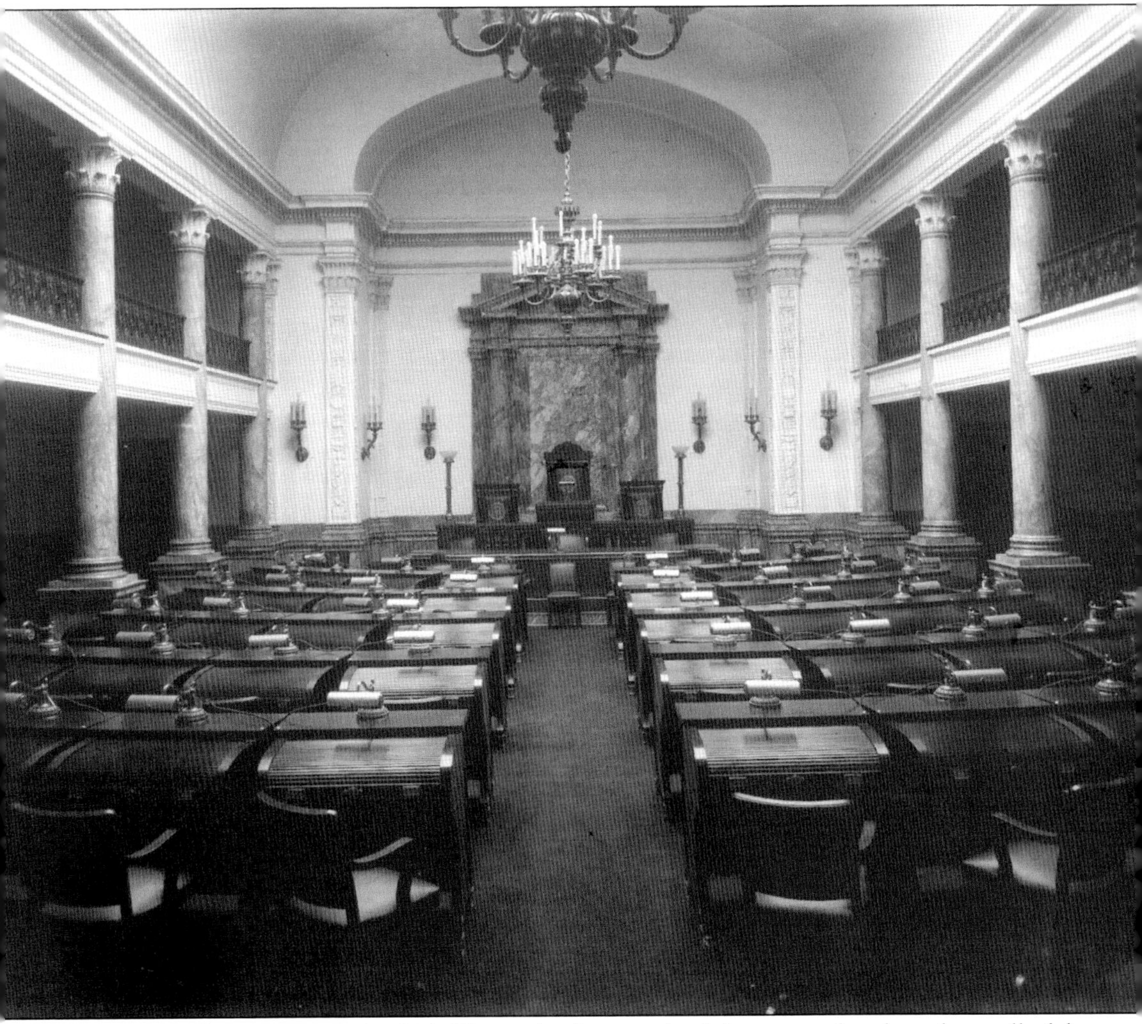

Senate Chambers, 1913–1914. This early photograph of the senate chambers shows all of the original furnishings, some of which are still in use. The two wonderful solid brass chandeliers were sadly removed in the 1960s. Photographs like this example are helpful in reproducing the original fixtures. The columns in the senate and the house chambers are made of scagliola, a popular faux marble decorative finish treatment in early-20th-century buildings. Scagliola is typically made by starting with canvas or burlap on a flat surface, and then plaster is applied to the surface of the material. Strands of silk or fine fabrics are then saturated in pigmented colors depending on the desired marble color. The strands are typically added in a crisscrossing, angled pattern. The strands are removed, and after plaster is formed to a mold, it is moved to be used as a column, wall, or other decorative element. The scagliola is finally sanded and smoothed to bring out the varied veins of color to imitate marble.

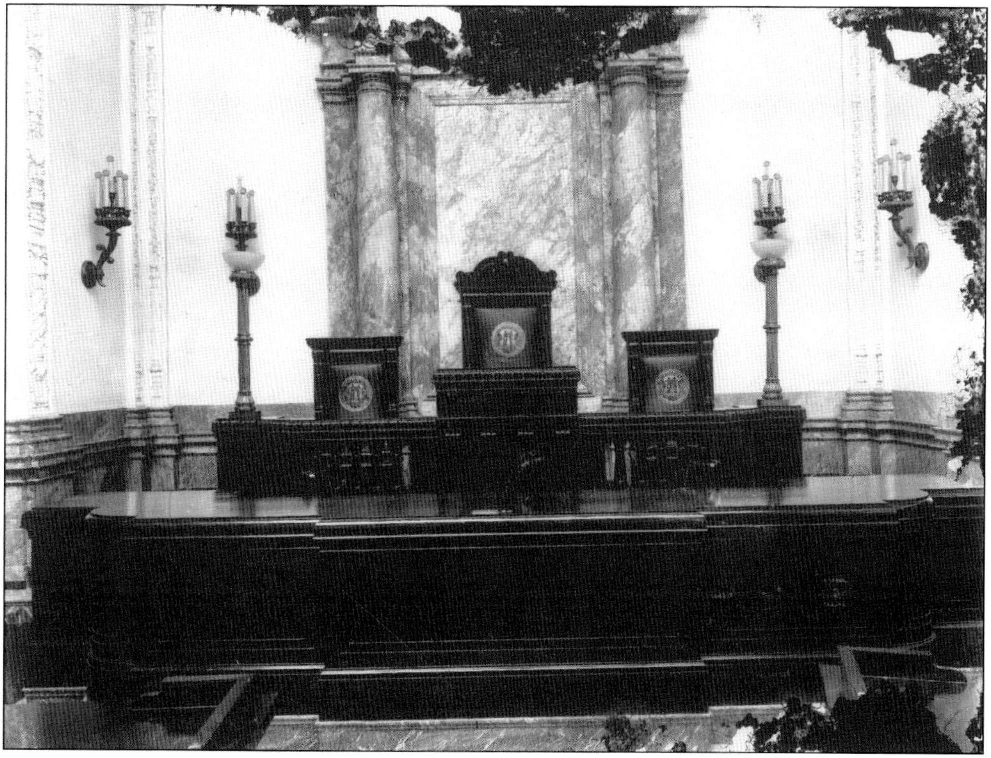

Senate Chamber Dais. This 1912 photograph of the senate chamber dais shows four original wall sconces and two light standards on the ends of the senate president's bench. The two light standards are not extant, while the four sconces are still in use today. The three large chairs behind the senate president's bench were made by Newton and Hart Furniture Company in 1908 and have been used for every senate president since 1910.

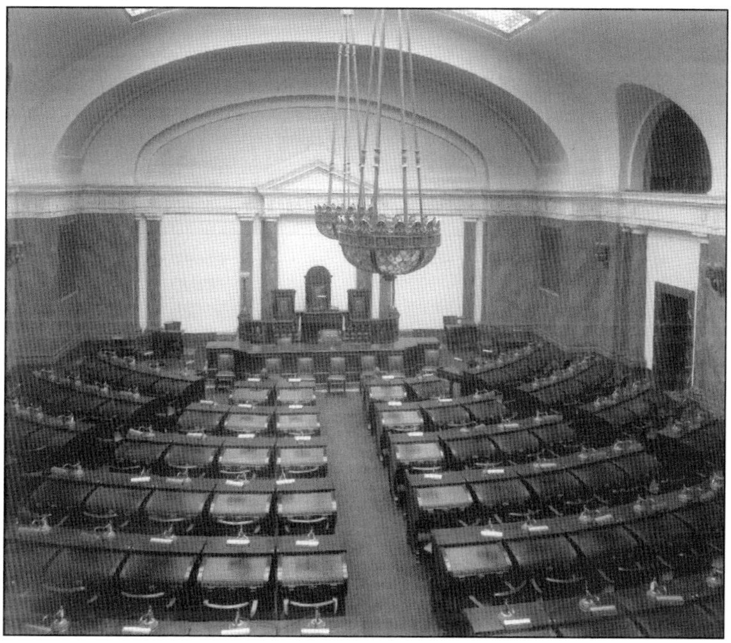

House of Representatives. The 1910 fixtures and furnishings are shown in this photograph. The need for better light and sound caused the pair of massive original ceiling pendants to be removed in the 1960s. Notice the continuity of the architectural design elements carried through the pendants to the decorative plaster below the cornice.

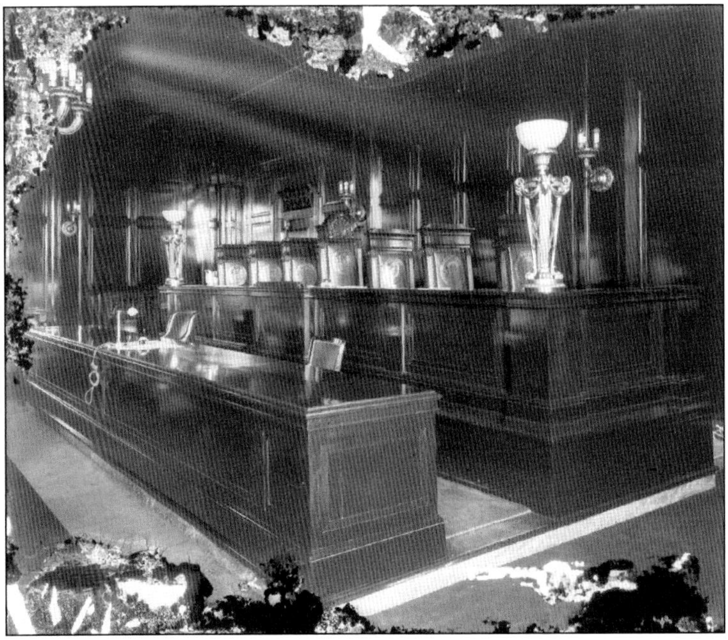

SUPREME COURT CHAMBERS. Originally the court of appeals chamber for the commonwealth, this space became the Kentucky Supreme Court chambers in the 1950s. Not shown in this 1912 image is the old Dutch hand-hammered metal ceiling. Another decorative finish treatment in the capitol, the plaster is lightly hammered and painted to imitate aged bronze.

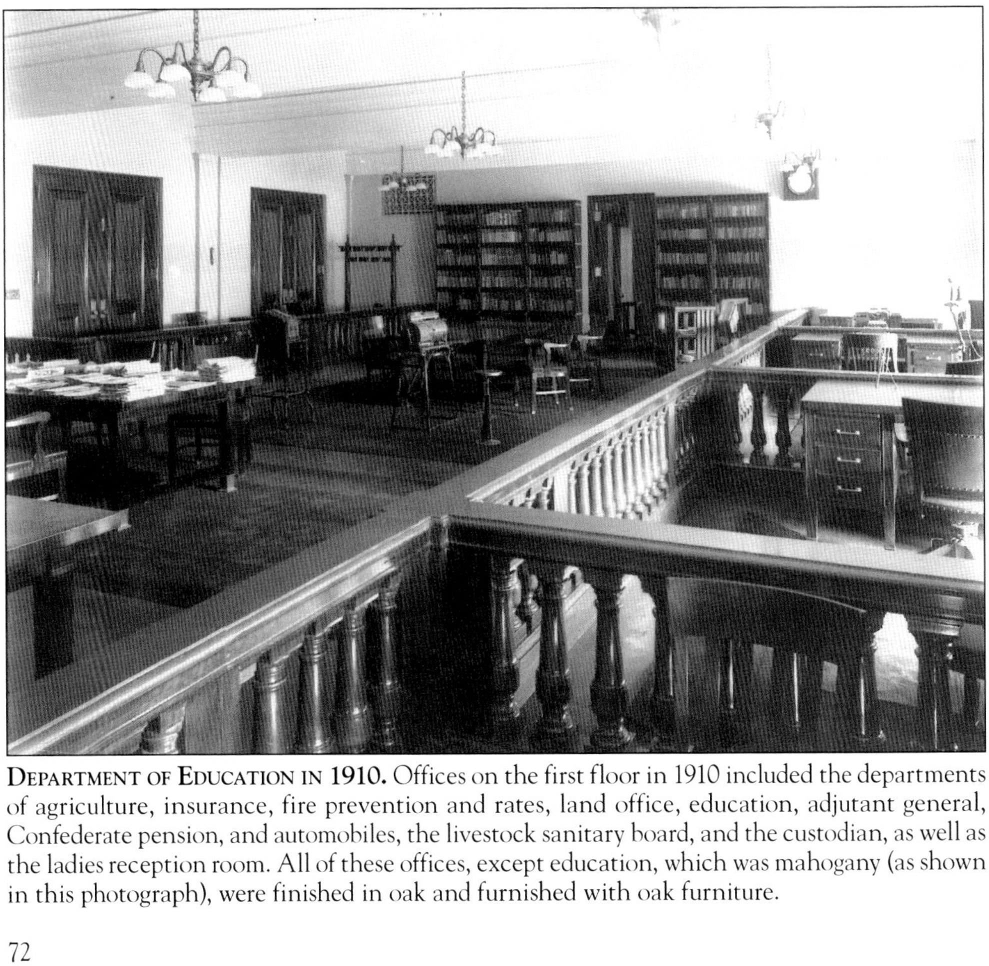

DEPARTMENT OF EDUCATION IN 1910. Offices on the first floor in 1910 included the departments of agriculture, insurance, fire prevention and rates, land office, education, adjutant general, Confederate pension, and automobiles, the livestock sanitary board, and the custodian, as well as the ladies reception room. All of these offices, except education, which was mahogany (as shown in this photograph), were finished in oak and furnished with oak furniture.

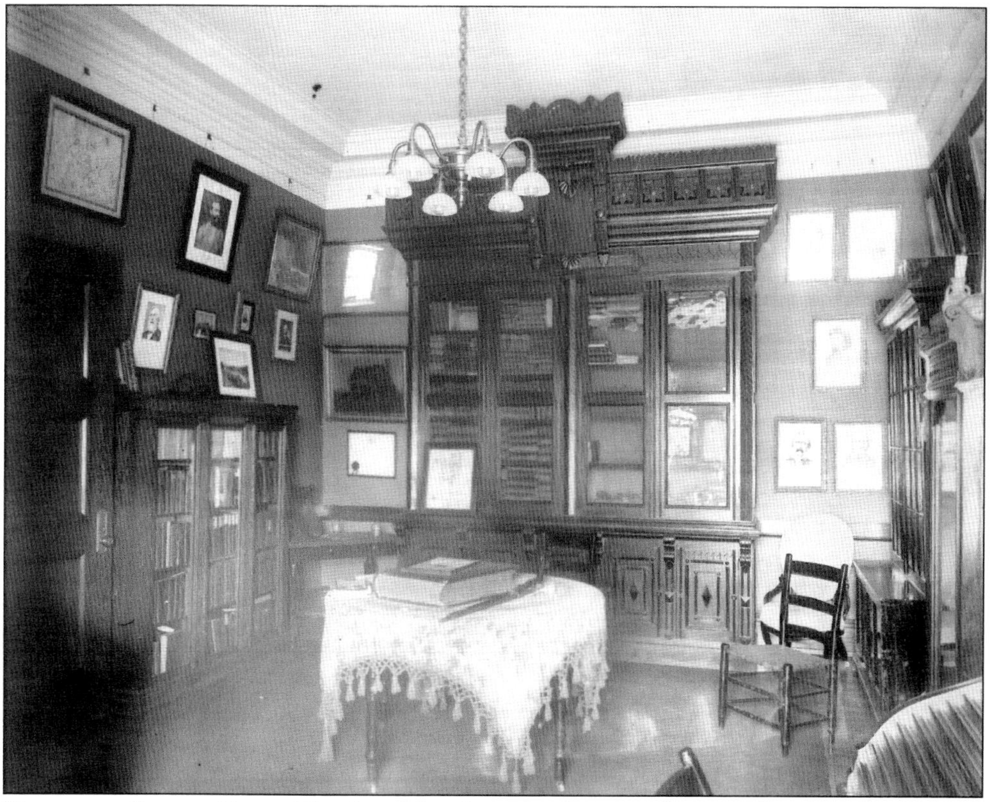

HISTORICAL SOCIETY ROOM. The chandelier shown in this 1910 photograph was one of the many original fixtures removed from the capitol in 1955. Several of the fixtures were used in the old governor's mansion until 2002. The massive bookcase was moved to the old capitol annex in 1955 also. The handsomely crafted piece now graces the lobby of the old capitol annex.

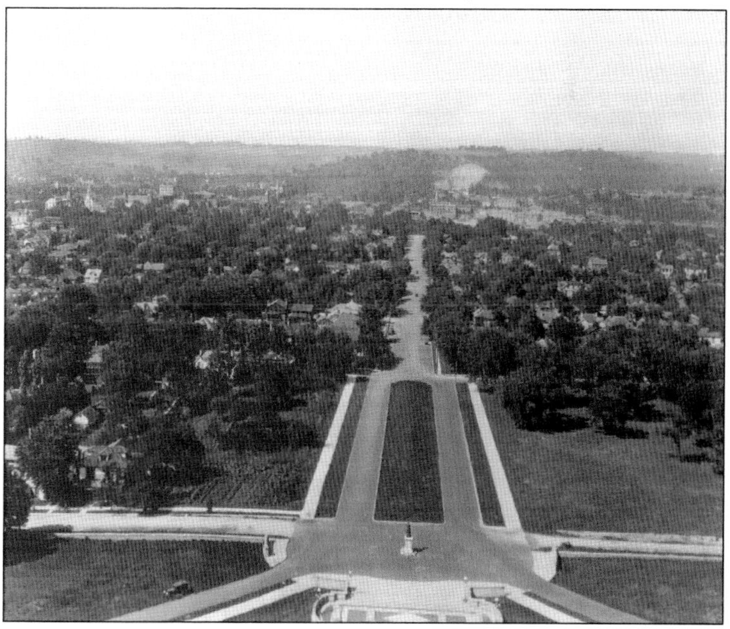

ROOM WITH A VIEW. This 1914–1915 photograph taken from the lantern in the top of the dome gives one a good idea of the view from this vantage point. In 1910, the climb to the top was reported as 78 spiral steps and a series of ladders resulting in a height too dizzying for most. (Courtesy of Division of Historic Properties.)

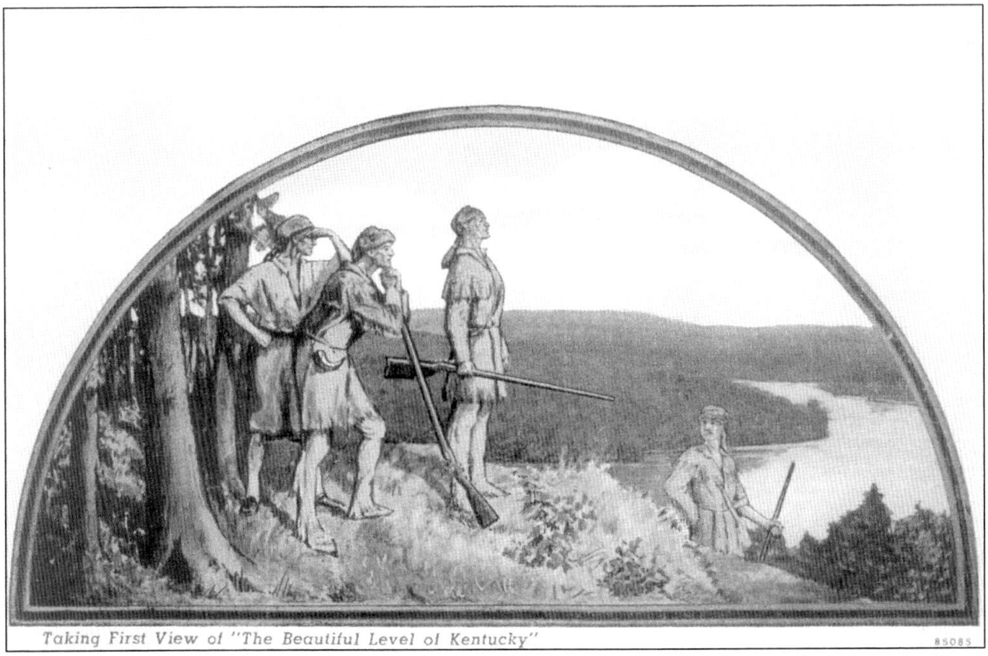

LUNETTE MURAL (EAST). This image of the east mural by T. Gilbert White in the Kentucky State Capitol is often contradicted. The setting is said to be Daniel Boone's first view of Kentucky from the Ohio River. However, people from Frankfort and others are partial to the claim that Boone is overlooking Frankfort from approximately his gravesite in the cemetery. (Courtesy collection of Scot Walters.)

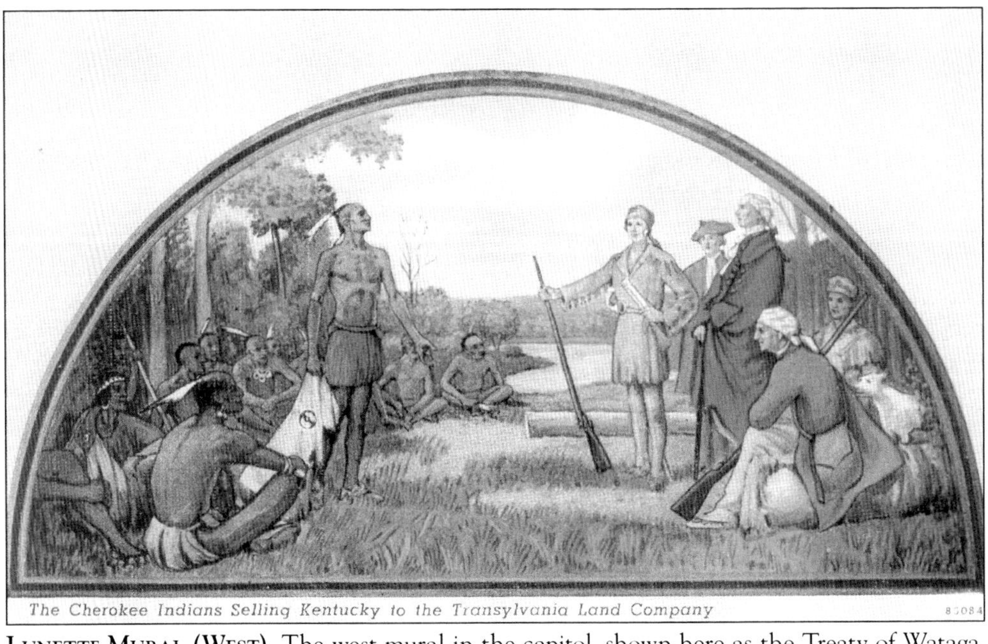

LUNETTE MURAL (WEST). The west mural in the capitol, shown here as the Treaty of Wataga, is purported to be the scene of the land transfer of Kentucky from the Cherokee Indians to the Transylvania Land Company. (Courtesy collection of Scot Walters.)

Six

ETERNAL LANDMARKS FOR FRANKFORT

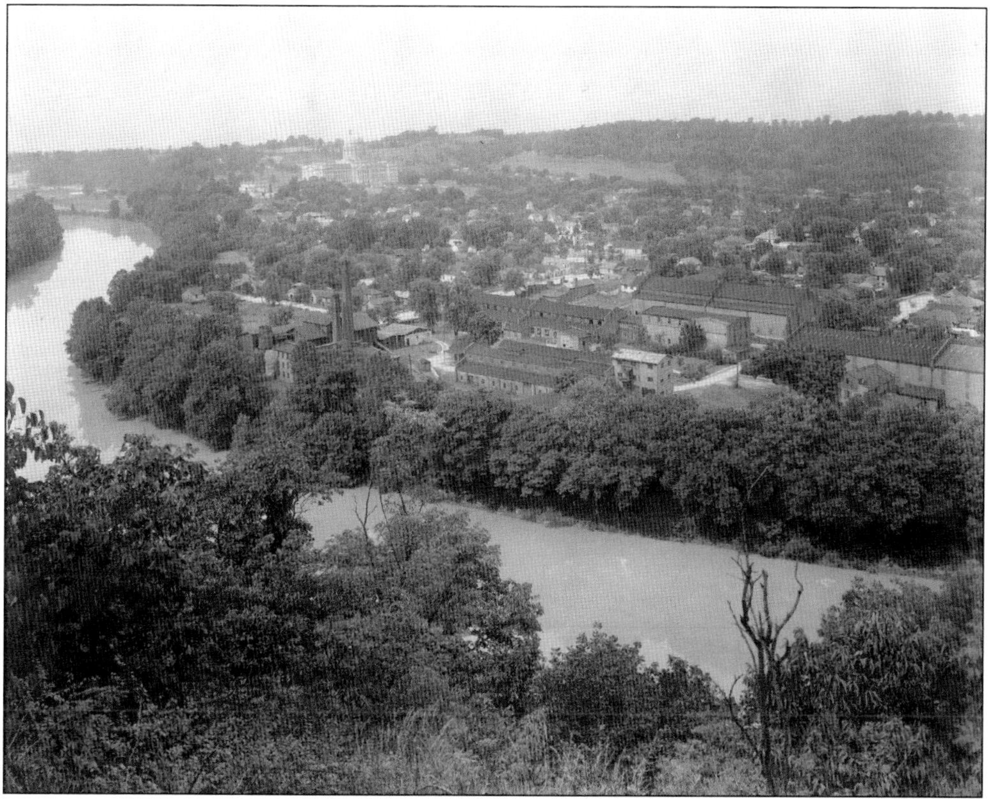

MARRIAGE OF THE LANDSCAPE AND BUILDING. This photograph, taken from the Frankfort Cemetery during the summer season after 1914, shows the Kentucky State Capitol beautifully blending into South Frankfort's landscape. The photograph also highlights one of the many distilleries along the Kentucky River, which later closed during Prohibition. Although the capitol building was a wonderful addition to Frankfort, as early as 1922 it was reported that the lack of foresight in anticipating future needs was a problem for the capitol building. Space was reported to be limited, offices were divided, and several state departments were moved back to the old capitol and annex across the river.

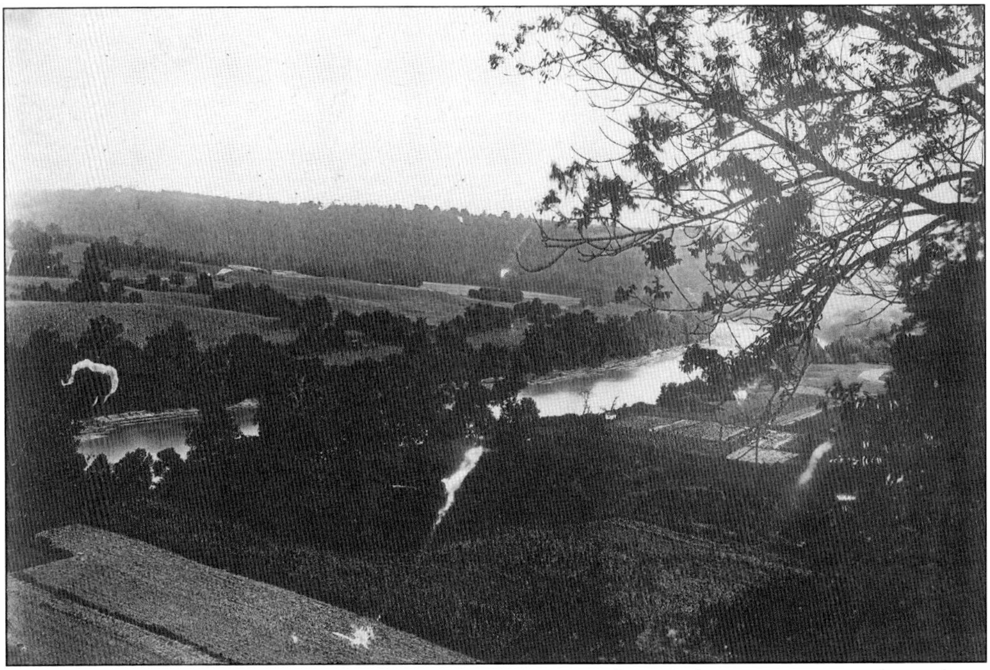

South Frankfort, 1890–1900. The previous photograph and the next image indicate how much South Frankfort grew from 1900 to 1920. This photograph, from before 1905, shows the Hunt property and surrounding landscape. (Courtesy of Division of Historic Properties.)

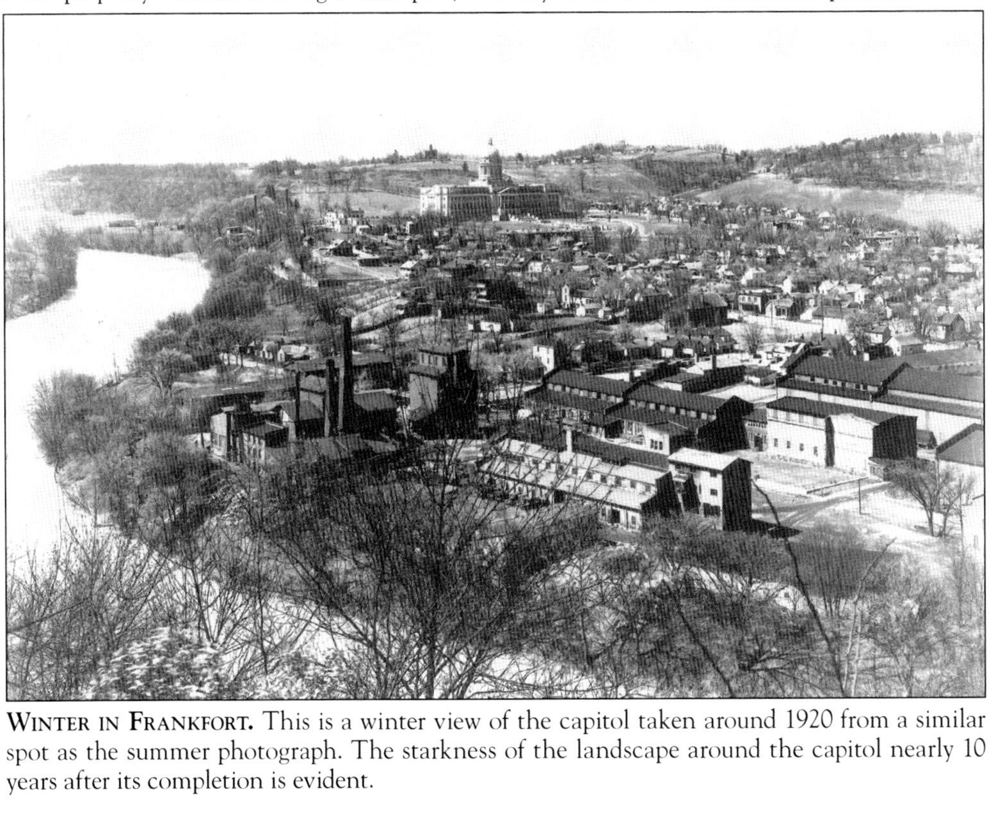

Winter in Frankfort. This is a winter view of the capitol taken around 1920 from a similar spot as the summer photograph. The starkness of the landscape around the capitol nearly 10 years after its completion is evident.

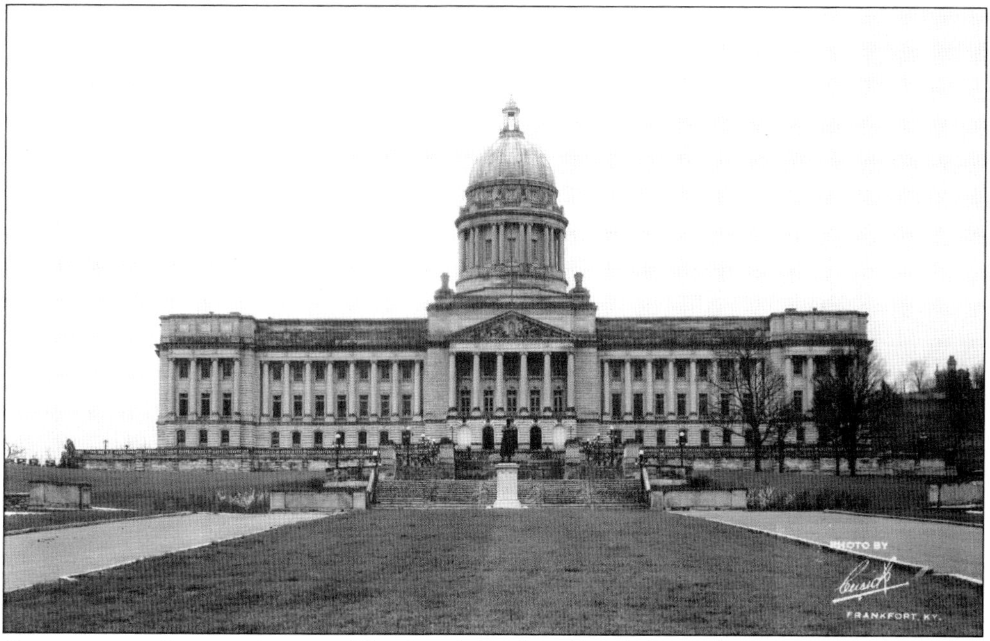

Capitol from Capital Avenue. The Cusick Studio of Frankfort took this iconic image of the new capitol after its completion around 1915. The exterior lights, minimal landscaping, and paved roads are present in the photograph.

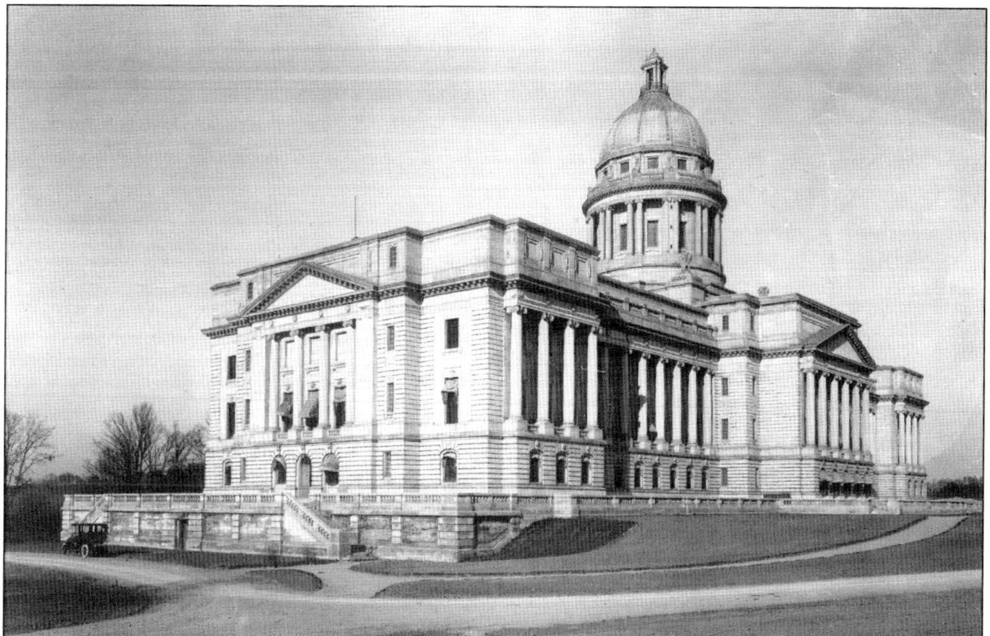

Where Does the Model T Park? This is a southwest view of capitol again by Cusick Studio around 1915. The car in the lower left corner of the photograph is a good visual of a glaring omission from the plans for the capitol grounds—parking spaces. Neither Olmsted Brothers' plan or architect Andrews's plan had included consideration for the horseless carriage. Popular opinion at the time viewed the automobile as a fad.

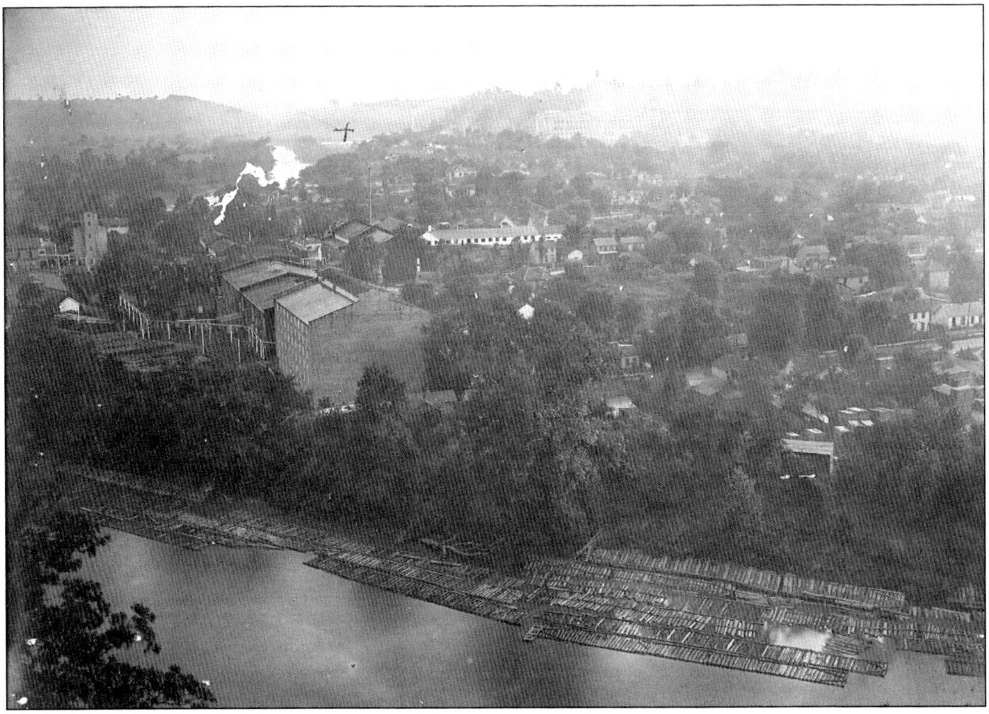

Cemetery Hill around 1912. This photograph predates the executive mansion's construction; however, it was at about the time discussions began on moving the aging and dilapidated executive residence across the river near the capitol. Gov. James McCreary indicated he was tired of traveling across the river to work in the new capitol building. (Courtesy of Division of Historic Properties.)

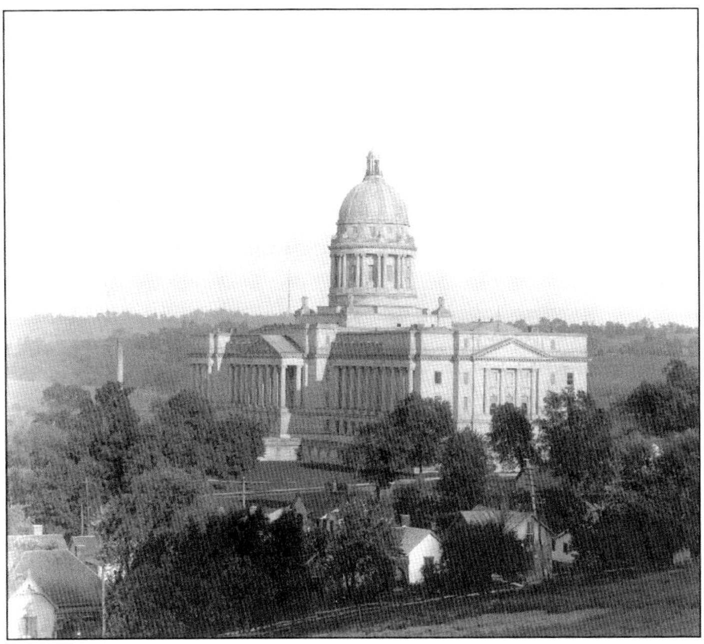

Old Louisville Pike around 1912. This view of the capitol showcases a feature on the great dome that was left off in a 1941 reconstruction. The original dome, as shown in this photograph, had decorative details traversing the 10 sections of the dome's terra-cotta tiles. In the reconstruction, it appears that the decorative element was omitted. (Courtesy of Division of Historic Properties.)

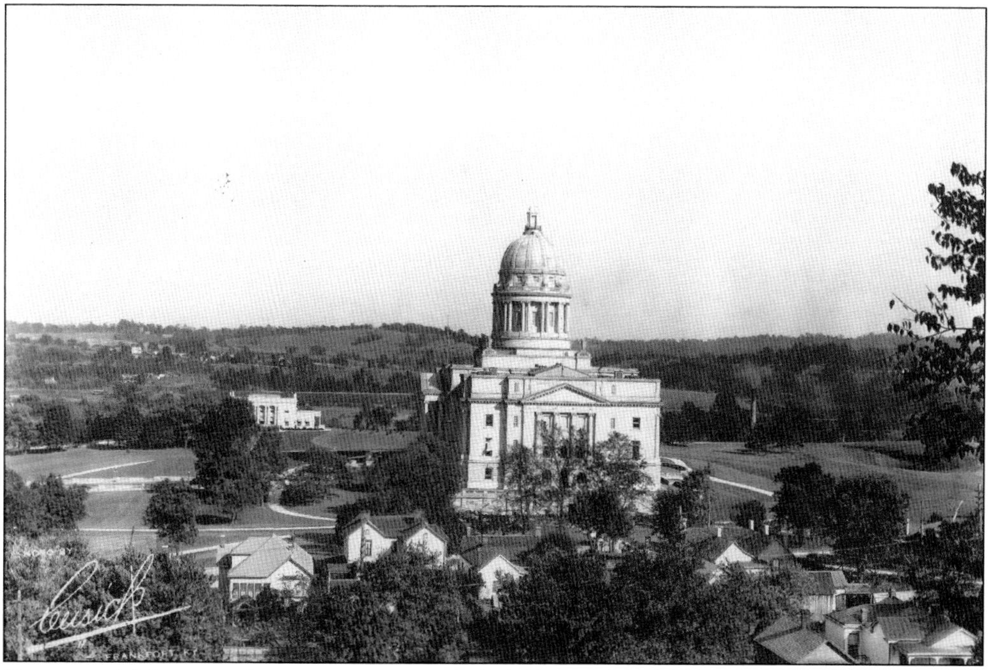

Governor's Mansion Complete around 1915. At a cost of under $93,000 for land and building, the governor's mansion finally joined the capitol building on the campus. With the completion of the mansion, the 44-acre site became one of the most picturesque capital cities in America.

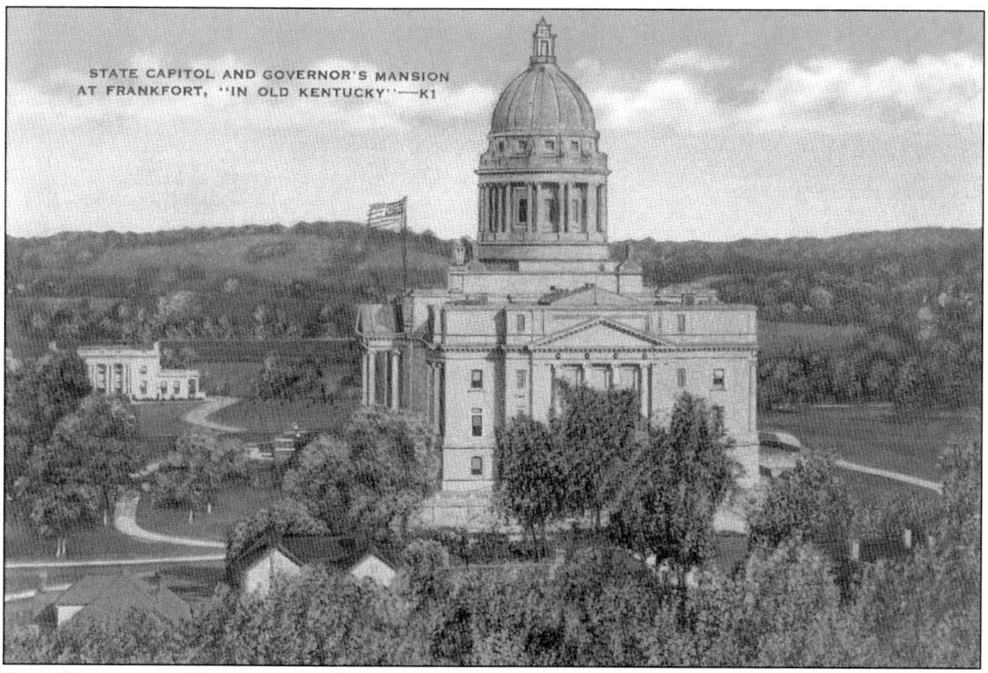

Old Kentucky. This postcard from around 1915–1920 shows both the completed governor's mansion and the new state capitol. The title "In Old Kentucky" probably refers to "My Old Kentucky Home." It is not known what K1 is in reference to. (Courtesy collection of Scot Walters.)

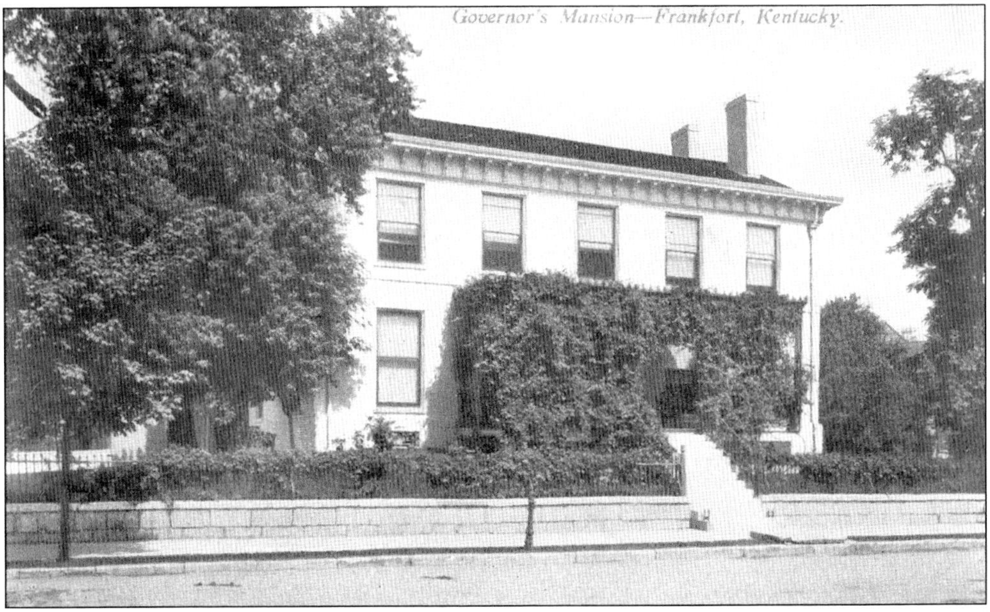

OLD GOVERNOR'S MANSION, 1915–1920. The old governor's mansion was virtually abandoned after Governor McCreary moved out in 1914. It is easy to understand the governor's reasons for wanting to build a new mansion for the commonwealth. Nearly 4,000 of the state's most hardened criminals were just across High Street at the state penitentiary. (Courtesy collection of Scot Walters.)

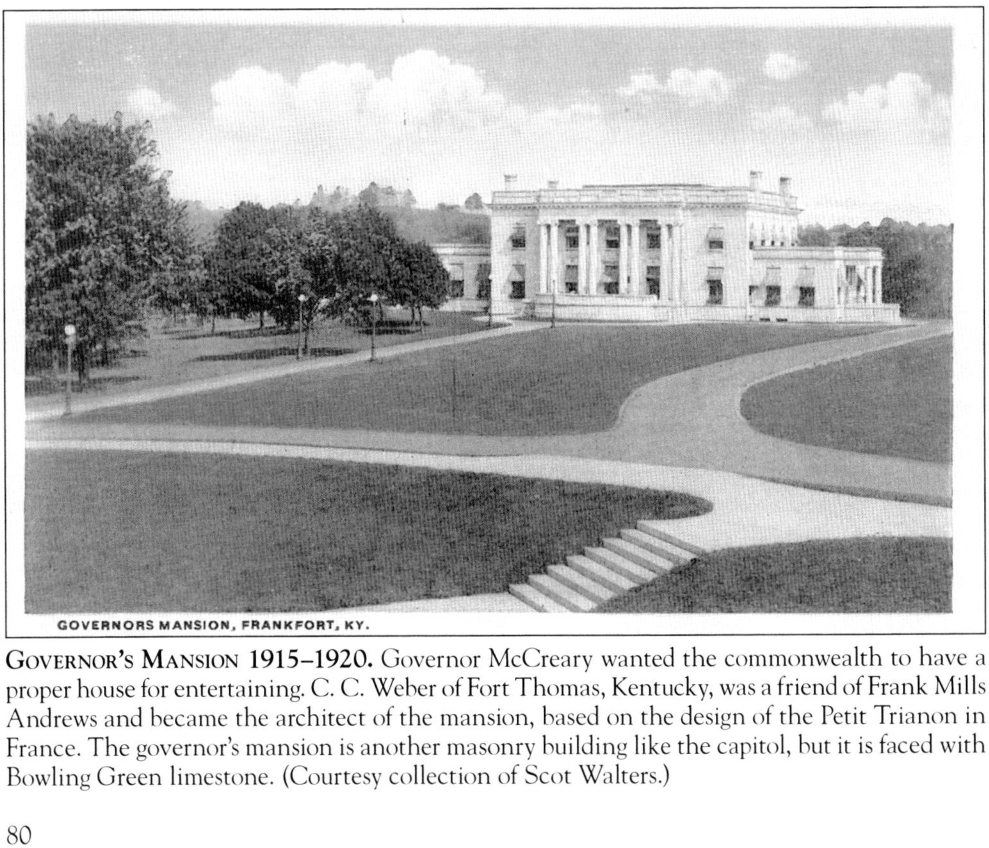

GOVERNOR'S MANSION 1915–1920. Governor McCreary wanted the commonwealth to have a proper house for entertaining. C. C. Weber of Fort Thomas, Kentucky, was a friend of Frank Mills Andrews and became the architect of the mansion, based on the design of the Petit Trianon in France. The governor's mansion is another masonry building like the capitol, but it is faced with Bowling Green limestone. (Courtesy collection of Scot Walters.)

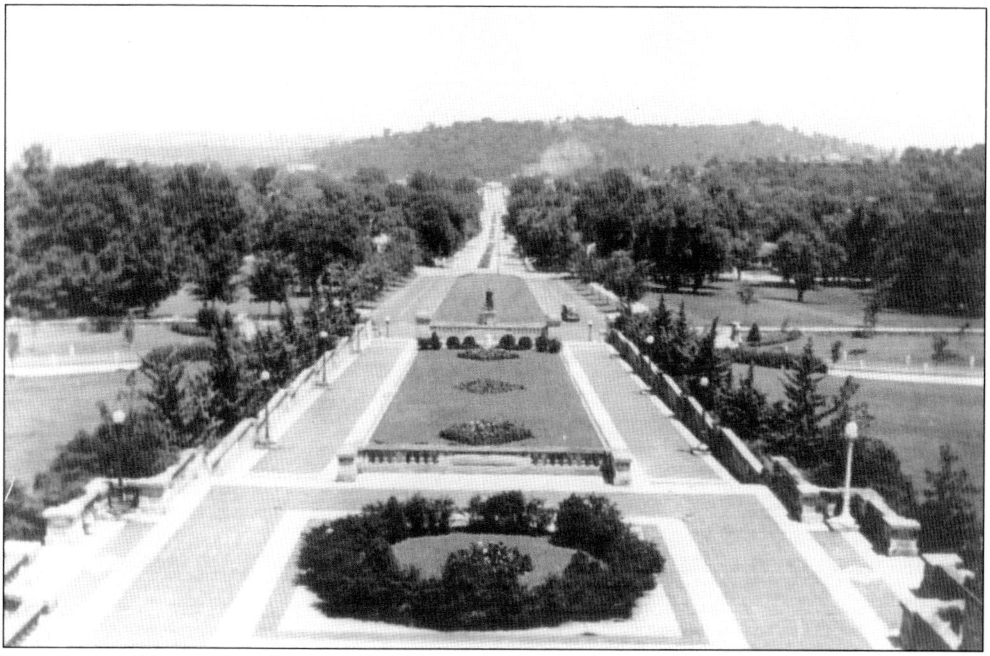

PROMENADE VIEW. This photograph, taken on September 1, 1939, presumably from the state reception room balcony, shows the impressive terraced promenade leading to two-lane Capital Avenue. By this time, the Capital Avenue bridge was complete, bringing even greater accessibility to South Frankfort and the capitol campus.

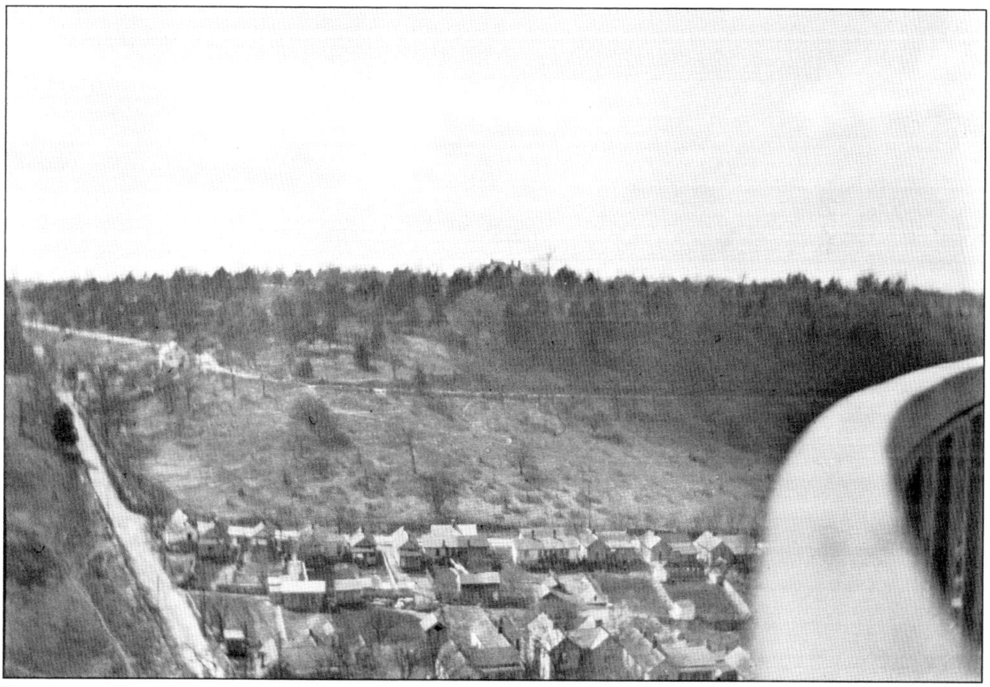

LANTERN VIEW NORTH. This series of photographs taken around 1910 from the new capitol's lantern shows the panoramic view from over 200 feet above the capitol grounds. The first image was taken looking directly north towards downtown Frankfort.

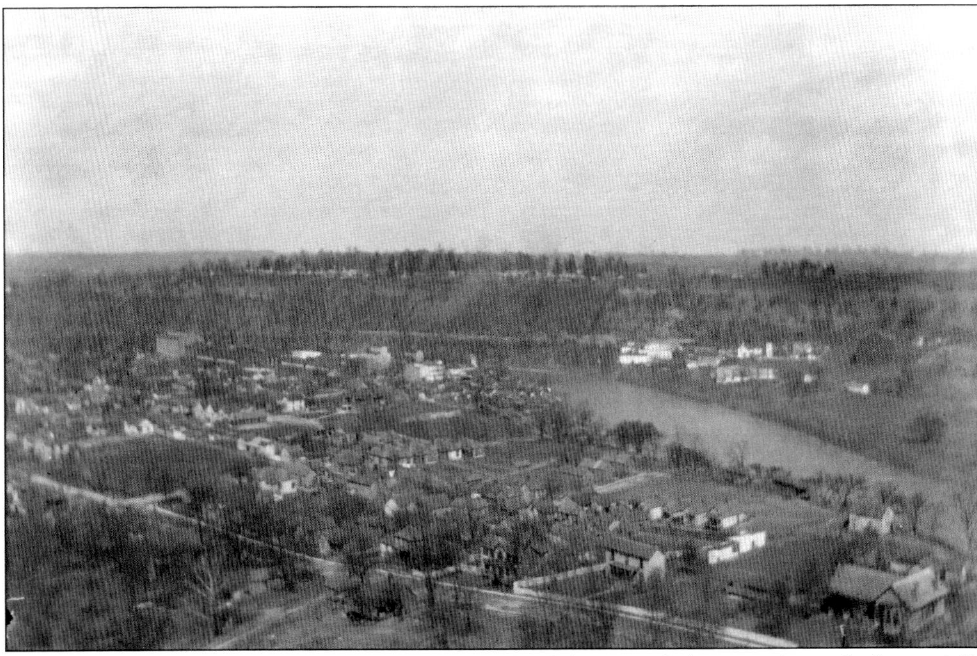

LANTERN VIEW WEST. The view from the west side of the capitol's lantern shows the beautifully laid out grounds, which were designed by the Olmsted Brothers landscape architecture firm. The rail of the lantern is visible in this historic 1910 photograph.

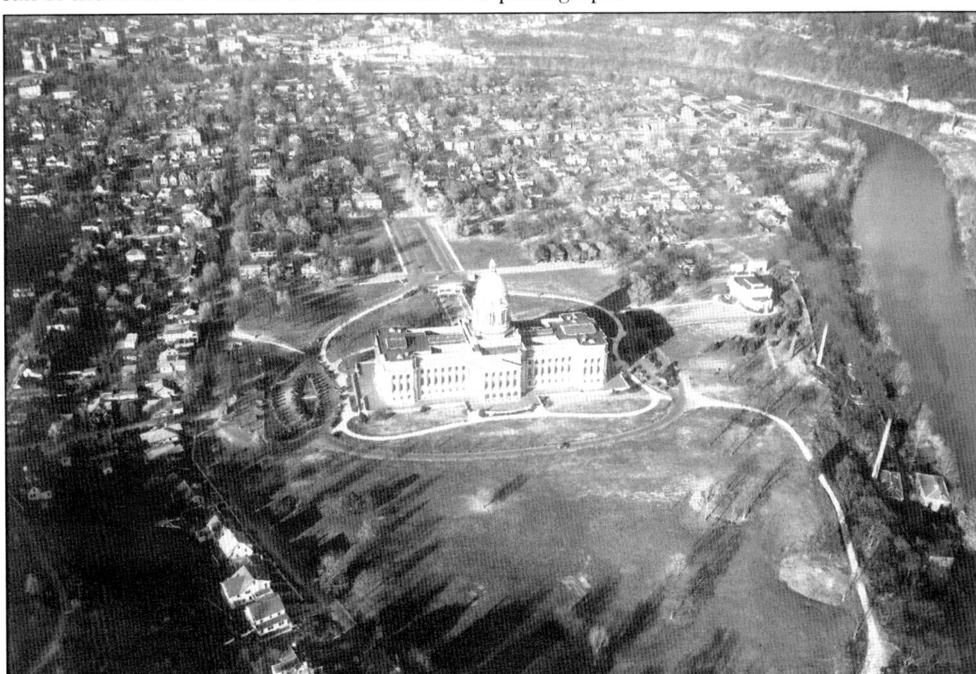

AERIAL SHOT, 1914–1925. This aerial photograph of the capitol grounds and governor's mansion looking north towards downtown Frankfort effectively illustrates the harmony of the capitol campus and the Kentucky River. The image also shows the parking problem at the capitol beginning to be solved, at least temporarily, by spaces on both ends of the building.

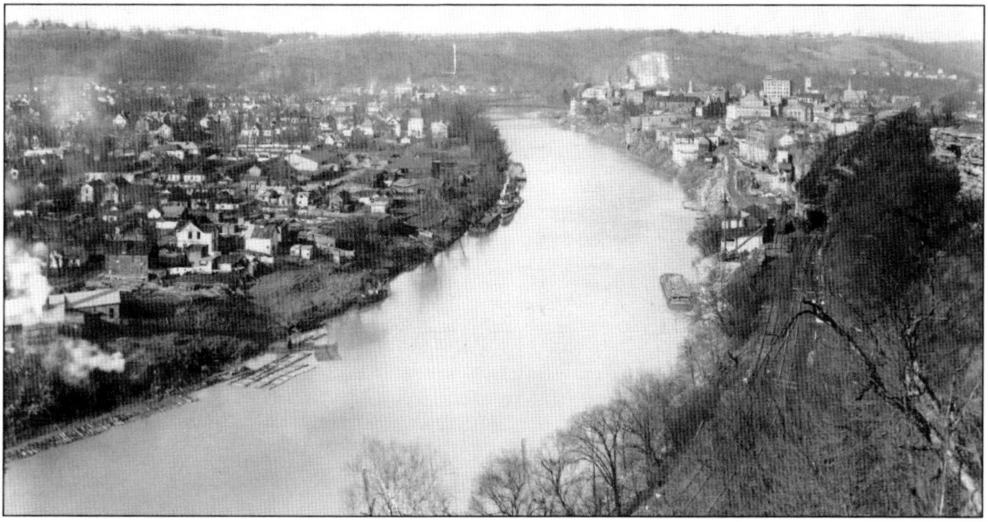

Kentucky River around 1927. The river is shown in this photograph taken by a well-known local photographer, H. A. Gretter, as it winds its way through Frankfort. The capitol building is not visible to the left of the image. In 1931, the Capital Avenue bridge would connect this part of South Frankfort to downtown.

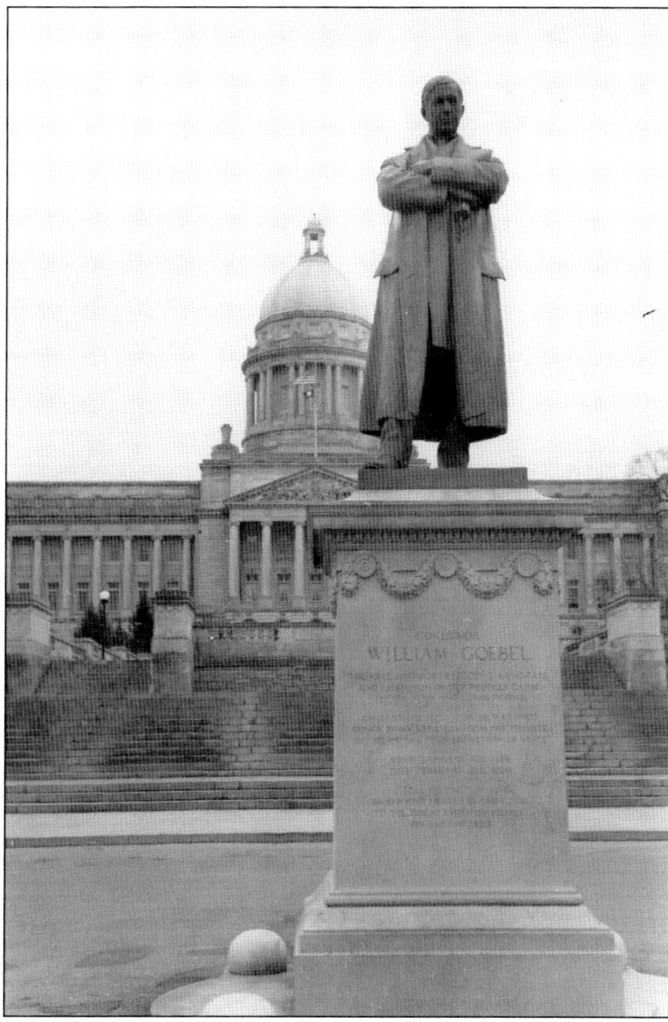

Gov. William Goebel. Kentucky's governor Goebel is the only governor ever to be assassinated in office. This statue by Charles Niehaus was erected in 1919 and placed in his honor. The statue stood at the capitol until the 1960s, when Gov. Bert Combs determined it was a traffic hazard. With no objection, it was moved to its current home on the old state capitol grounds near where Goebel was shot.

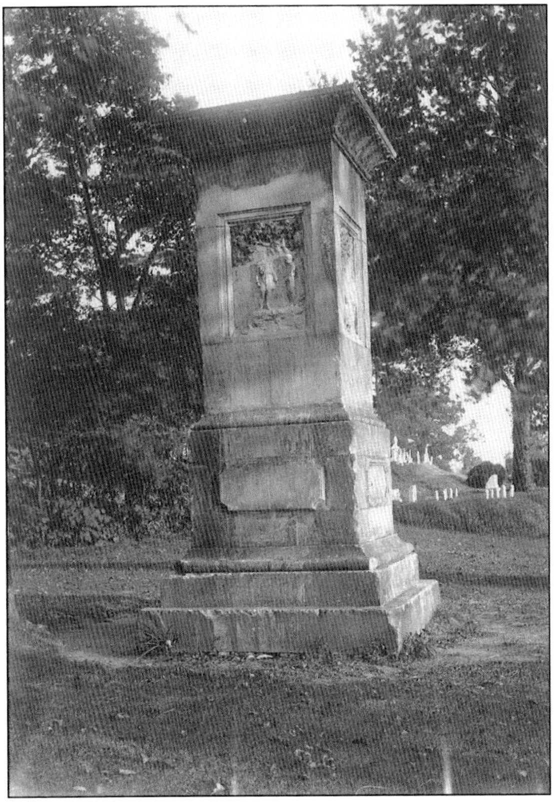

DANIEL BOONE GRAVESITE. Daniel Boone's gravesite in the Frankfort Cemetery, also known as Kentucky's Westminster, is the location of many of the photographs seen earlier that were taken of the capitol. This image was photographed around 1900, prior to the installation of the iron fence that now encloses the site. (Courtesy of Division of Historic Properties.)

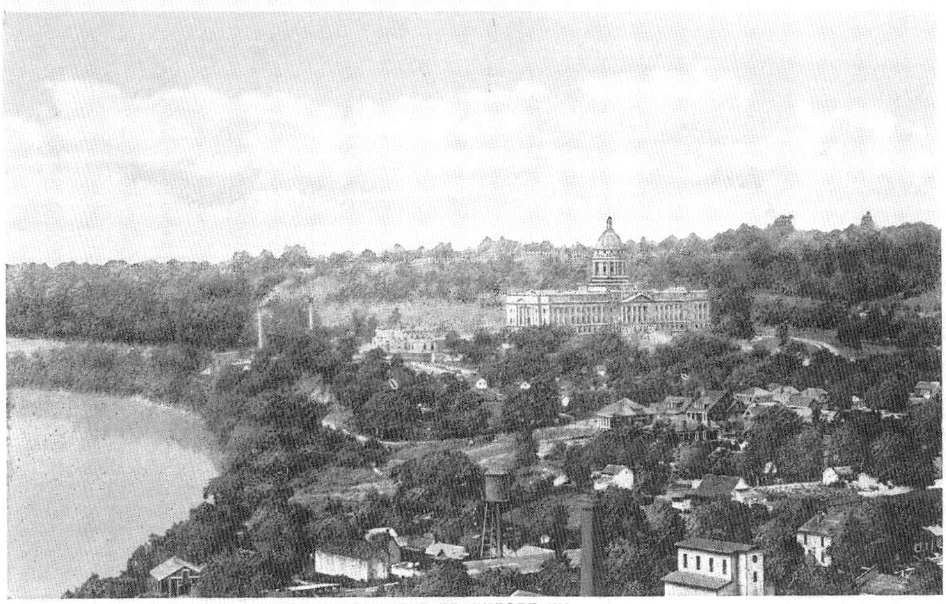

STATE CAPITOL FROM DANIEL BOONE MONUMENT, FRANKFORT, KY.

VIEW FROM DANIEL BOONE'S GRAVESITE. This early-1900s postcard shows both the new capitol and governor's mansion along with some of the long-gone industry along the banks of the Kentucky River. (Courtesy collection of Scot Walters.)

KENTUCKY CAPITOL/HIGH BRIDGE POSTCARD. This postcard image of two celebrated landmarks in Kentucky was included because it is a treat today to read the boastfulness of its language. Obviously the postcard and its message were written sometime after 1910. (Courtesy collection of Scot Walters.)

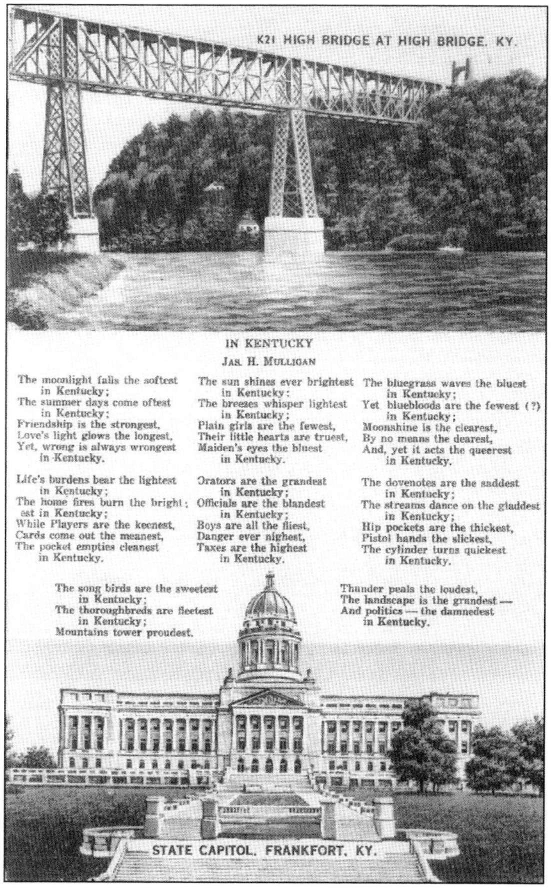

CAPITOL NORTH ENTRANCE. This is a visitor's description of the new capitol in 1910. "Entering the grounds at Todd Street is an avenue 360 feet wide, with a beautiful grass plot in the center, while asphalt driveways and concrete walks run along each side. The grounds have been handsomely graded, slope away gracefully from the front of the building and sides of the approach, and in their summer dress of bluegrass are beautiful indeed." (Courtesy collection of Scot Walters.)

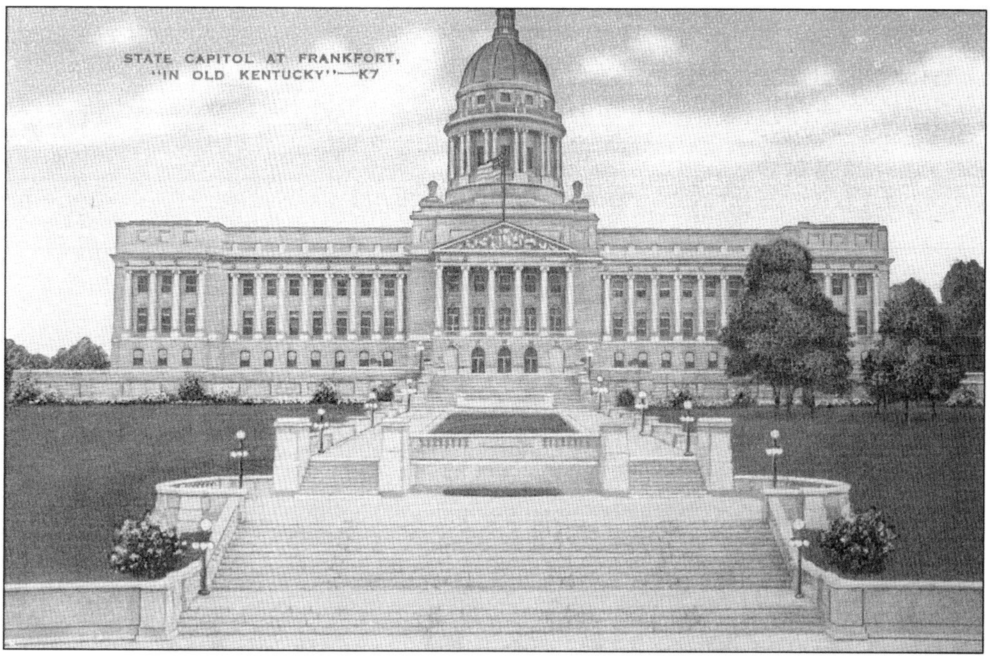

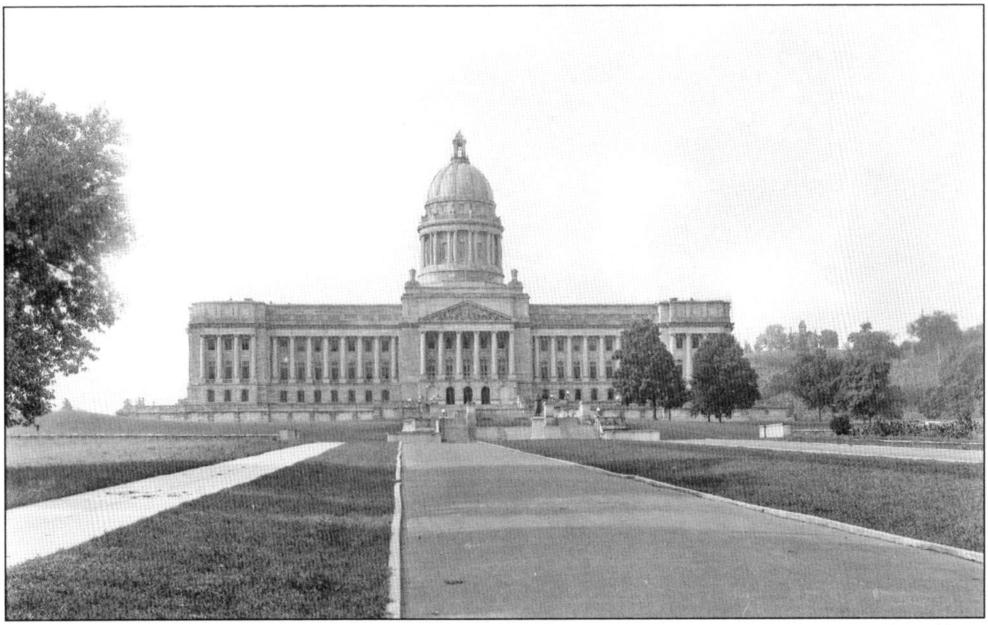

Commonwealth's Capitol. Although many images of the north entrance of the capitol building have been shown in this book, this photograph is of interest aside from the architecture. The 1915 photograph appears to show Kentucky's cash crop of the time, tobacco, planted on the right side of Capital Avenue. (Courtesy of Caufield and Shook Studio Collection, Ekstrom Library Special Collections, University of Louisville.)

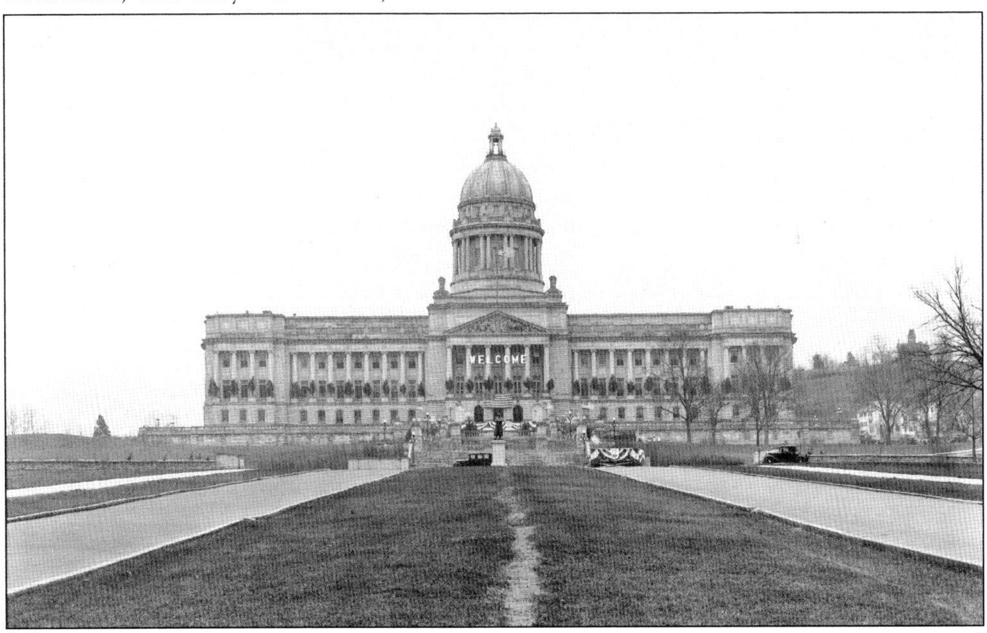

Welcome, 1931. The Kentucky State Capitol Building is all decked out for the inauguration ceremony for Gov. Ruby Laffoon. This photograph shows a welcome banner on the front facade of the building, and a closer examination reveals that all along the second floor ledge, there are trees in dirt balls—presumably to be planted in honor of the new governor. (Courtesy of Division of Historic Properties.)

Seven

The Capitol and People 1910–1940

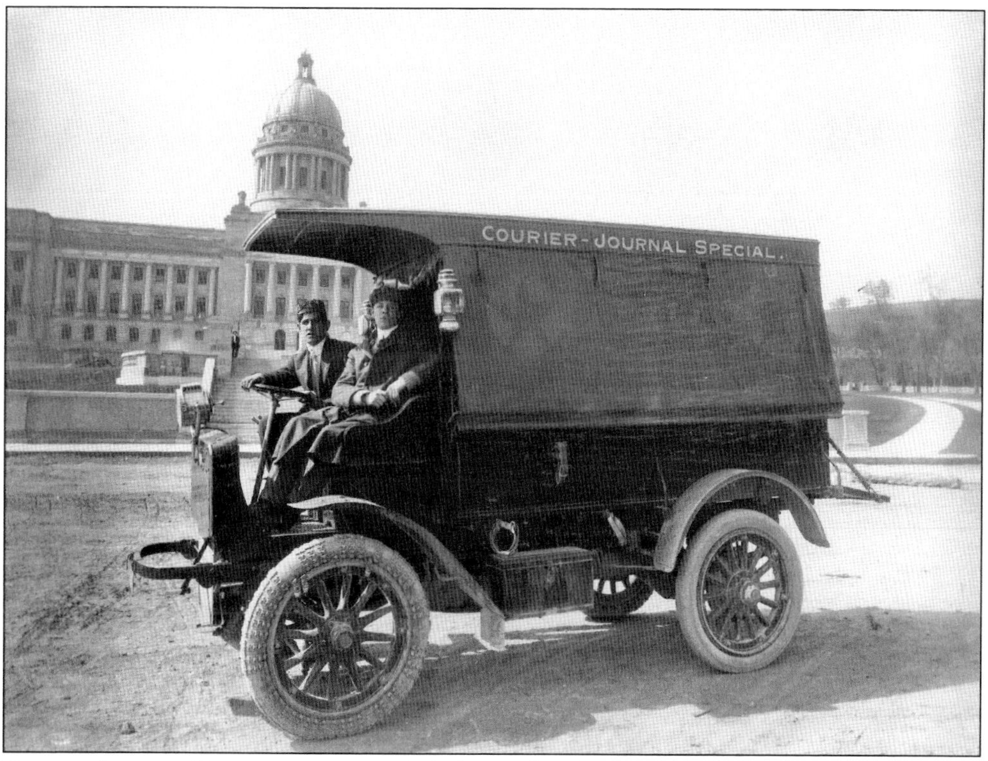

Courier-Journal Delivery around 1910. Soon after the new capitol opened in Frankfort, the rest of the state began to embrace the commerce opportunities presented by having the capitol centrally located in Frankfort. The automobile was starting to be used more as a transportation method, and trips from Louisville and Lexington were shorter as roads improved. This 1910 photograph of a Louisville *Courier-Journal* Autocar delivery truck indicates such with "Commercial and Daily Delivery Louisville, Shelbyville, and Frankfort."

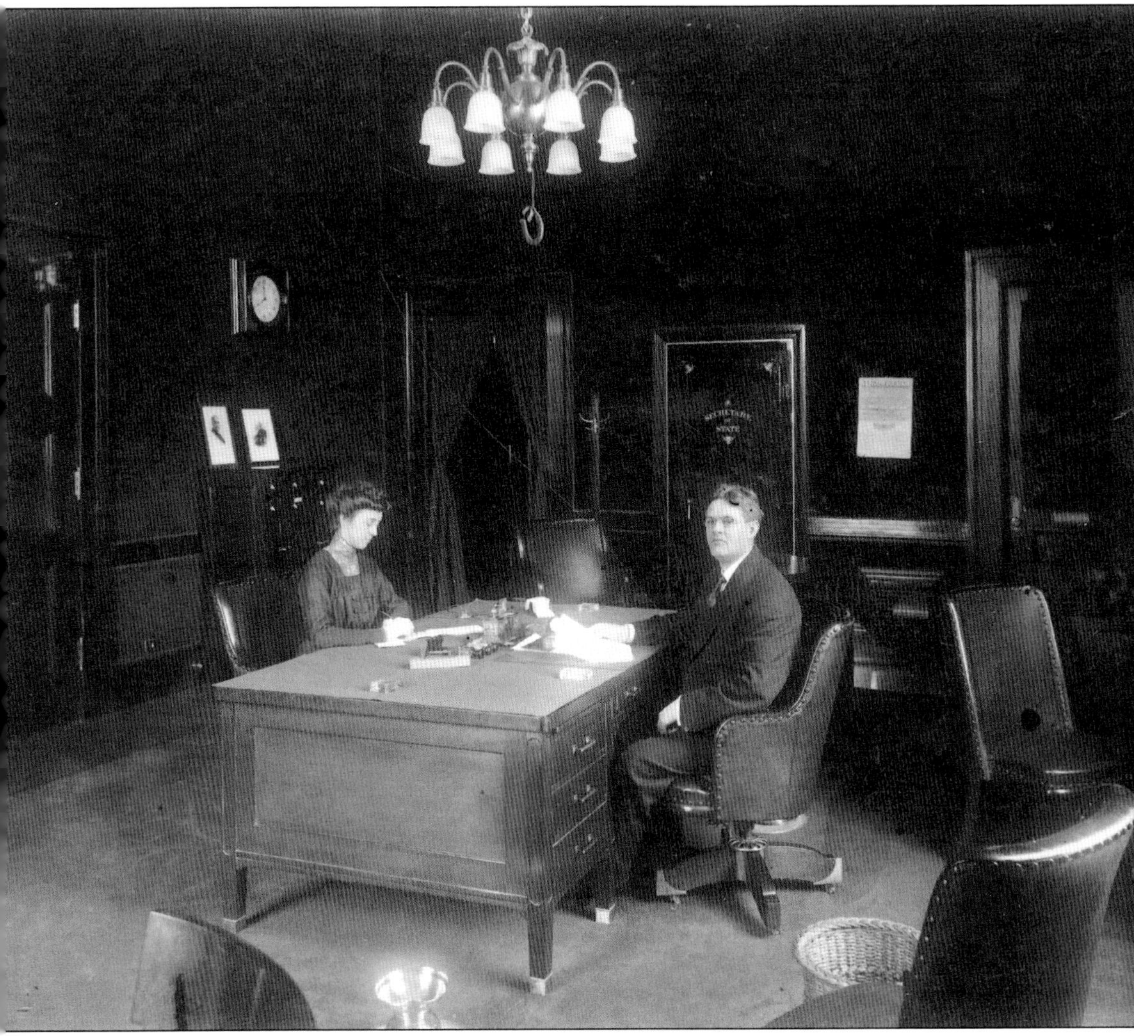

SECRETARY OF THE COMMONWEALTH. The initial state official to occupy the new building was Dr. Ben L. Bruner, secretary of state, shown here posing in his new office. The photograph shows a horseshoe for good luck dangling from the chandelier, and his stenographer, Minnie Lee McDaniel, coyly looks down at her work. It is recorded that Secretary Bruner moved in on July 26, 1909, at least seven weeks before other state officials. By December 1, 1909, all of the major departments had moved into the building. The first legislative session in the new capitol occurred in January 1910, even though the building was formally dedicated several months later.

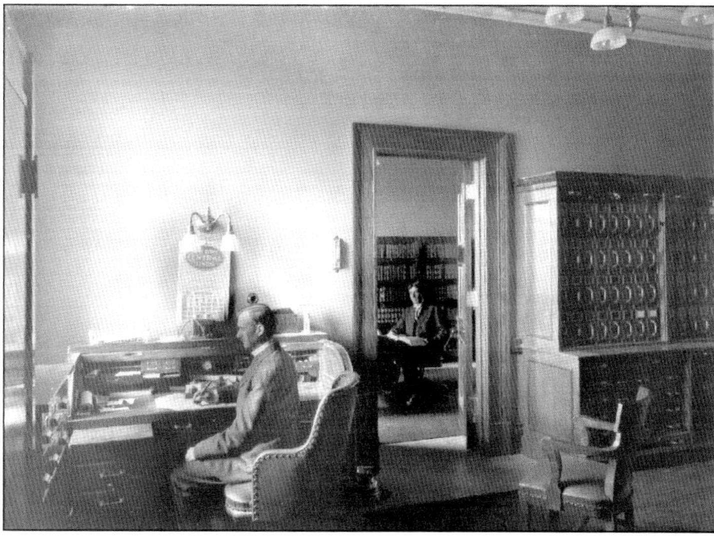

NOVEMBER 1909. Two unidentified men are shown working in the original new capitol offices with all original fixtures and furnishings. The calendar in the background indicates it was November 1909, which was about the time staff were moving into offices.

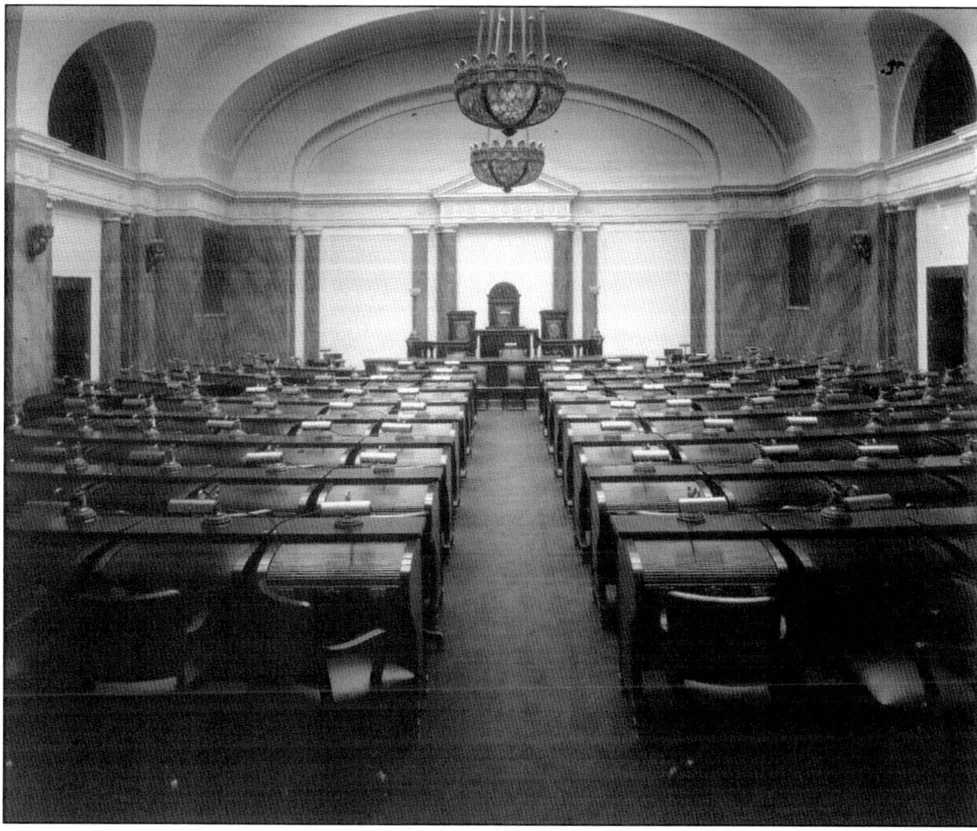

BLANK CANVAS. The Kentucky House of Representatives is pictured in this 1910 photograph. Discussions of ornament and decorative arts for the new capitol continued for many years after the building was complete. In 1910, Governor Willson was scheduled to meet with a classmate of his at Harvard, Frank Millett, to discuss mural decorations for the capitol. Millett was a talented muralist and had worked in many public buildings in the United States. It is not known whether Millett made it to Kentucky, as he died on the *Titanic* in 1912.

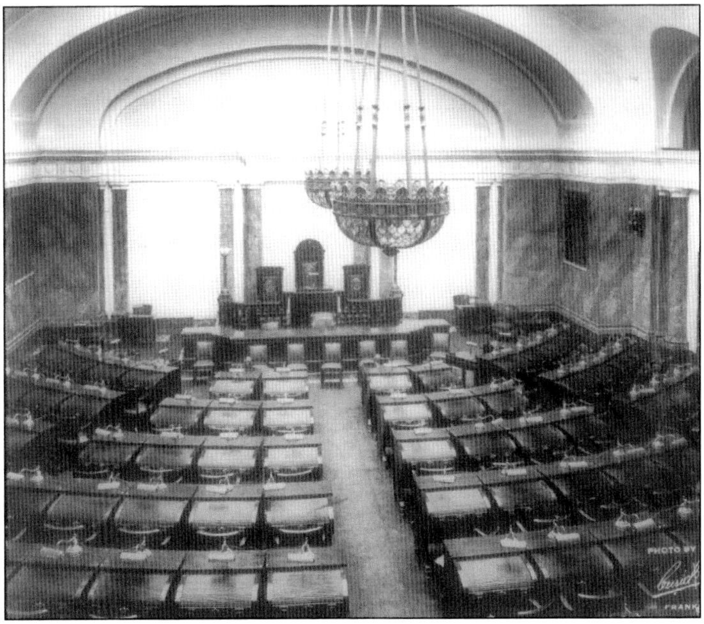

House of Representatives, 1910. This photograph shows the original rolltop desks and furnishings in the house chambers. The desks and much of the furniture are still in use today.

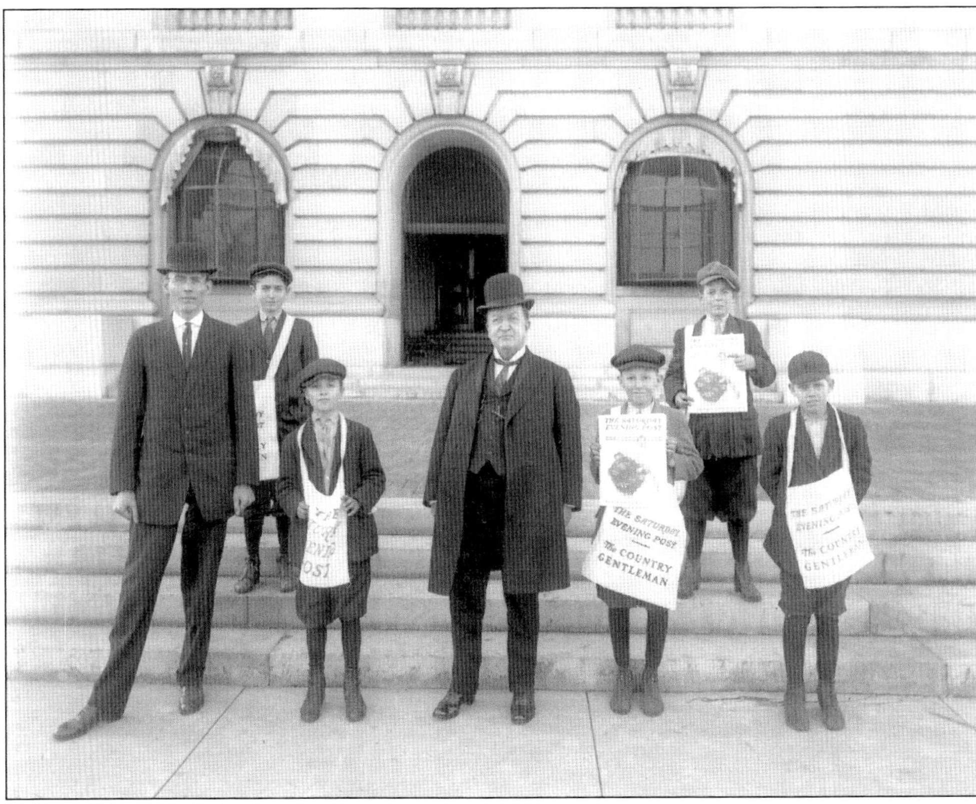

Governor Willson around 1911. Governor Willson is pictured at the new capitol's east entrance with several unidentified children selling the *Saturday Evening Post*. The east entrance is now known as the governor's entrance because of its proximity to the governor's mansion. (Courtesy of Division of Historic Properties.)

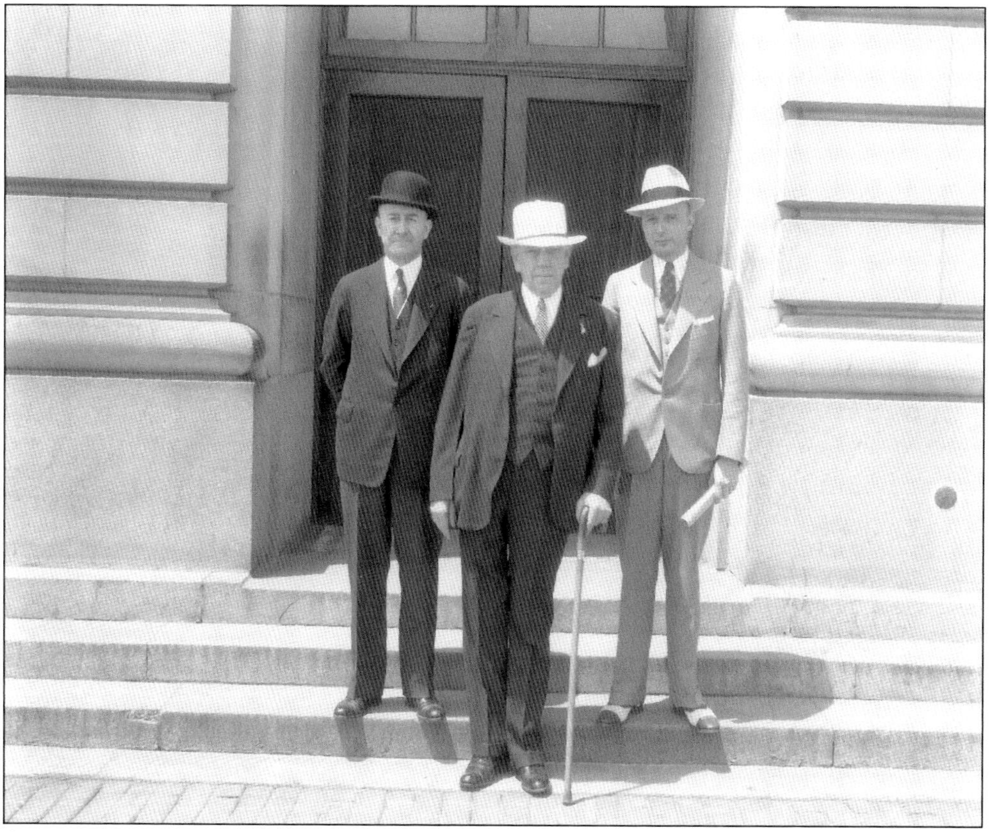

GOVERNOR AND STAFF, 1931–1935. Governor Laffoon is seen here outside the east entrance of the new capitol. Photographs like this are important not only because of Kentucky's gubernatorial history, but also because they show features that have been lost or removed from the capitol building. In this image screen doors are shown, which were later removed.

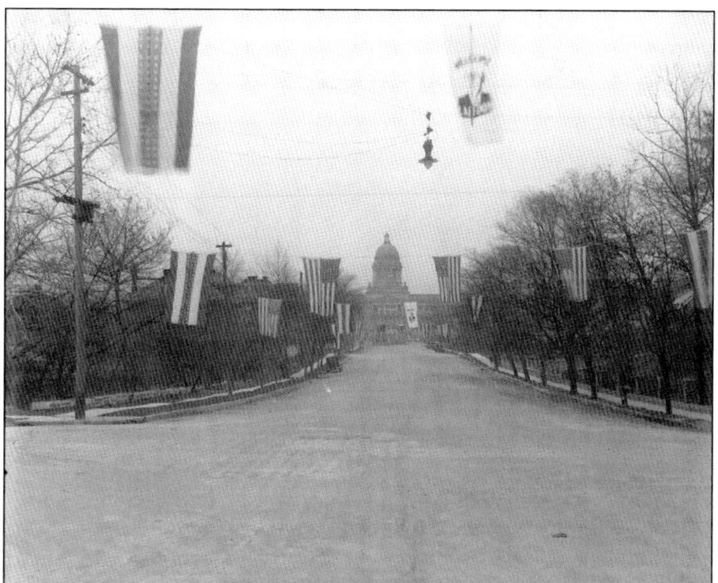

CAPITAL AVENUE. Flags and banners traverse Capital Avenue in anticipation of the inauguration parade for the newly elected Governor Laffoon. The upper center of this 1931 photograph shows a cartoon of Laffoon's image with "welcome" framing his head.

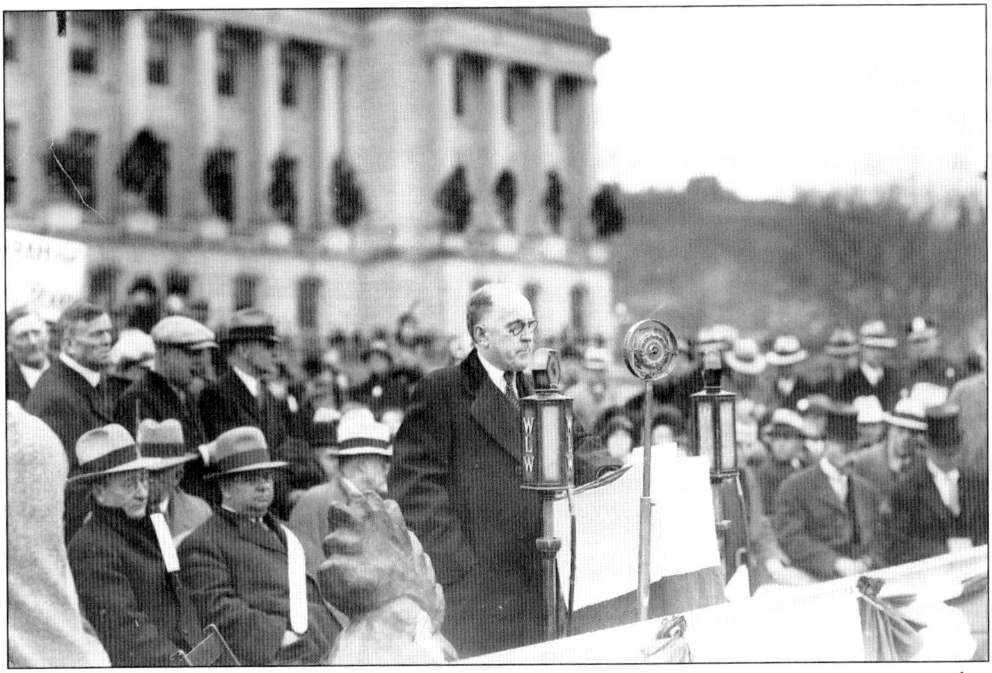

Gov. Flem Sampson's Valedictory. The photograph shows Governor Sampson giving his valedictory speech prior to Laffoon taking office in 1931. In the background, trees are situated under each Ionic column on the second level of the capitol; later they were planted on the grounds.

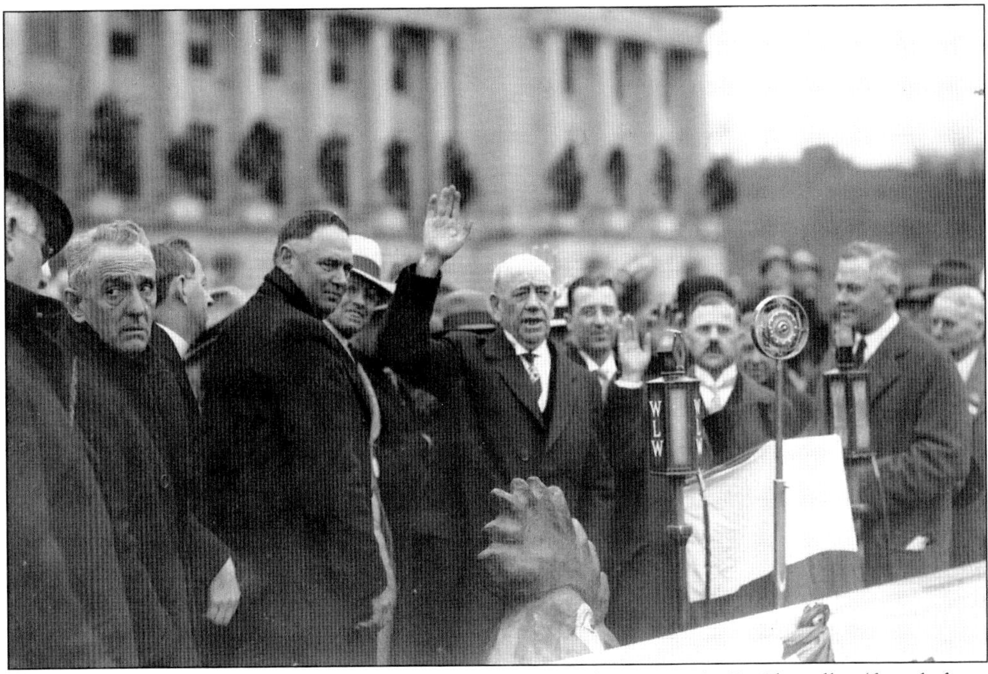

Laffoon and Chandler. Governor Laffoon (center) and Lt. Gov. A. B. Chandler (fourth from left) are taking the oath of office as administered by Chief Justice Richard P. Dietzman. There is a large rooster symbol for Kentucky's Democratic Party in the lower center of this 1931 photograph. WLW Radio broadcasted the event to listeners around the commonwealth.

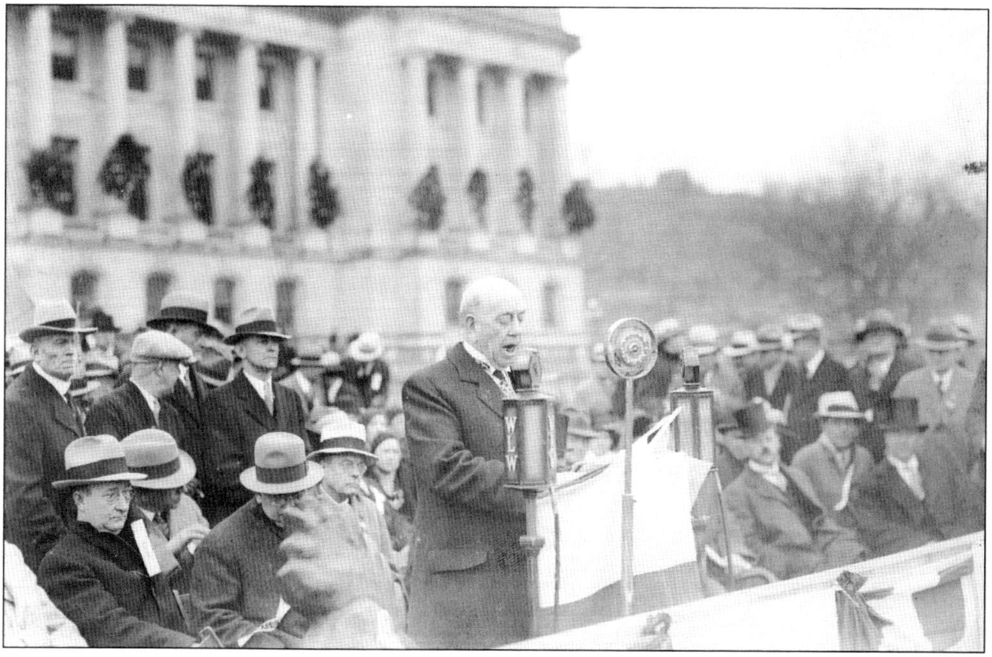

GOVERNOR LAFFOON'S INAUGURAL ADDRESS, 1931. Seated to the right of Governor Laffoon are C. W. Hay, chairman of the executive committee, and L. W. Morris, master of ceremonies. To the left are Chief Justice Richard P. Dietzman and Lt. Gov. A. B. "Happy" Chandler.

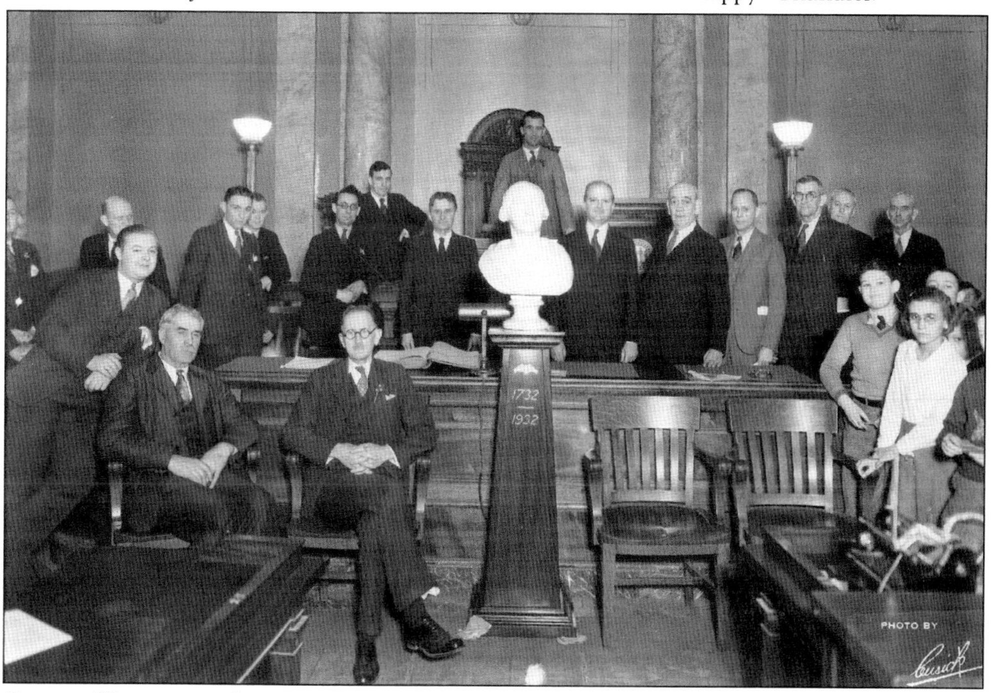

GEORGE WASHINGTON'S 200TH. Congressman Virgil Chapman presents George Washington's bust to Governor Laffoon in the presence of Kentucky legislature in this 1932 photograph. The bust does not exist in the capitol today; however, the wooden pedestal with 1732–1932 engraved on it is still retained in the Kentucky Division of Historic Properties archival storage.

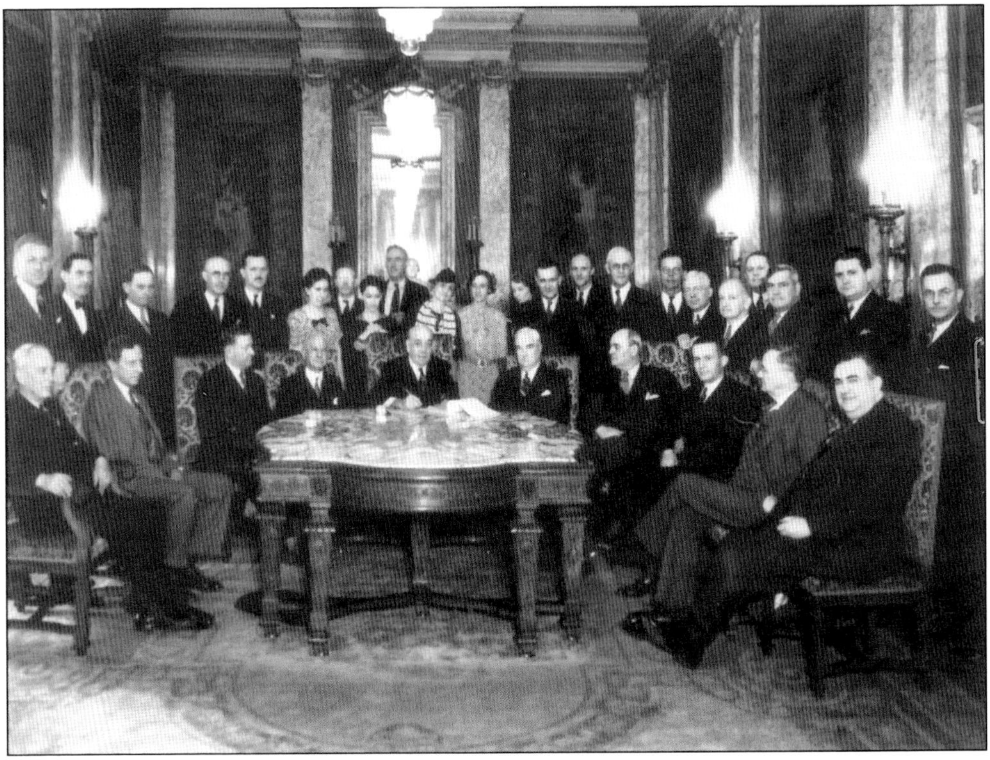

Historic Occasion. In 1910, the capitol's state reception room was decorated with impressive furnishings and fixtures to serve as a formal room for the governor to conduct commonwealth business. In this photograph, Governor Laffoon is seen between 1931 and 1935 with a group formally signing a bill into law. (Courtesy of Division of Historic Properties.)

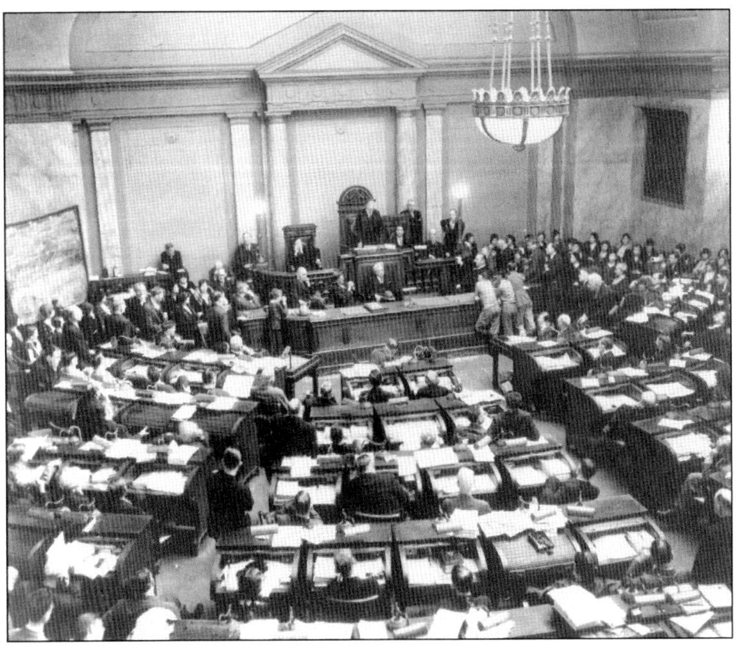

Speaker of the House. The speaker of the house addresses a full group of busy lawmakers in this 1930s photograph. By this period, as this image shows, some simple stenciling had been added to the house chambers and hand-painted "united we stand, divided we fall" figures were painted by an unknown artist. (Courtesy of Division of Historic Properties.)

BACK OF HOUSE. This photograph, taken in 1934 for a special session of the Kentucky House of Representatives, is evidence of the stenciling that was added in the arches and archways of the house gallery. The concrete floor was originally covered in carpet, as it is today. The photograph shows a fairly significant hole in the carpet to the left of the description. (Courtesy of Division of Historic Properties.)

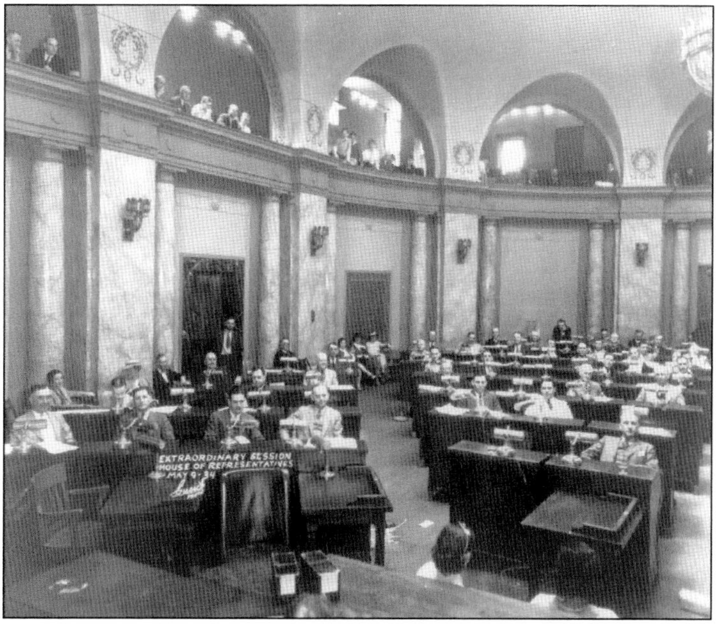

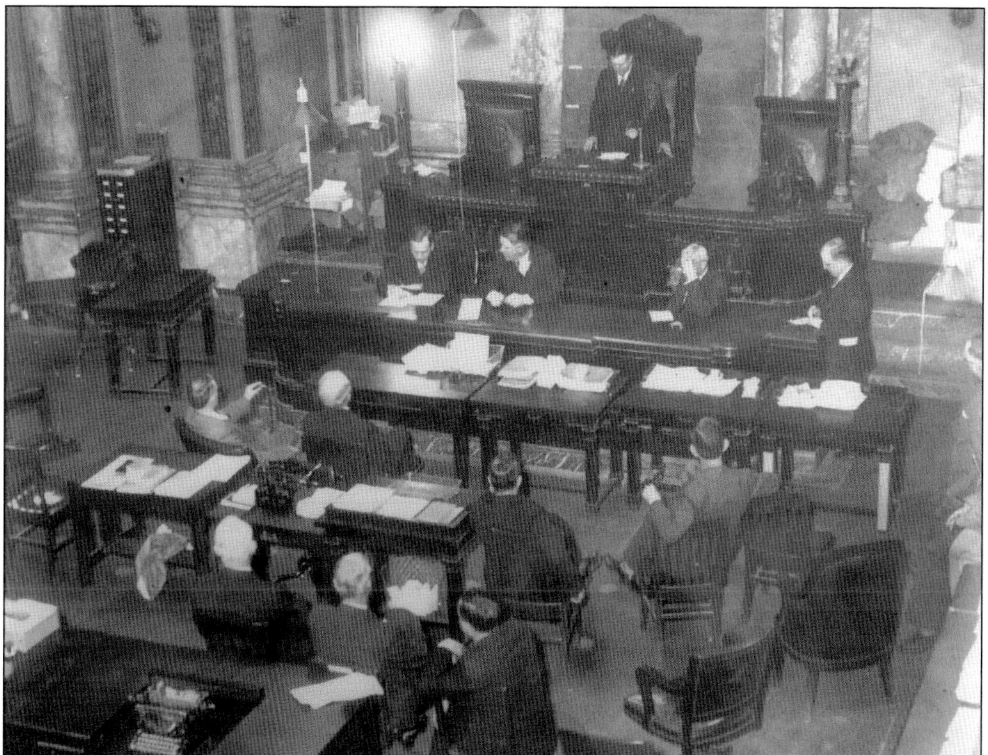

NOT ENOUGH LIGHT. It seems from reviewing early work photographs of the new capitol that proper light was always an issue, especially on cloudy days. In this 1930s photograph, auxiliary lighting is shown hanging from chandeliers with strings to turn on and off. Shades have also been removed from light standards to allow more light. (Courtesy of Harold Post Collection, Ekstrom Library Special Collections, University of Louisville.)

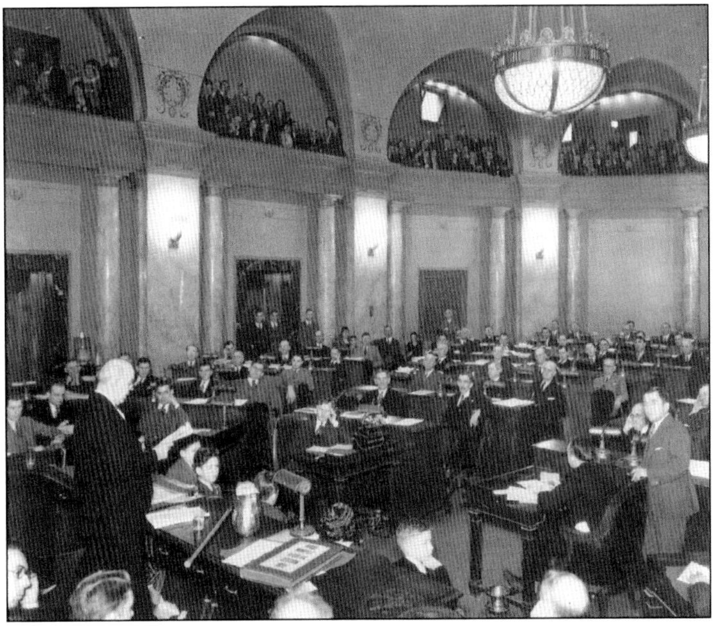

HOUSE REGULAR SESSION, 1932. Although this angle of the house chambers was shown in an earlier image, this 1932 photograph shows a full house gallery of unidentified spectators with Governor Laffoon addressing legislators. The photograph also illustrates the stenciling in between the arches, which curiously has little relationship to the architecture of the capitol. (Courtesy of Division of Historic Properties.)

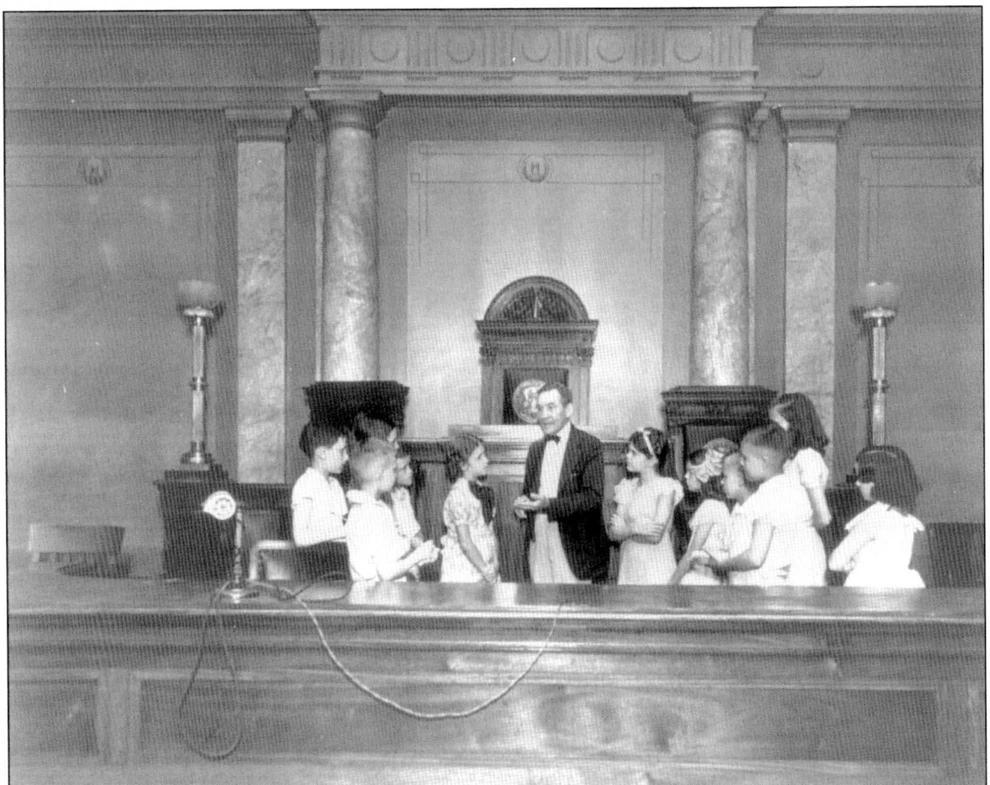

LEGISLATOR WITH SCHOOLCHILDREN. Kentucky's legislators have a long-standing history of spending some of their time to help the commonwealth's schoolchildren understand the three branches of government. This photograph from the 1930s shows an unknown legislator having a session with unidentified children. (Courtesy of Division of Historic Properties.)

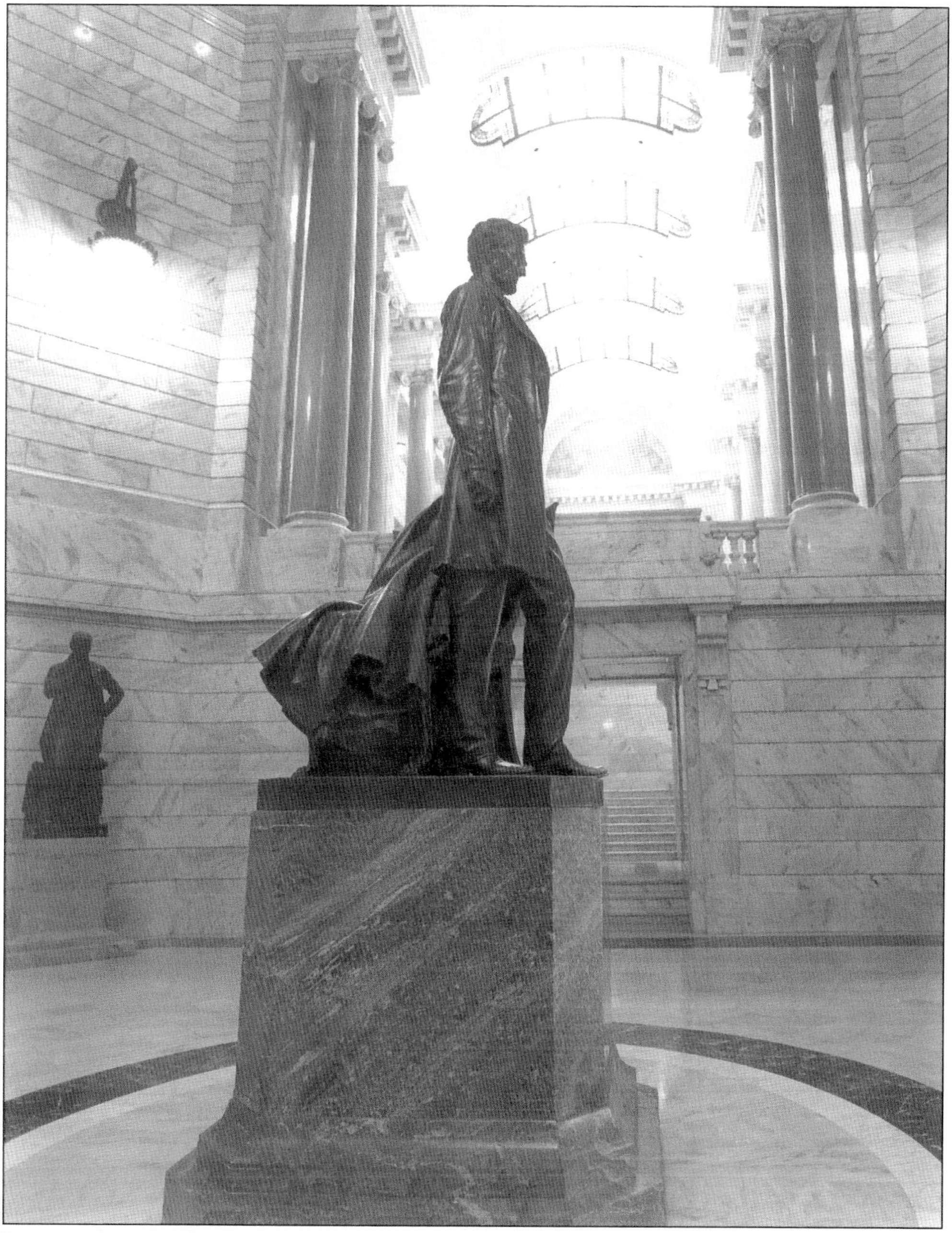

LINCOLN STATUE, CAPITOL ROTUNDA. Although the Abraham Lincoln statue in the capitol was the first unveiled in 1911 by President Taft, it would not be the last. Over the next 50 years, four more statues of influential Kentuckians were installed. Henry Clay and Ephraim McDowell were both unveiled in 1930 as plaster models for the original bronzes in the U.S. Capitol's Statuary Hall in Washington, D.C. On December 10, 1936, Governor Chandler was present at the unveiling of a statue of Kentucky-born Jefferson Davis. The white Carrara marble statue, sculpted by Fredrick Cleveland Hibbard, was donated by the United Daughters of the Confederacy. Finally Alben Barkley, the former vice president from western Kentucky, was enshrined with a bronze statue in 1963. (Courtesy of Division of Historic Properties.)

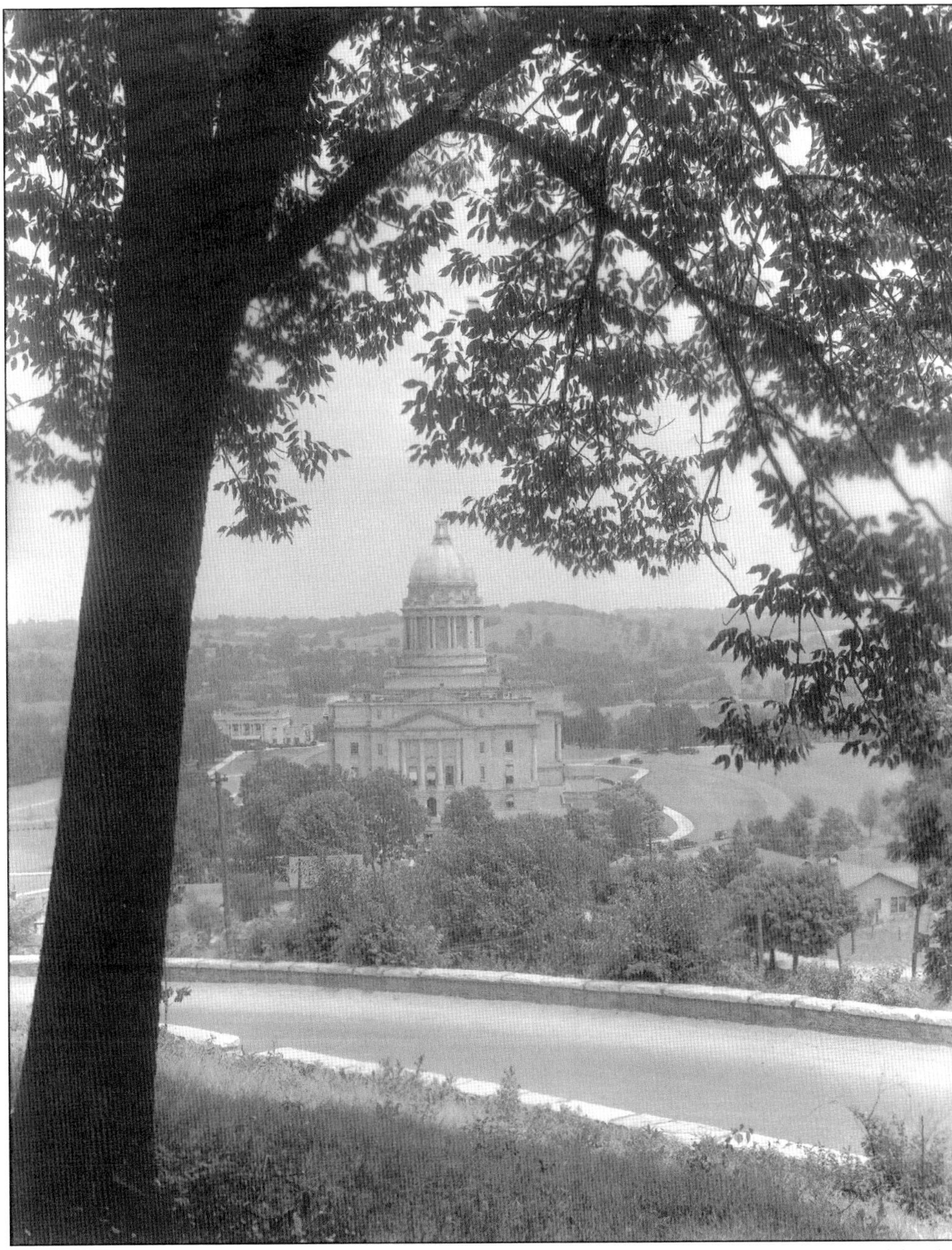

View of the Capitol, 1920–1925. This photograph from Louisville Hill shows the need for the transformation of the capitol grounds to cater to the automobile. Cars of 1920s vintage are parked on both sides of the capitol in the grass and under shade trees without parking spaces. (Courtesy of Caufield and Shook Studio Collection, Ekstrom Library Special Collections, University of Louisville.)

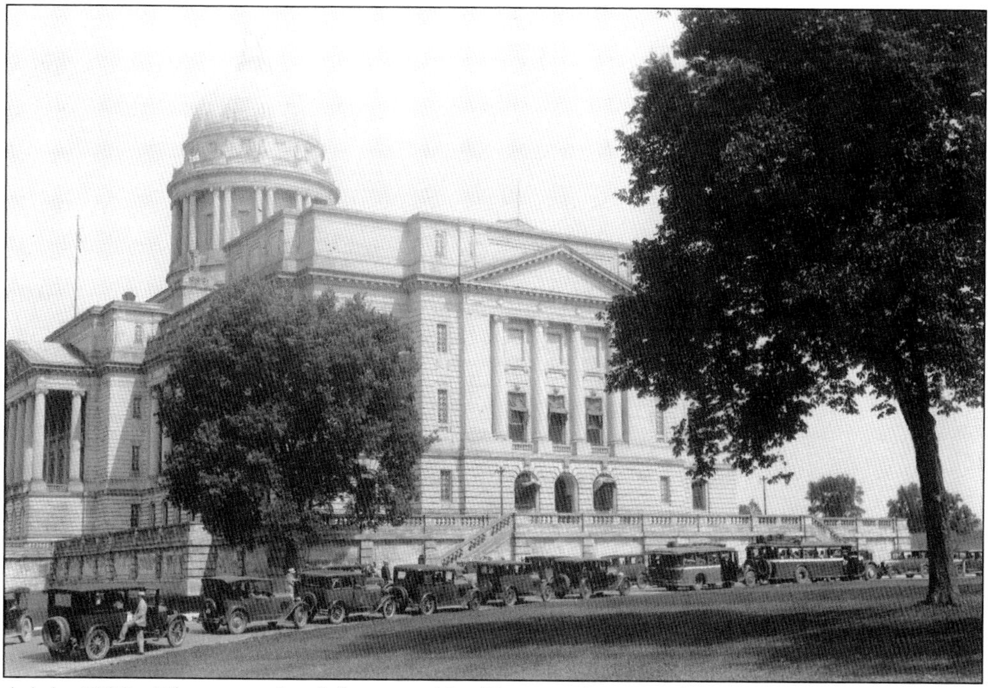

AAA, 1930s. The west side of the capitol building is taken over by a line of automobiles from the American Automobile Association's (AAA) trip to the capitol in Frankfort. Because there were no parking lots yet, vehicles just lined the edges of Capital Avenue.

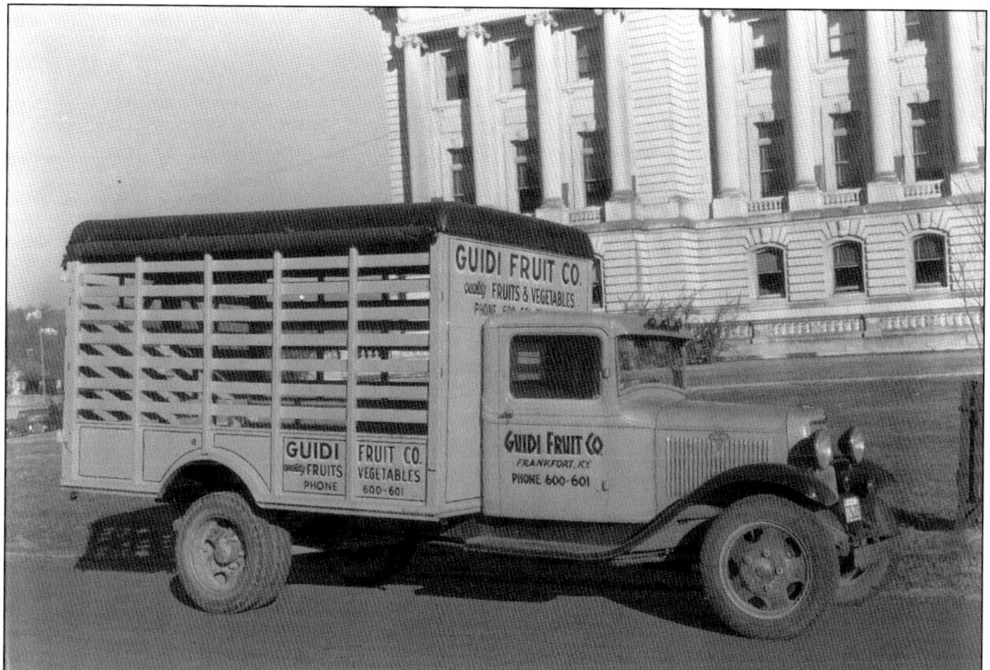

Guidi Fruit Company in the 1930s. As the automobile age evolved, trucks began to serve the capitol. In this photograph, a truck with covered racks from the Guidi Fruit Company is making a delivery.

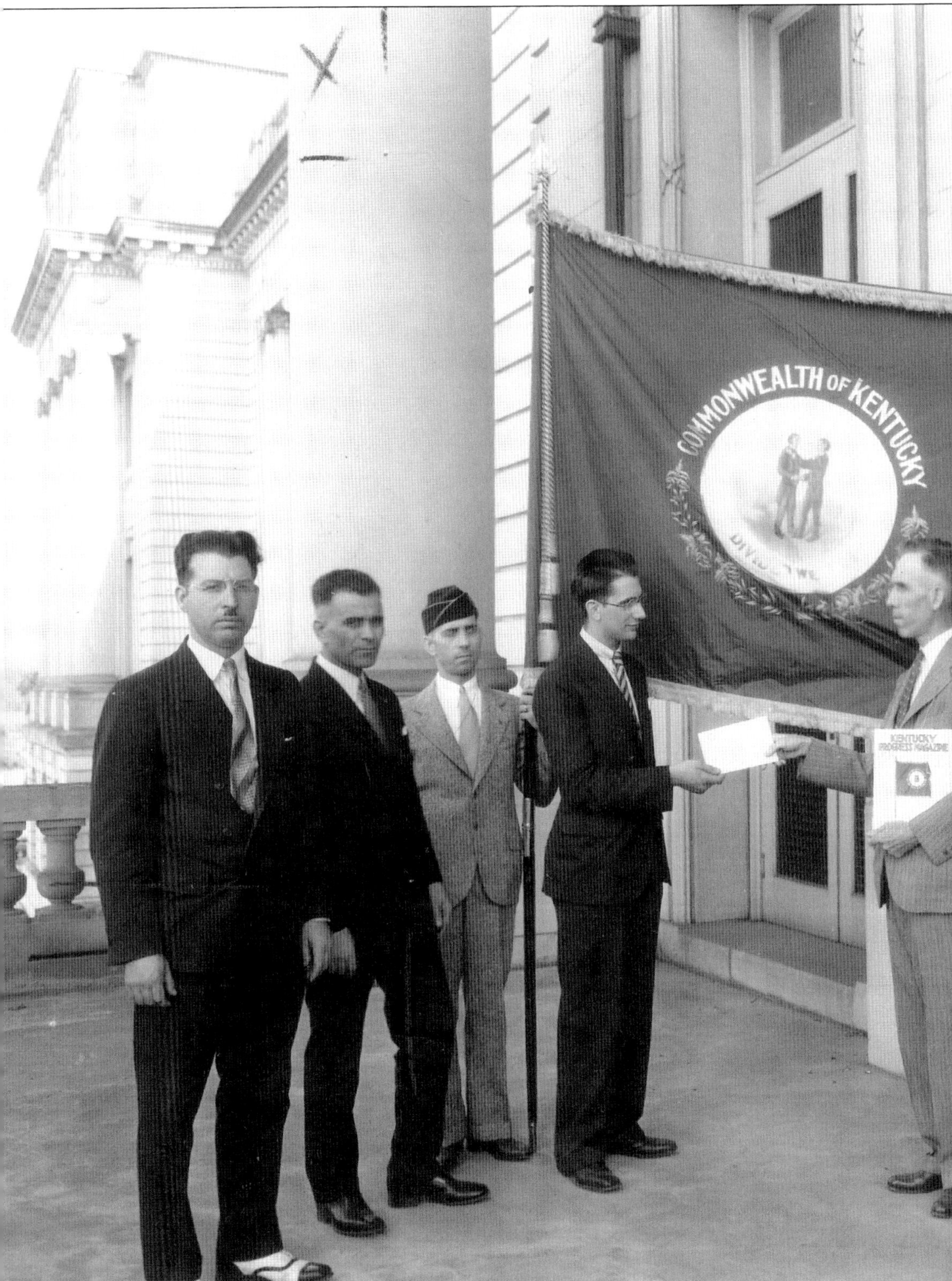
COMMONWEALTH OF KENTUCKY
KENTUCKY PROGRESS MAGAZINE

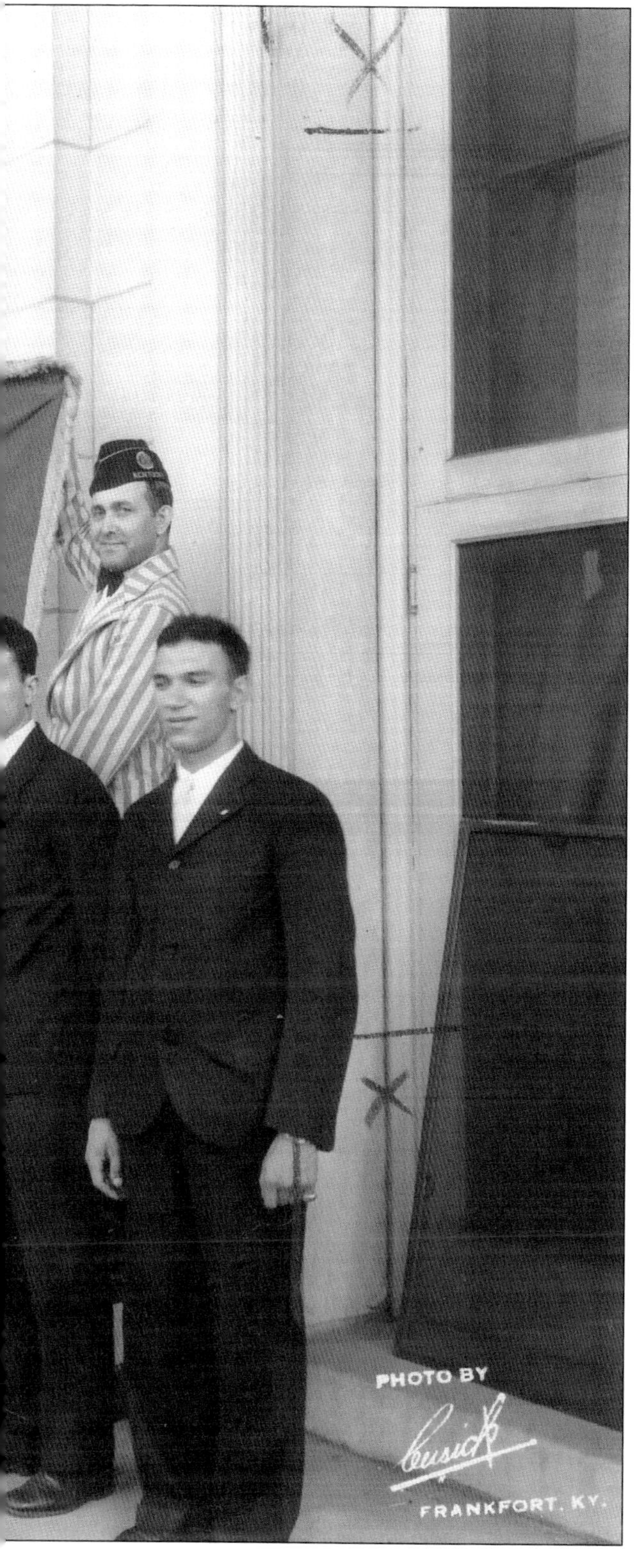

Original Commonwealth Flag. In this 1930 photograph taken from the state reception room balcony, the original commonwealth flag is headed to Athens, Greece, for the American Legion Post. The official flag was sent to be part of a celebration in Greece. The seal on the original flag shows two gentlemen shaking hands, each with a hand on opposite shoulders. The official seal is now recognized as the frontiersman (Daniel Boone) shaking hands with the gentleman. The people in the photograph are, from left to right, Louis Constant, George Georgantas, Nicholas Gianacakes, Louis P. Maniatis, C. Frank Dunn, B. S. Skenderis, James Gianacakes, and George C. Callis.

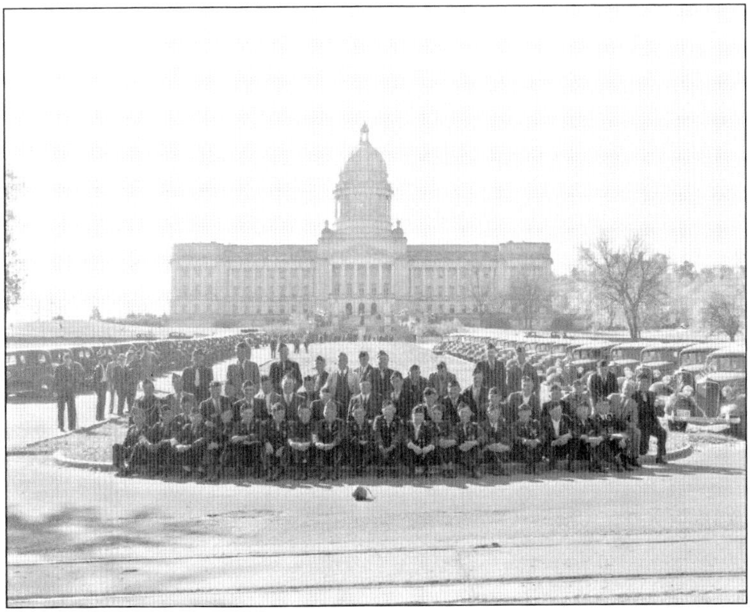

American Legion, 1930s. Dozens of American Legion members are seen in front of the capitol's north entrance on Capital Avenue. Legion members on motorcycles and automobiles are posed for the perfect shot in front of the capitol in this 1930s photograph.

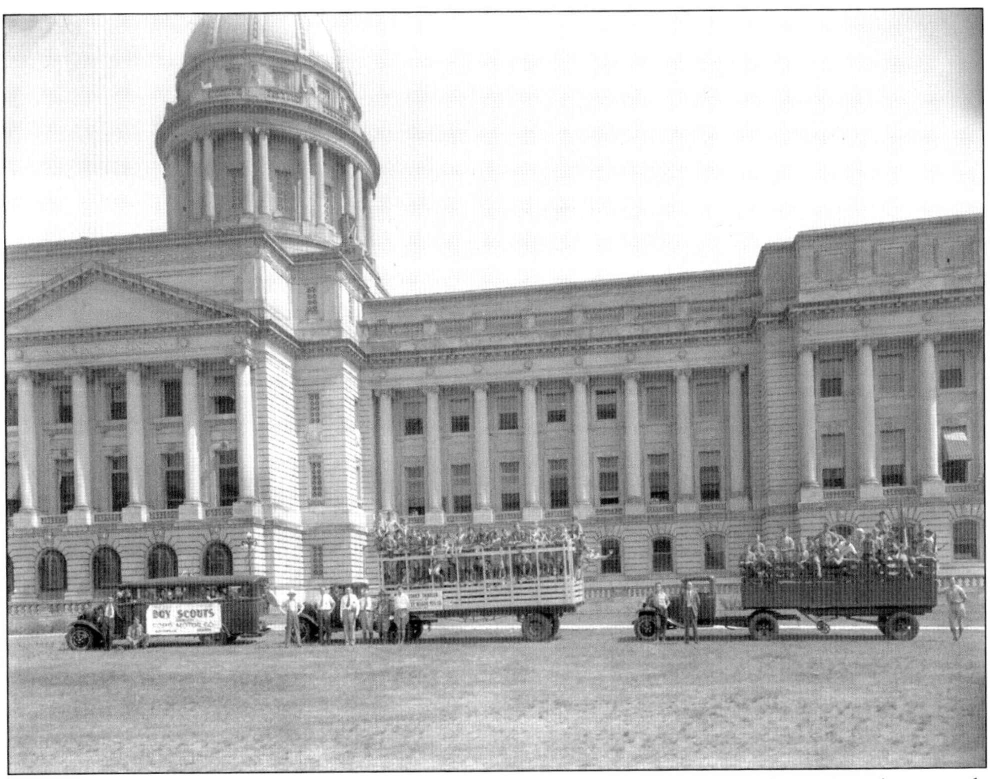

Boy Scout Day. Ford trucks made in Louisville, Kentucky, are shown in this 1930s photograph loaded with scores of Boy Scouts for their annual visit to the capitol. At that time, it was common to drive vehicles nearly up to the front entrance to take photographs or let passengers out.

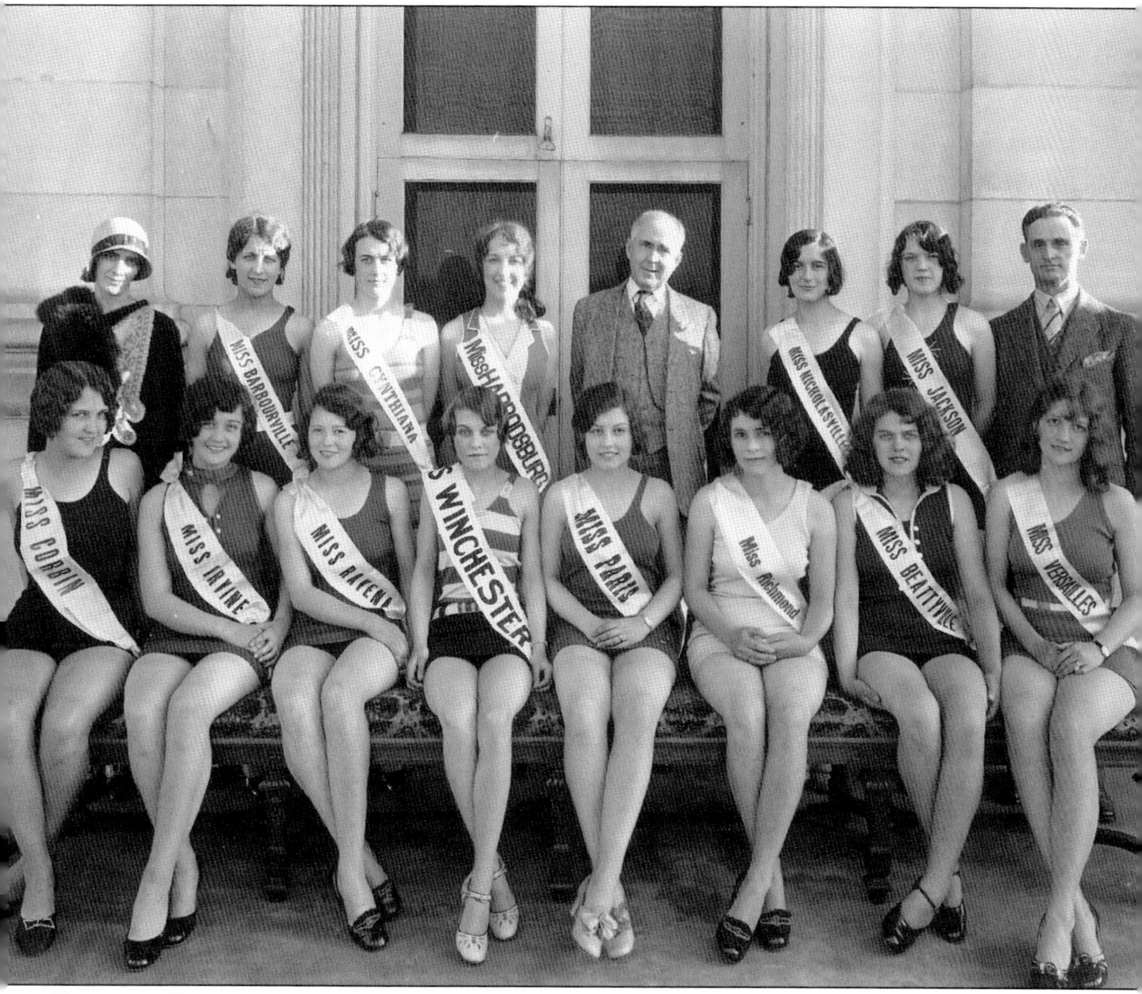

Kentucky Bathing Beauties, 1928–1931. Gov. Flem D. Sampson is shown outside the state reception room with 13 "Kentucky Bathing Beauties," as noted on the back of the photograph. Pictured here are, from left to right, (first row) Miss Corbin, Miss Irvine, Miss Ravenna, Miss Winchester, Miss Paris, Miss Richmond, Miss Beattyville, and Miss Versailles; (second row) possibly a female chaperone, Miss Barbourville, Miss Cynthiana, Miss Harrodsburg, Gov. Flem Sampson, Miss Nicholasville, Miss Jackson, and an unidentified gentleman. It appears at that time that it was an acceptable practice to take the state reception room furniture outside on the balcony for photographs. The ladies are sitting on two benches from the room.

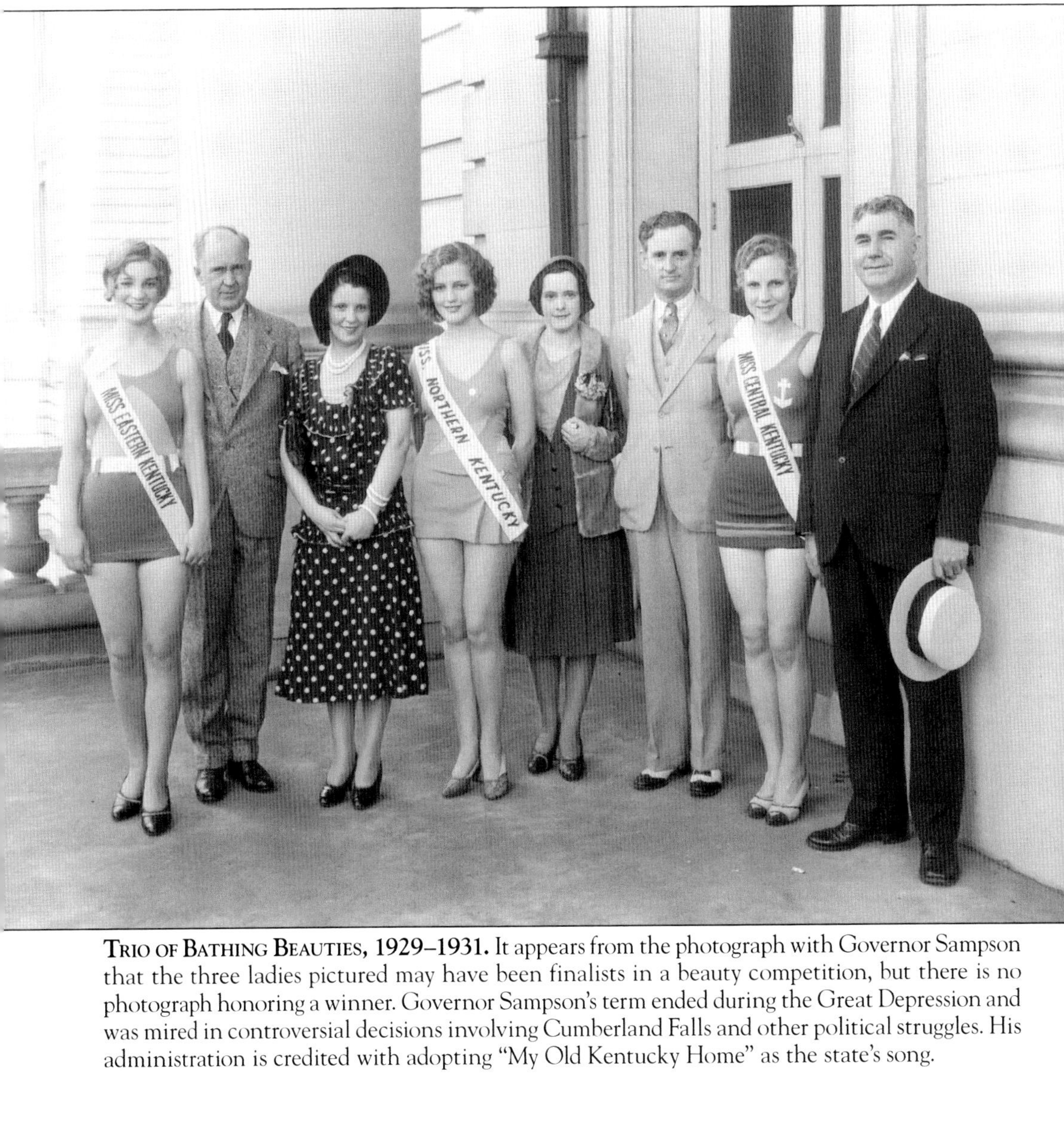

Trio of Bathing Beauties, 1929–1931. It appears from the photograph with Governor Sampson that the three ladies pictured may have been finalists in a beauty competition, but there is no photograph honoring a winner. Governor Sampson's term ended during the Great Depression and was mired in controversial decisions involving Cumberland Falls and other political struggles. His administration is credited with adopting "My Old Kentucky Home" as the state's song.

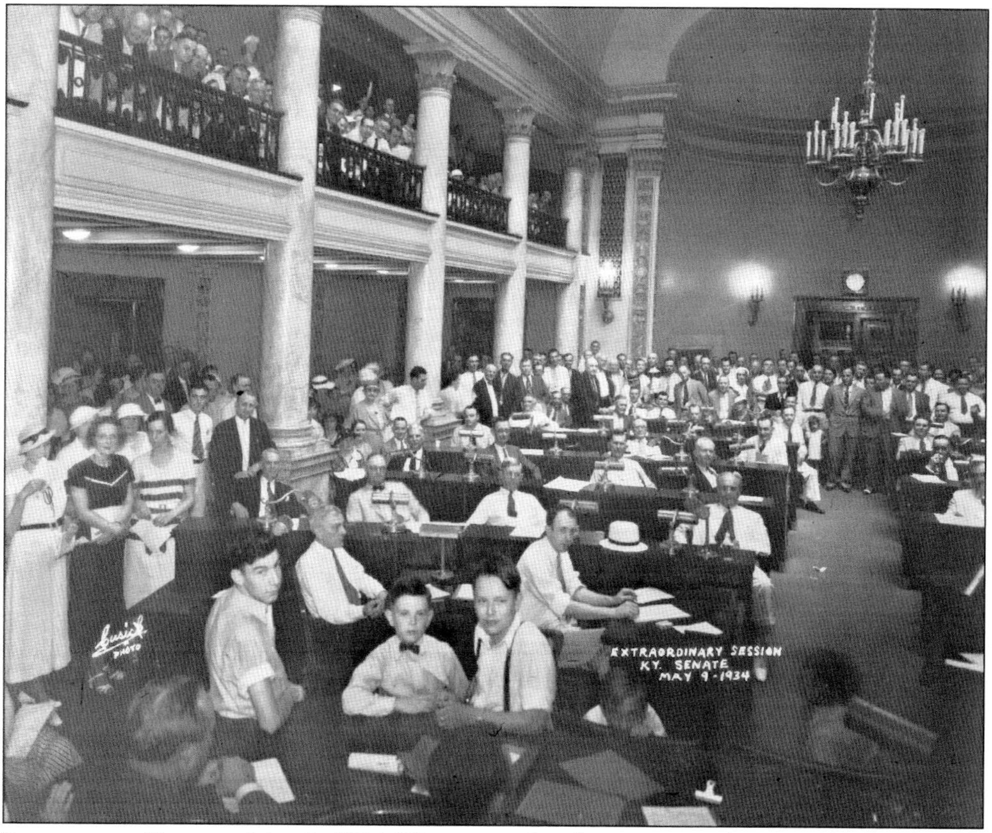

SENATORS AT DESKS ON MAY 9, 1934. The senate chamber is seen in this 1934 photograph; the senators still work at these desks today. Original chandeliers, which were large, solid brass fixtures from the Mitchell Vance Company, are shown. The scagliola, discussed earlier as a decorative treatment to imitate marble in the senate chamber, is a sienna color in the photograph.

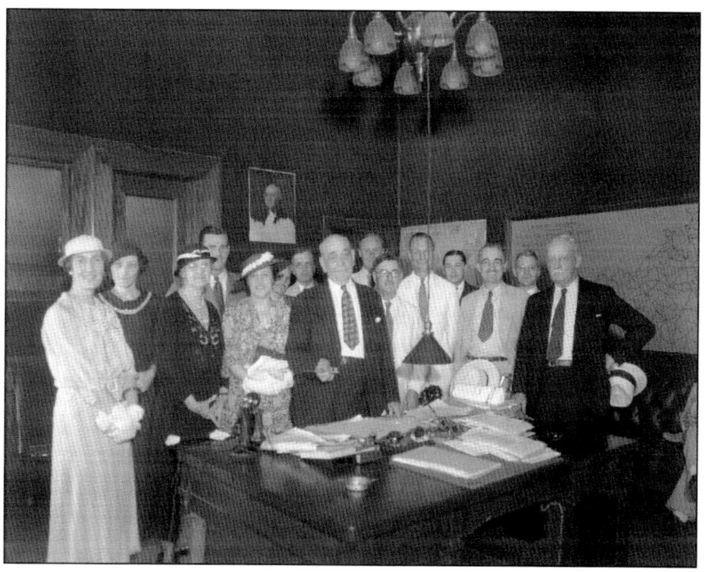

REPEAL OF THE 18TH AMENDMENT. In this 1934 photograph, Gov. Ruby Laffoon is signing a bill in the governor's office. He was signing the bill to repeal the 18th Amendment and end Prohibition in Kentucky. Governor Laffoon must have had troubles seeing in the capitol, as there is also as a makeshift light fixture hanging down from the chandelier above.

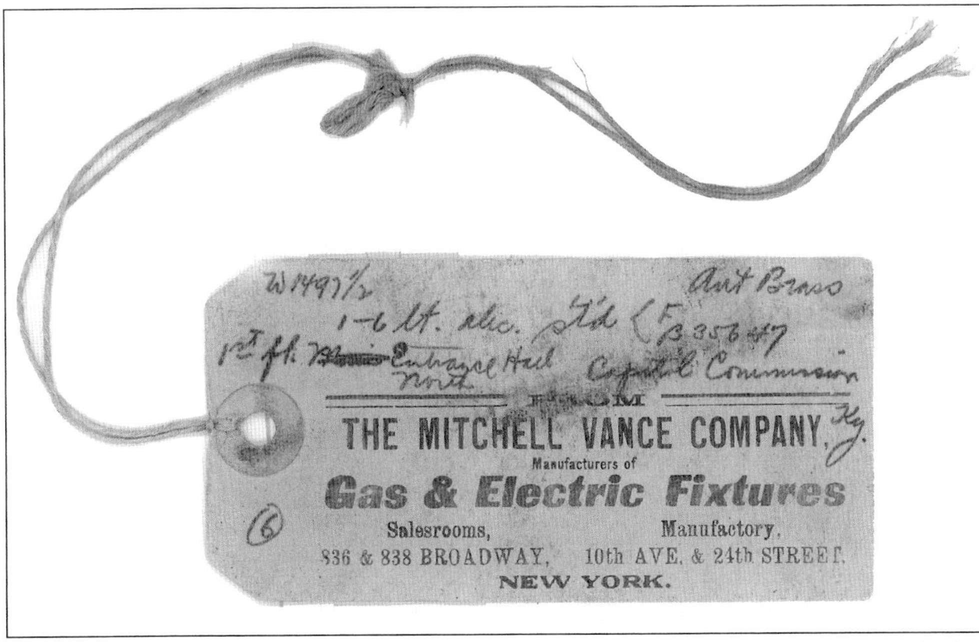

MITCHELL VANCE COMPANY. The Mitchell Vance Company of New York City provided all of the original interior fixtures in the Kentucky State Capitol for a cost of $15,775.75. Many of the surviving fixtures have been restored in recent years, and the tag pictured was found inside one of those fixtures. The tag is dated to 1909. (Courtesy of Division of Historic Properties.)

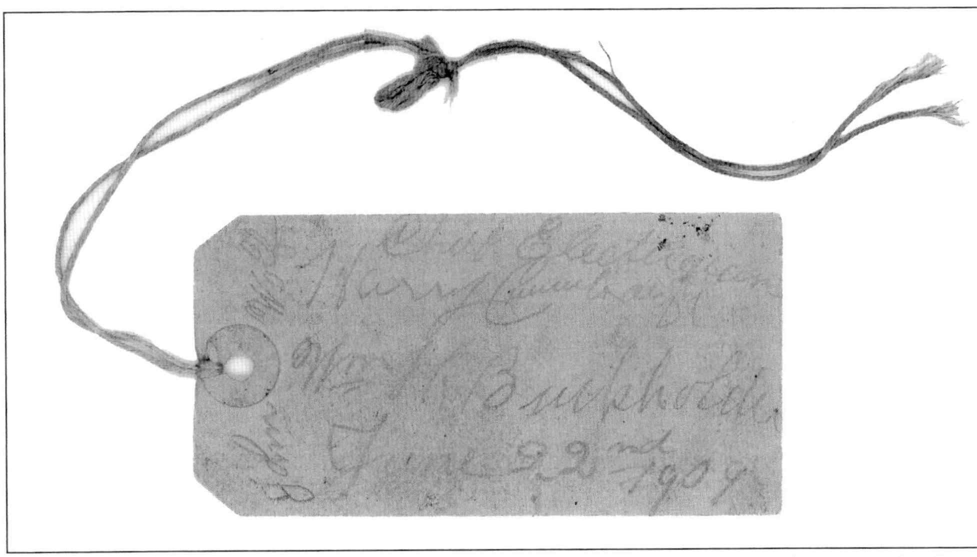

LEFT BEHIND. Obviously proud of installing something of permanence in the Kentucky State Capitol, three men who installed two large light standards in the north entrance of the building signed the back of the Mitchell Vance tag on June 22, 1909. The names are John Wolf, William Burkholder, and chief electrician Harry C. (the rest is not quite clear). (Courtesy of Division of Historic Properties.)

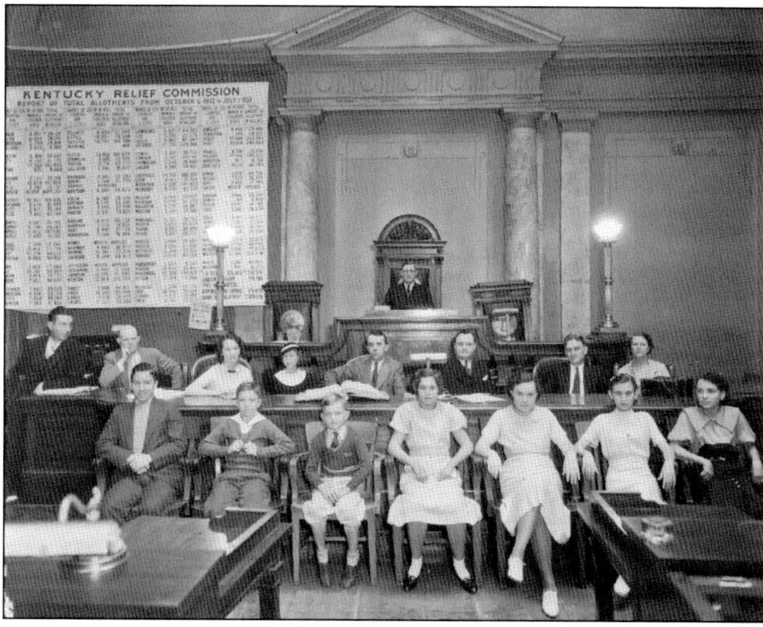

PAGES FOR THE HOUSE. This photograph, taken in 1934 according to the board on the left side, shows the speaker of the house with several pages. The young people have a long-standing tradition for delivery and pickup of legislative documents and communications throughout the capitol campus.

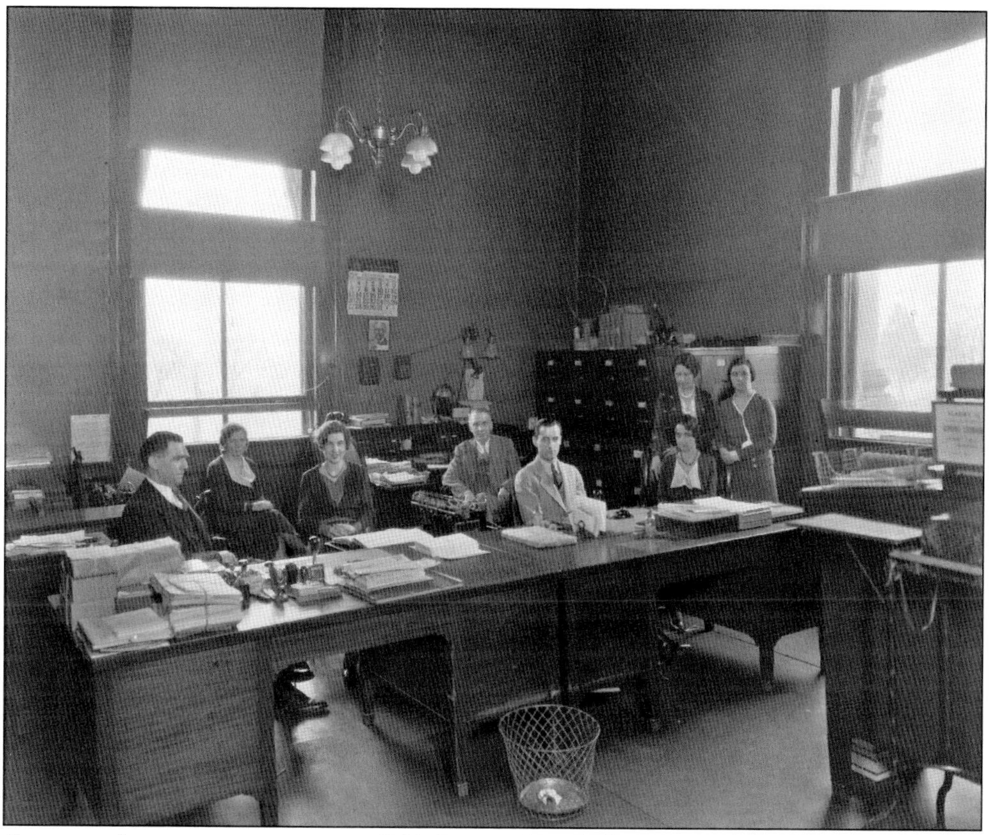

COURT OF APPEALS OFFICE AROUND 1931. Five unidentified women and three unidentified men are shown at desks in the office for the court of appeals, which would later become the Kentucky Supreme Court.

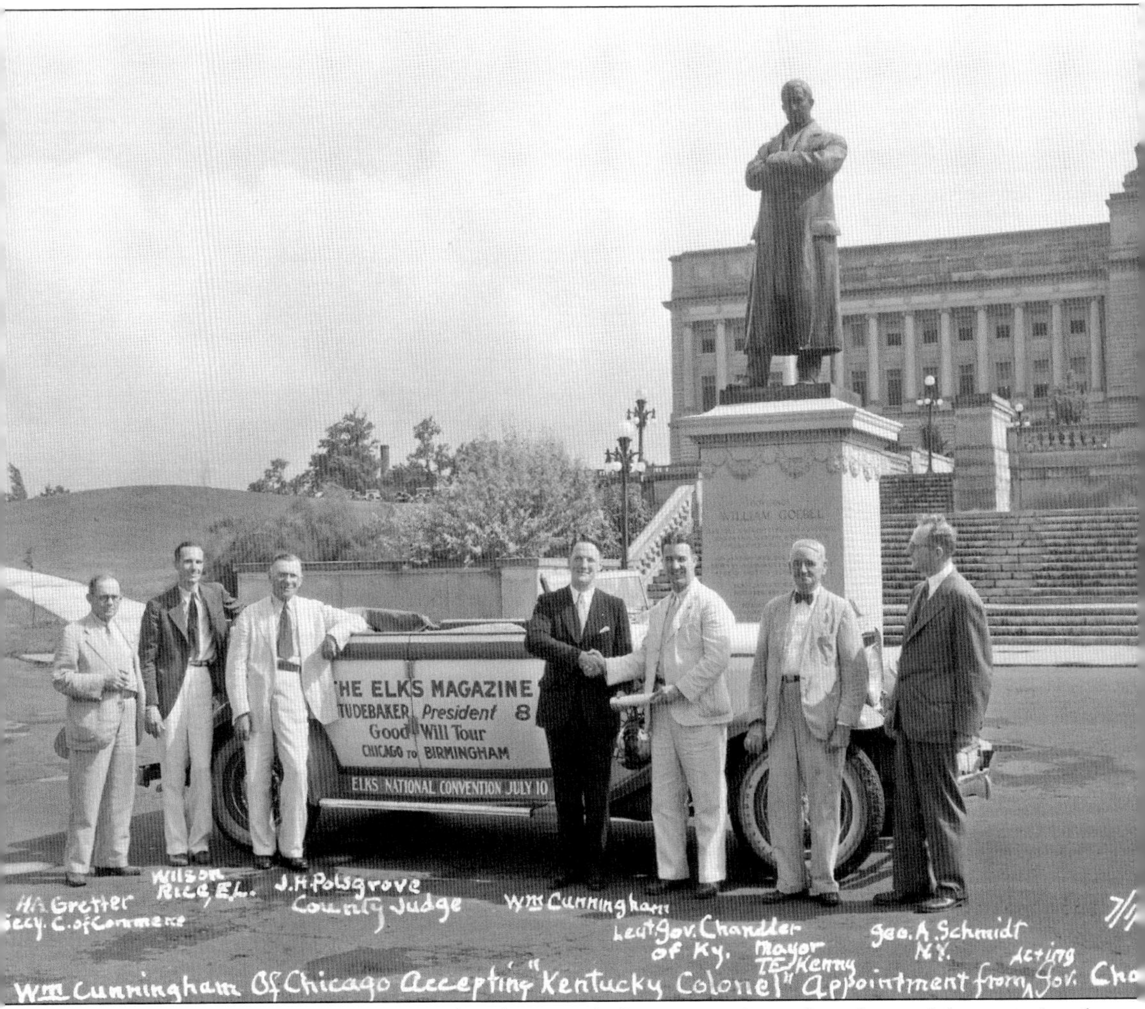

Elks Magazine around 1932. This photograph shows several people in front of the capitol and Goebel statue. Pictured here are, from left to right, H. A. Gretter (secretary of commerce), Wilson Rice of Elks Lodge, J. H. Polsgrove (Franklin County judge), William Cunningham (mayor of Frankfort), A. B. Chandler, T. E. Kenny, and George A. Schmidt (New York). William Cunningham is accepting the Kentucky colonel appointment from acting governor A. B. Chandler. It looks as though the Elks Lodge group was stopping at the capitol on a national promotional tour following the Great Depression as the nation struggled to rebuild its economy.

Elks Group. Groups frequently visit the capitol and pose for formal shots as a memory of their visit. Elks Club members are shown in this 1934 photograph on the north entrance steps.

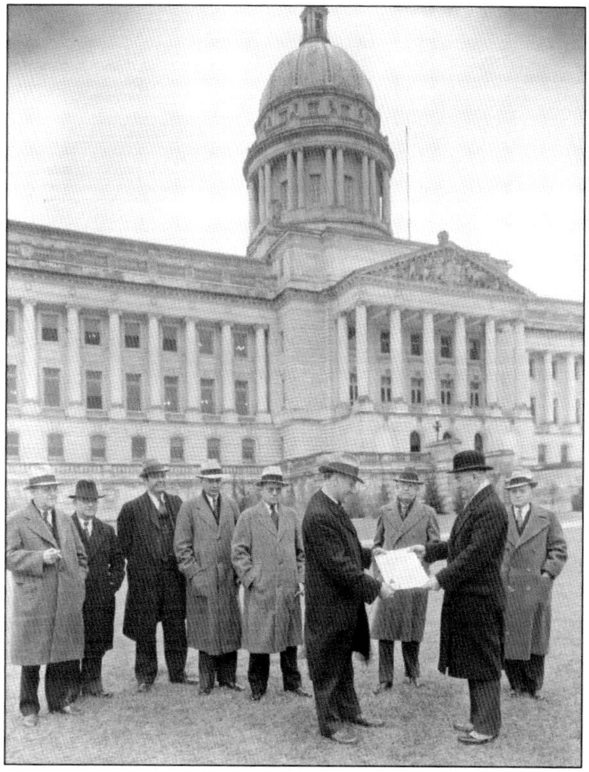

Float Truck. Pictured in this photograph is a 1932 truck from A. C. Morris Chevrolet Sales and Service in front of the capitol's north entrance. The truck is decorated like a parade float.

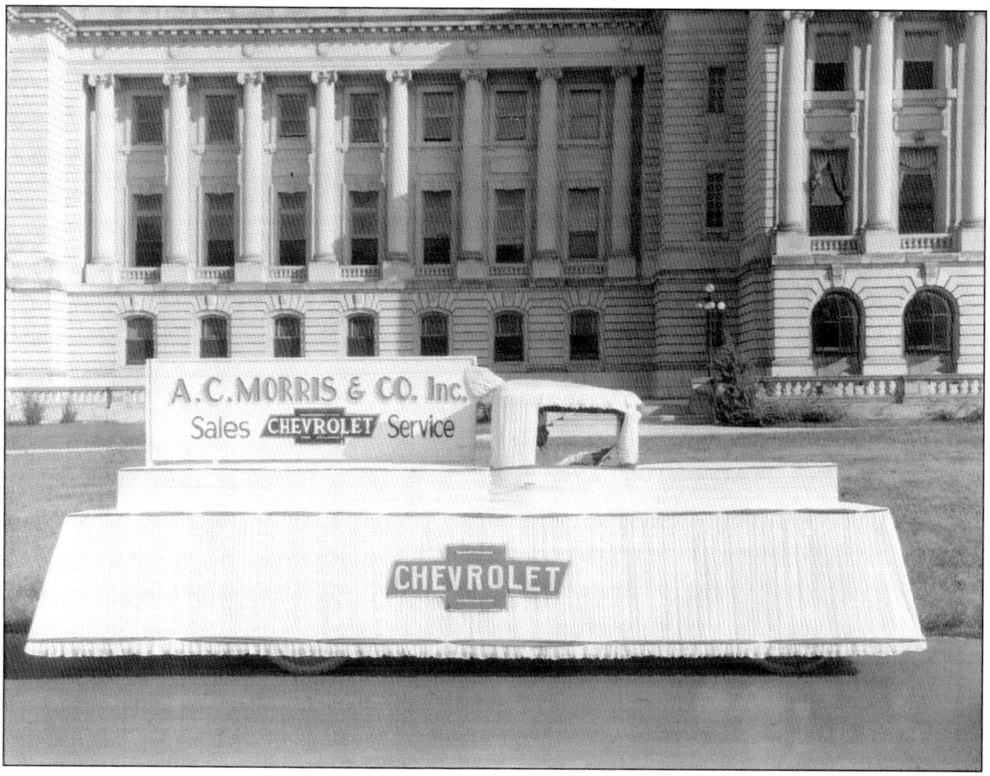

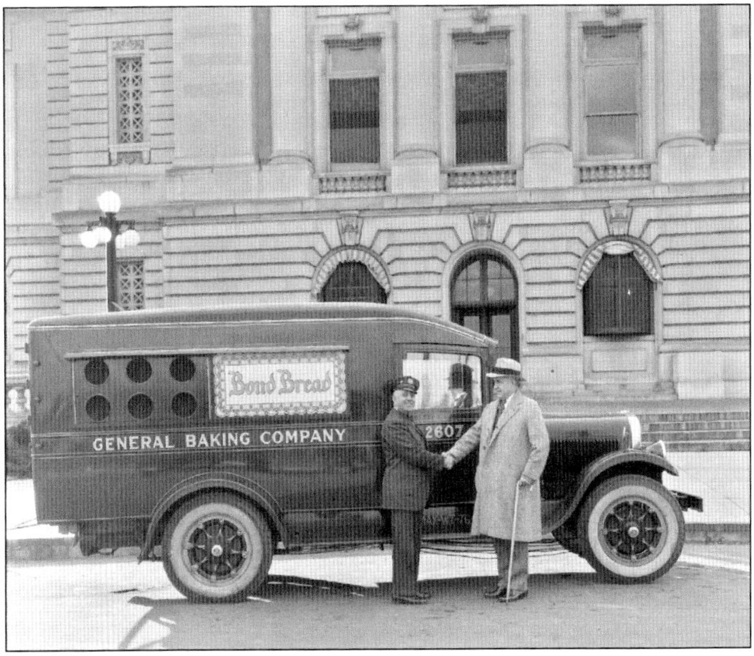

GENERAL BAKING COMPANY. Gov. Flem D. Sampson and a bread delivery truck advertising Bond Bread are pictured in this 1931 photograph on the south side of the capitol. Bakeries became essential during the Great Depression.

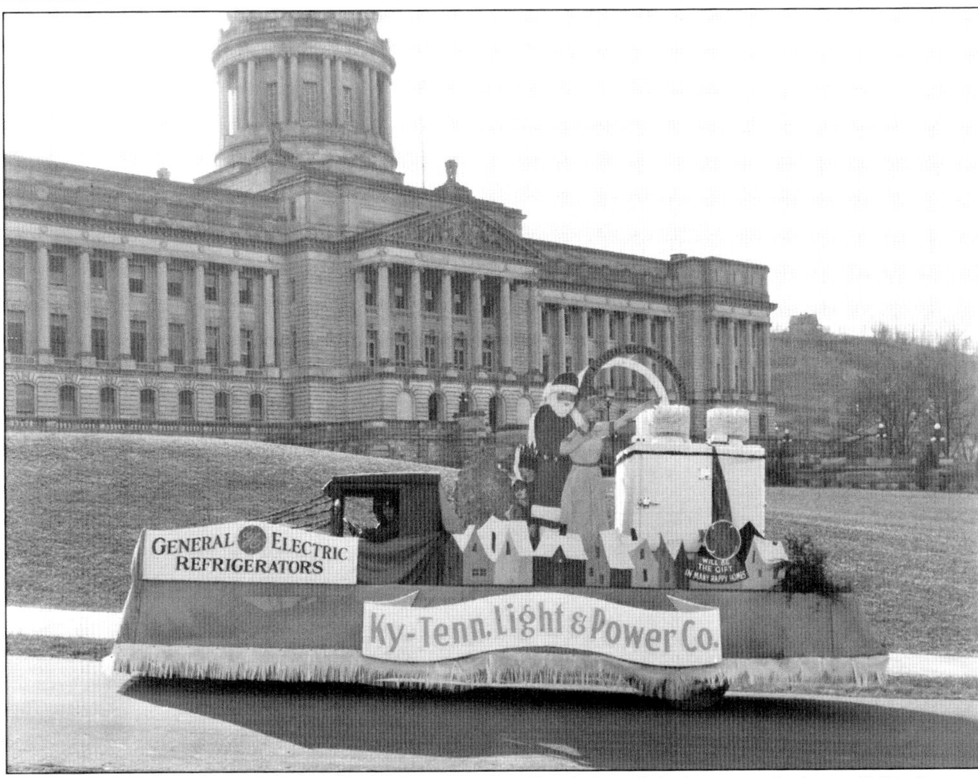

KENTUCKY-TENNESSEE LIGHT AND POWER, 1930. This beautiful photograph from 1930 shows a float passing by the northeast side of the capitol building. The float from Kentucky-Tennessee Light and Power Company is also promoting using General Electric refrigerators, which were made in Louisville, to keep things cold and use more electricity.

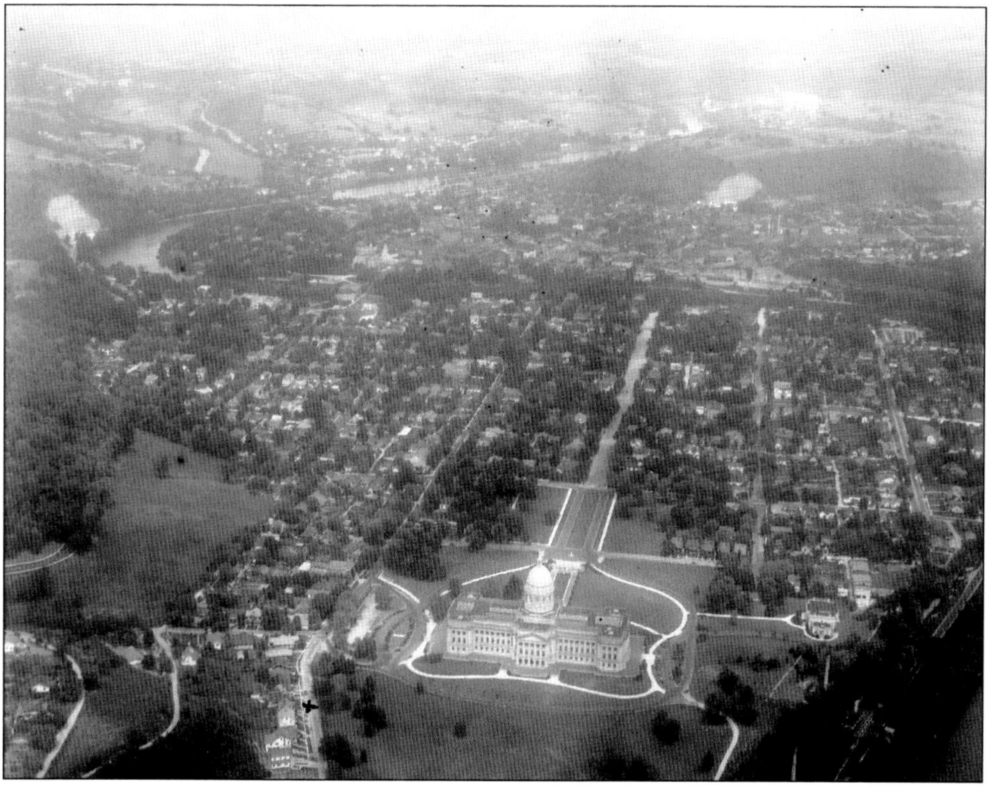

Aerial View, 1930–1935. The need for parking by 1930–1935 required the capitol to adjust grounds to accommodate parking lots on the east and west sides. As shown in this aerial view from the south looking north, the driveways and walkways around the capitol had become more defined and were paved. However, the basic landscape plan of 1908 remained the same.

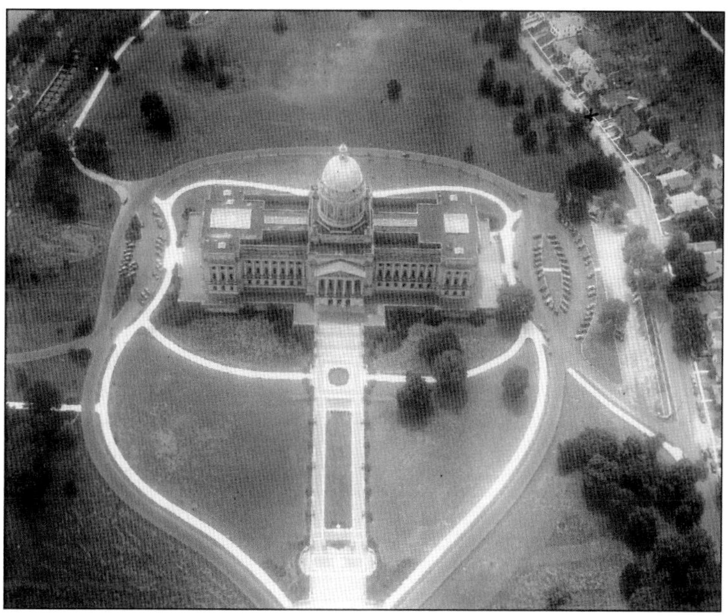

Sparse Campus. This image shows a closer view of the evolution of the capitol grounds since 1910. The graceful promenade is highlighted as well as the added parking spaces for automobiles. Landscaping appears to be sparse and sporadic, although several campaigns involving planting trees had occurred by this time.

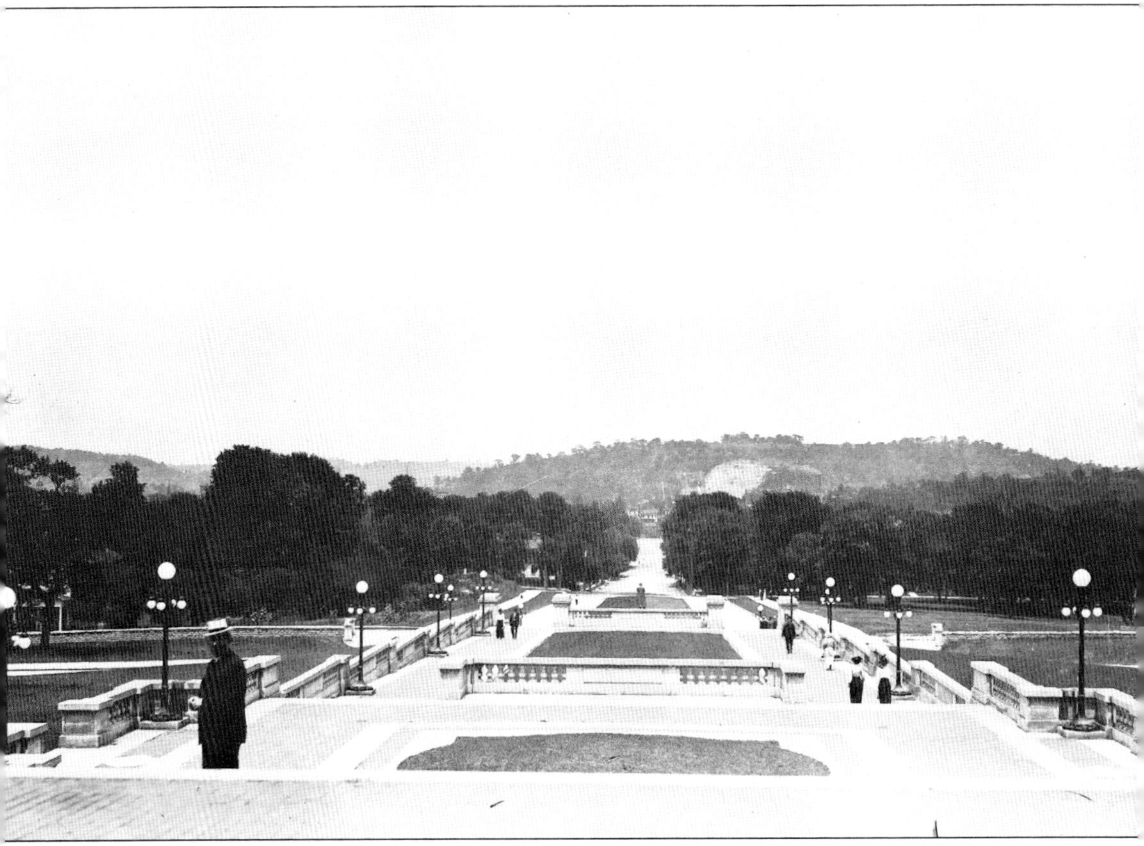

PROMENADE, 1930–1935. The approach to the capitol is often photographed looking up the steps to the capitol's facade. The view looking down the steps and towards Capital Avenue and downtown Frankfort is equally impressive for connecting the landscape of Frankfort with the capitol. The promenade features three terraces with solid Vermont granite steps framed in limestone balustrades with brick pavers. Many events, inaugurations, rallies, announcements, and protests have taken place on the promenade, shown here around 1930–1935.

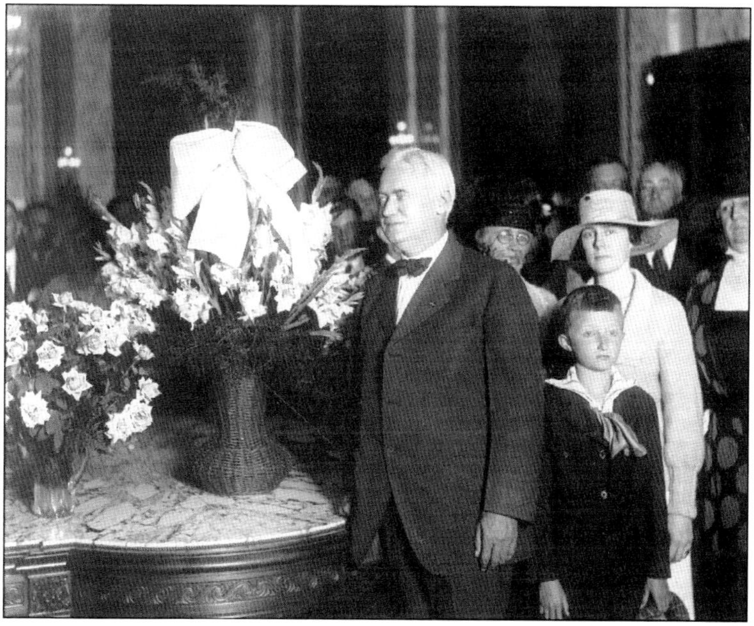

Gov. C. M. Harris. The state reception room has been the scene of many important meetings, bill signings, and even parties since 1910. This photograph from 1919 shows Gov. C. M. Harris holding an event in the celebrated room.

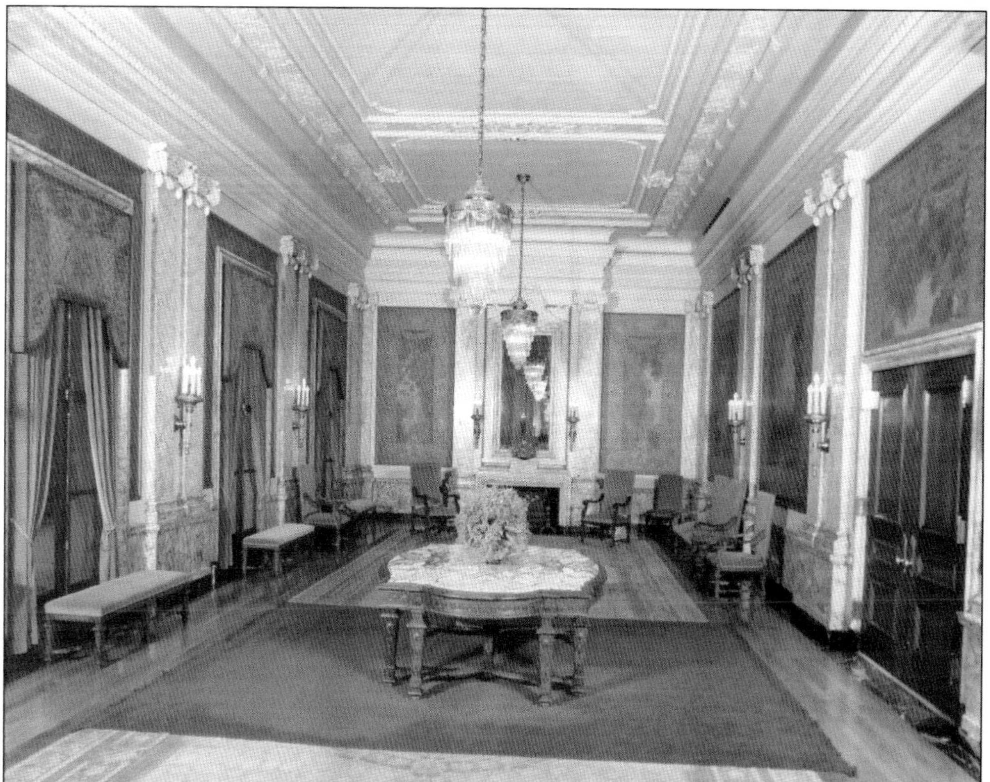

State Reception Room, 1940–1950. As shown in this photograph, the years were not kind to the state reception room's delicate finishes and furniture. There were stories of the massive table being used as a lunch area for capitol workers in the 1950s and 1960s. In the 1990s, the room was restored to its original grandeur.

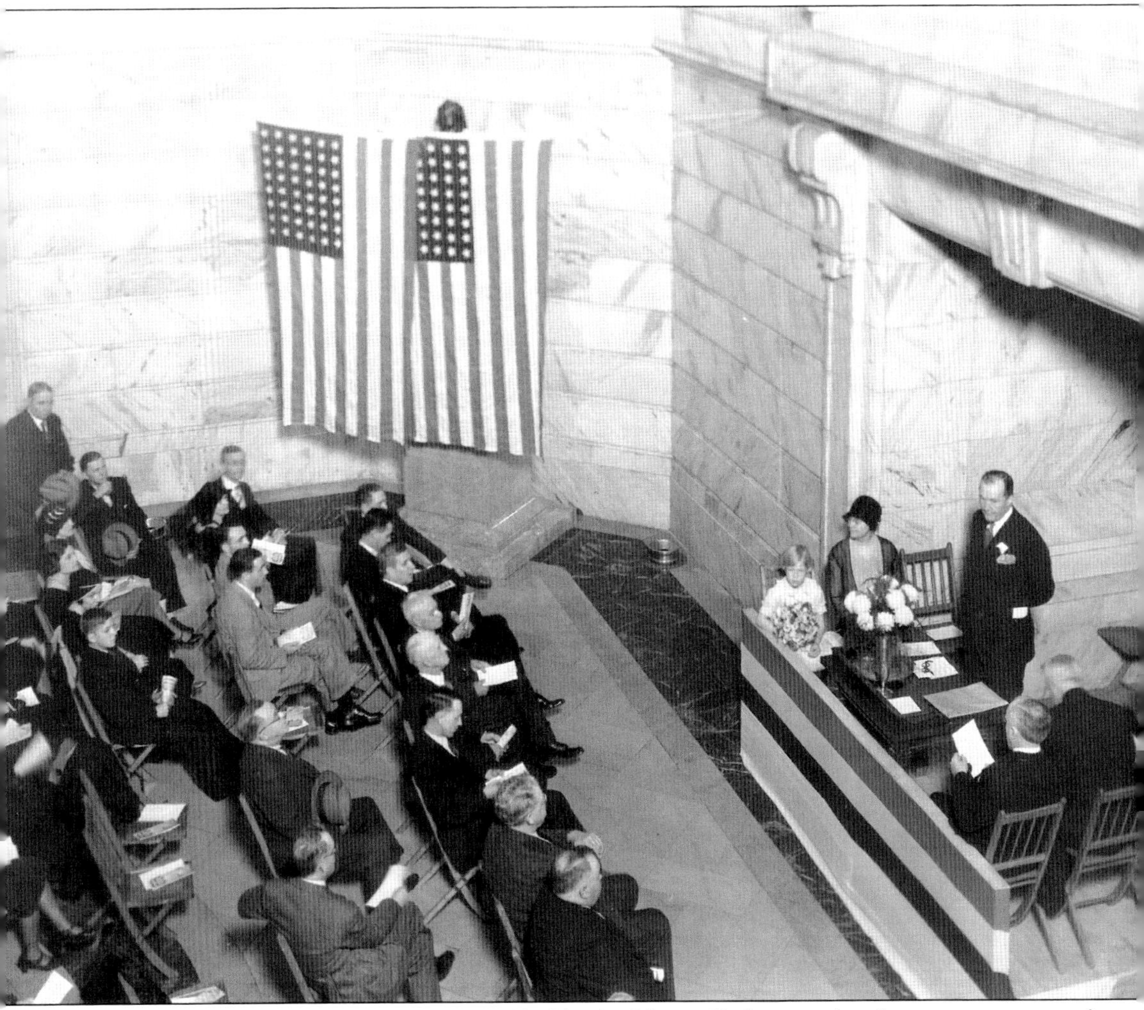

Henry Clay Statue Covered. In 1928, Charles Henry Niehaus sculpted two statues, one of Henry Clay and the other of Dr. Ephraim McDowell, to display in the statuary hall of the U.S. Capitol. The statues were a gift from wealthy Kentucky philanthropist Isaac Bernheim. Dr. Arthur T. McCormack, secretary of the state board of health, was present in Washington, D.C., for the unveiling of the McDowell statue. Niehaus made a generous offer to donate his plaster model of the McDowell statue to McCormack for the Commonwealth of Kentucky. Soon after Niehaus offered the McDowell sculpture model, he also offered the Henry Clay plaster model. The Clay statue is shown here in 1930 before its unveiling in the Kentucky Capitol rotunda.

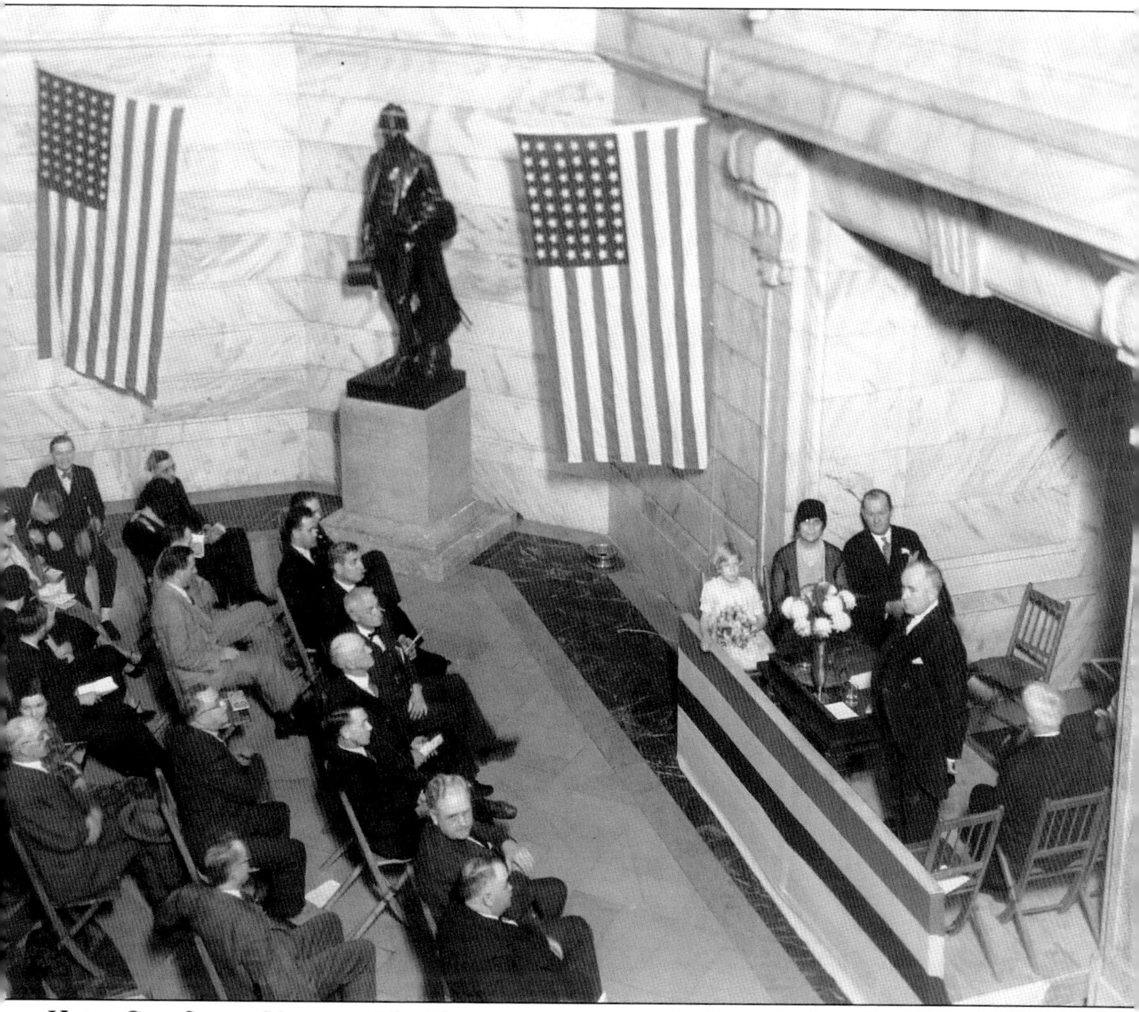

Henry Clay Statue Unveiled. The Clay statue was given to the Kentucky State Bar Association, who also donated the model to the commonwealth. The McDowell statue was unveiled in the rotunda by Gov. Flem Sampson on November 15, 1930, and the Henry Clay statue was unveiled four days later, as shown here, by parting two U.S. flags with 48 stars on November 19, 1930. Both statue models were painted to look like bronze.

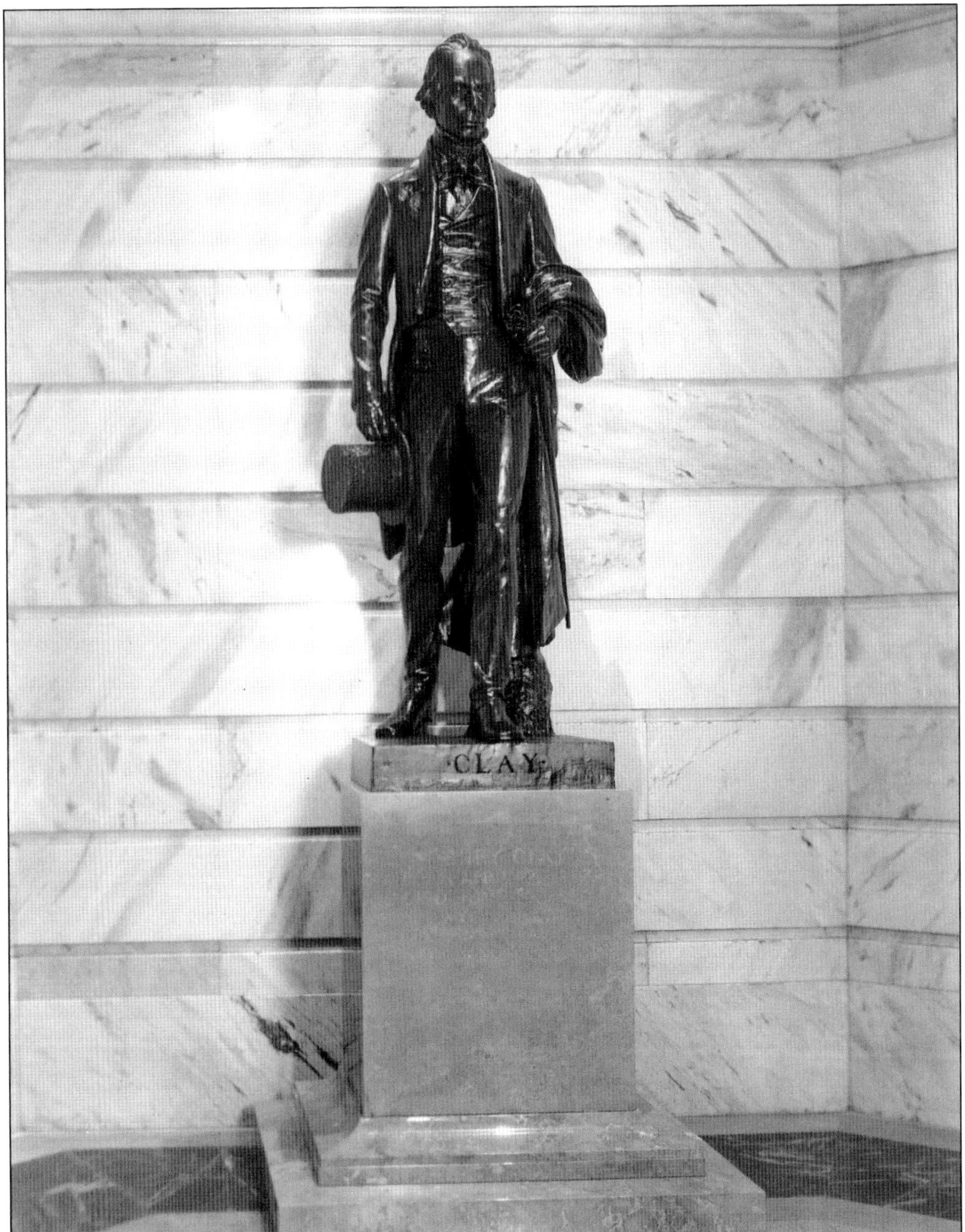

Henry Clay's Legacy. Henry Clay's life in Kentucky began in 1797, when he moved to central Kentucky from Virginia at age 20. He served in the commonwealth as a statesman, attorney, and farmer. Clay was elected to the Kentucky General Assembly in 1803, eventually earning enough influence to be selected by the Kentucky legislature to serve as U.S. senator for two terms. He was later elected as a member of the U.S. House of Representatives. In 1957, a senate committee chaired by John F. Kennedy named Henry Clay as one of the five greatest senators in U.S. history. Henry Clay is commonly referred to as "the Great Compromiser" for his astute political skills. Clay was known for his ability to negotiate treaties and settlements and for his eloquent skills as an orator.

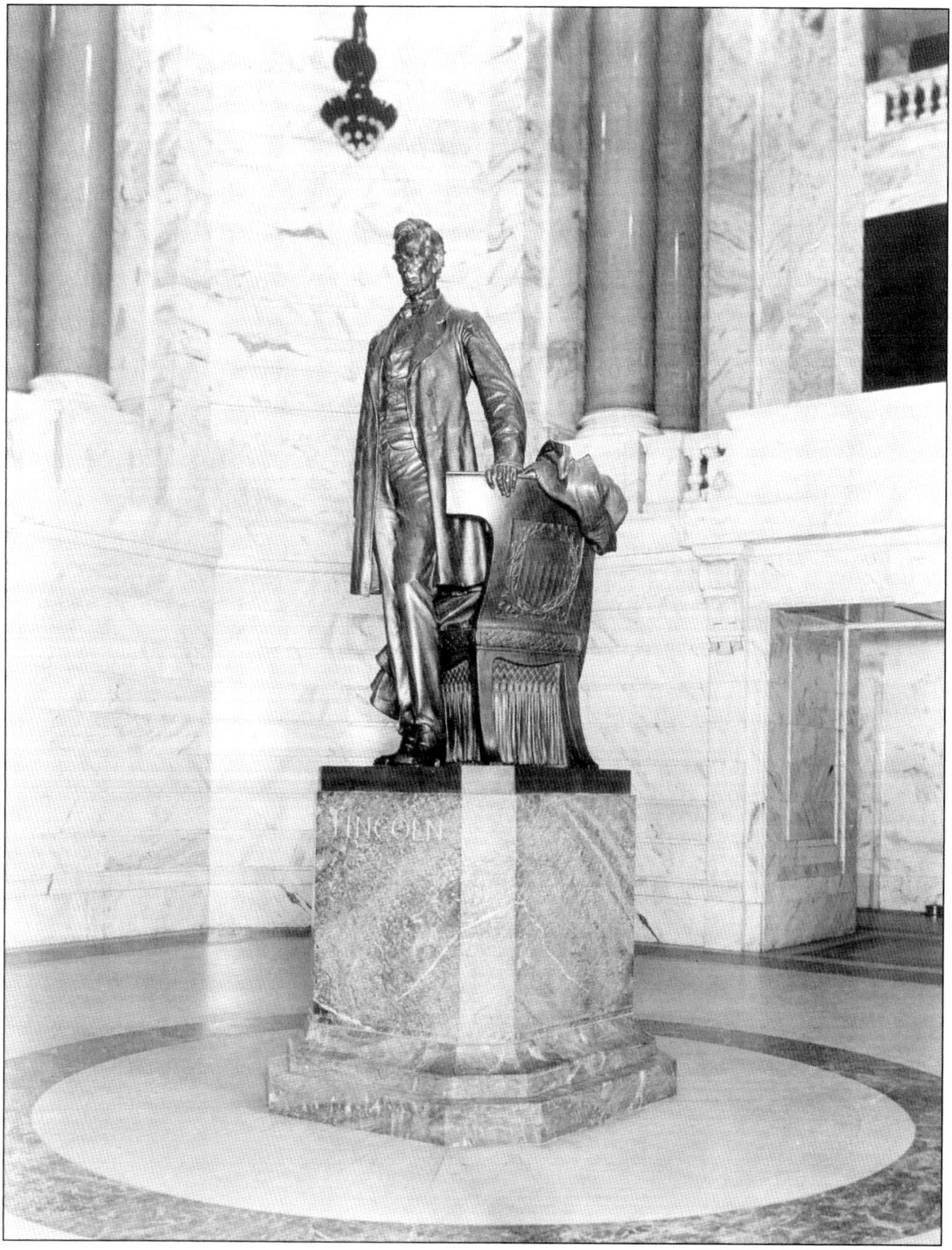

Abraham Lincoln. This 1915 photograph of the Lincoln statue in the capitol rotunda shows how Lincoln's left boot looked before a time-honored tradition began in the capitol—rubbing Lincoln's boot for good luck. The rubbing of Abe's boot by hundreds of thousands of visitors to the capitol has not caused any damage. With proper waxing and occasional repatination, Lincoln just has a very shiny boot tip. (Courtesy of Division of Historic Properties.)

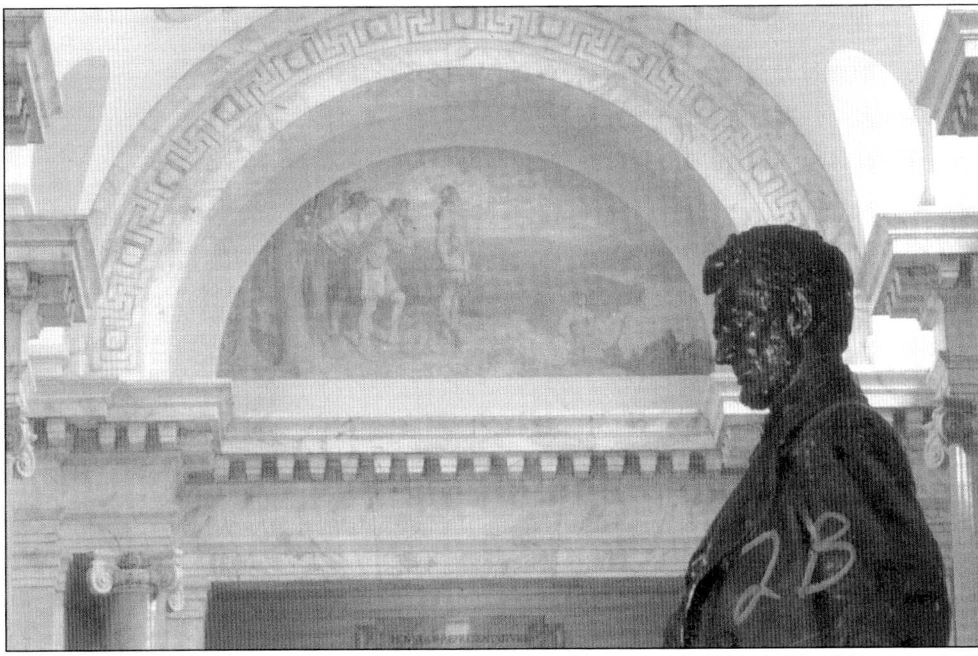

LINCOLN AND BOONE. This is a creative photograph taken around 1900–1930 of the great hall, as Abraham Lincoln's face almost appears as though it is much closer to the Daniel Boone mural. The face is actually 150 feet or more away from the mural. (Courtesy of Division of Historic Properties.)

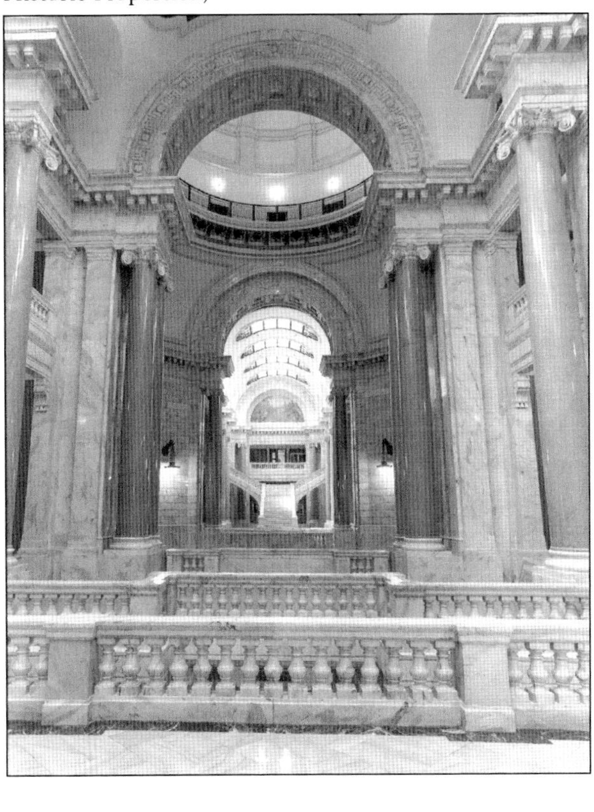

GREAT HALLS AND ROTUNDA AROUND 1915. In early 1924, a report in the Louisville *Courier-Journal* suggested that mural decorations be installed in the new capitol, including the areas shown in this photograph. "The building itself has never been finished in accordance with the specifications for its interior embellishment. These call for the design of mural decorations to harmonize with the classical lines of the building." A budget of $100,000 was estimated for this work that would make the building "second to none in the country." (Courtesy of Division of Historic Properties.)

Eight

NEW PRIORITIES FOR A NEW COMMONWEALTH

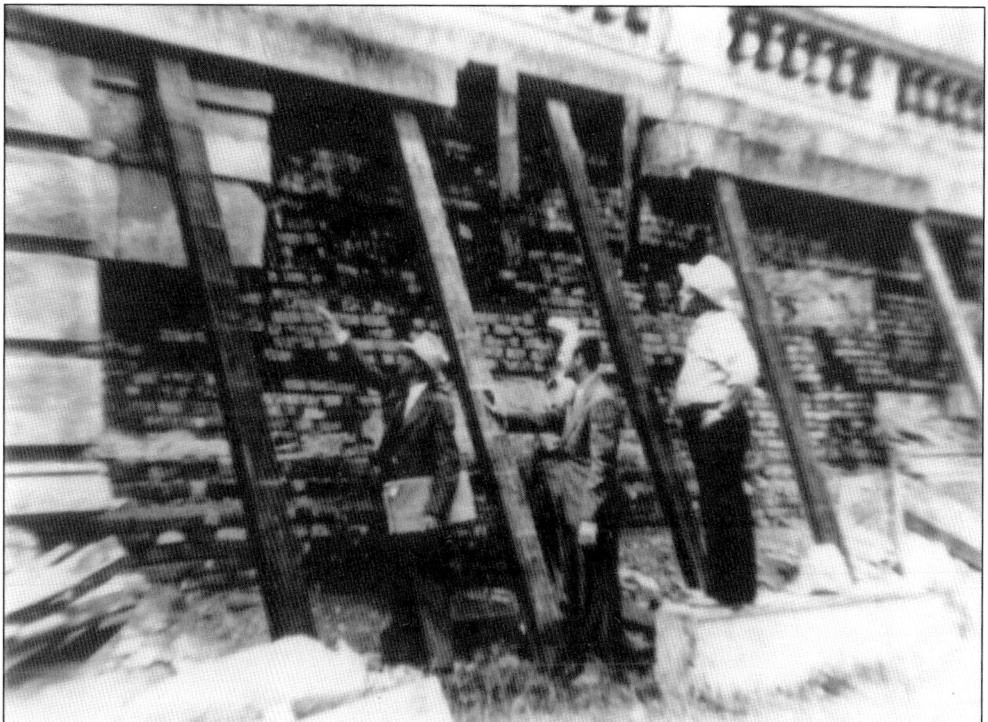

POOR CONDITIONS ON TERRACE AROUND **1940.** By the 1940s, the capitol building was starting to show not only its age but also that some of the construction was poorly done. Newspaper reports in April 1940 described the extent of the problems at the state capitol building. The problems reported included: loose stone veneer panels in the rotunda and great hall spaces; exterior stone that needed repointing; and retaining walls around the terrace perimeter that needed repair, as shown in this 1940s photograph. The masonry terrace walls were collapsing. It was determined that they would be replaced with concrete and the original limestone veneers reattached. (Courtesy of Division of Historic Properties.)

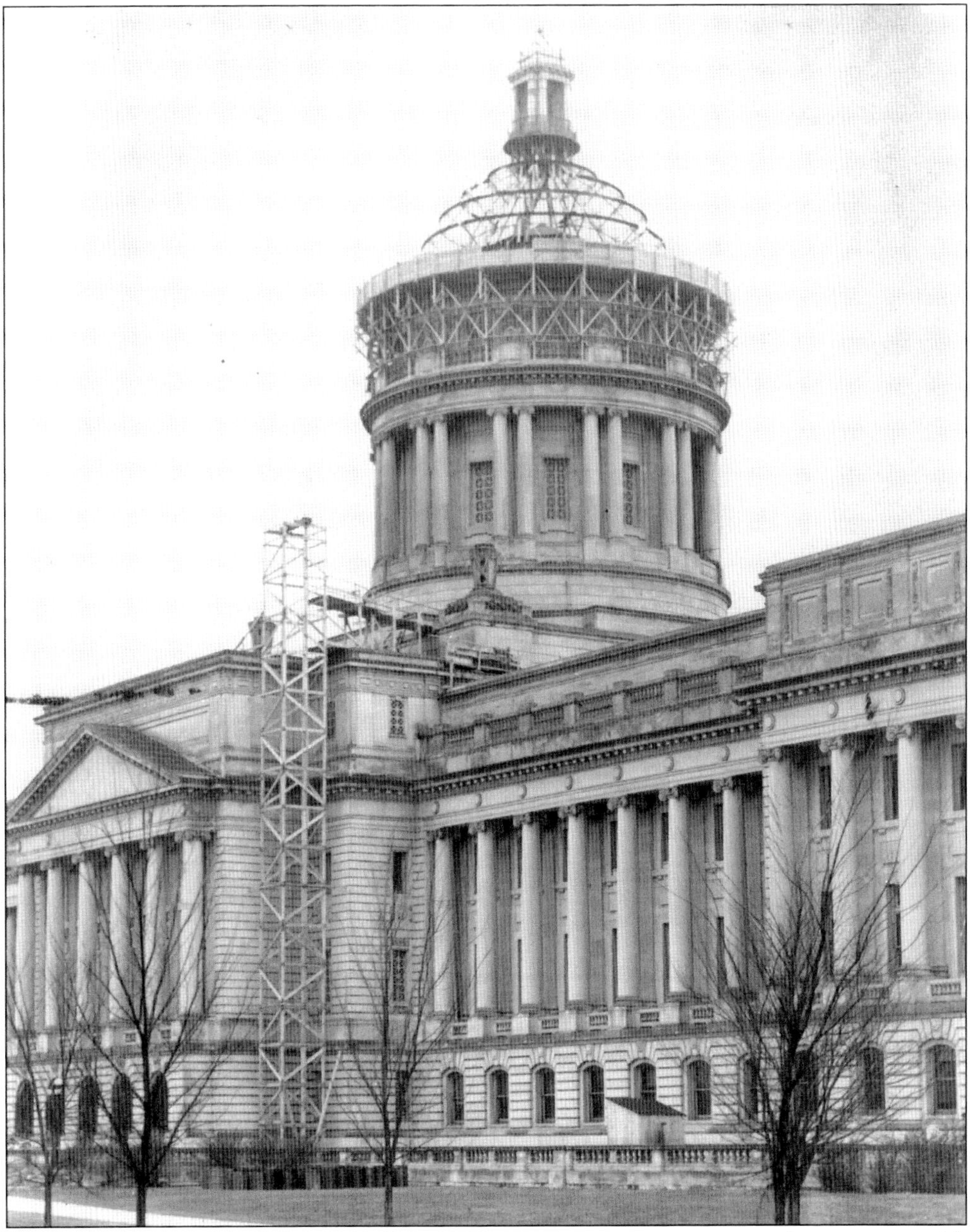

Dome Reconstruction. Throughout the 1930s, reports from newspapers across the commonwealth wrote about the deteriorated condition of the capitol's dome, which some feared was in danger of collapsing, causing the rotunda to be closed to the public. The interior plaster dome was deteriorated and weakened, and it was thought that the plaster might collapse. When the heavy wooden frames were erected around the statuary, the rotunda was closed to the public. Repair work to the dome, shown in this 1941 photograph, included removal and replacement of the terra-cotta cladding (excluding the lantern at the apex of the dome) and interior plaster dome. Portions of the steel structure that were severely corroded were replaced as well as reinforced with concrete. Additional steel members were added for reinforcement. The interior ornamental plaster dome was replaced to replicate the original design. (Courtesy of Division of Historic Properties.)

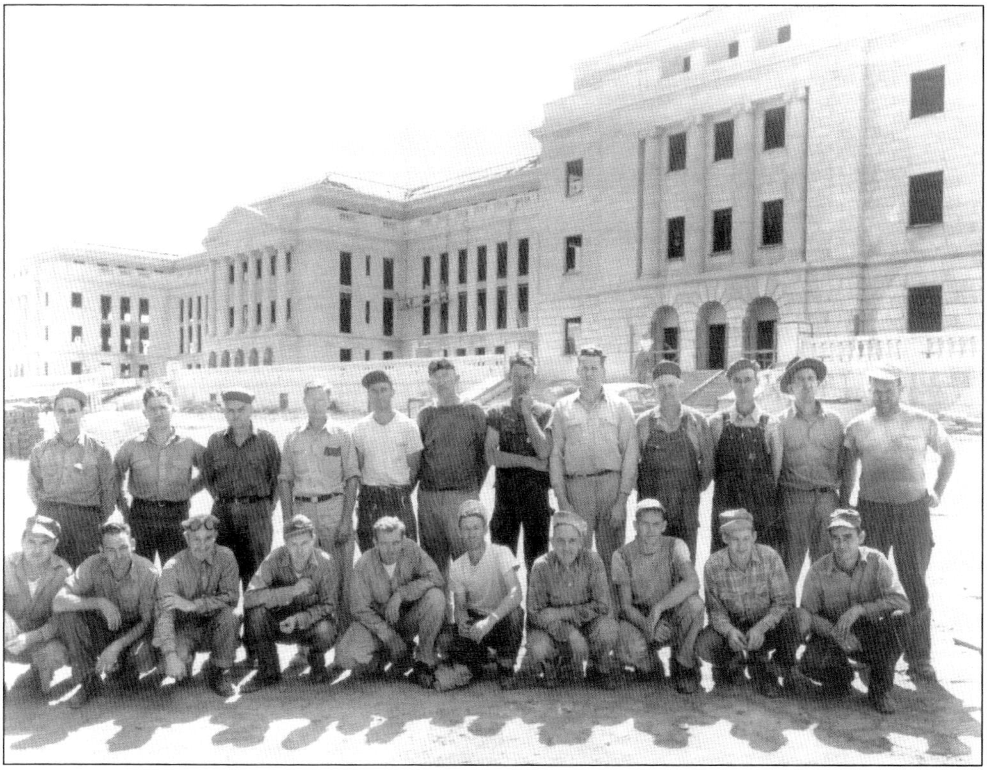

SPACE RELIEF. When the Kentucky State Capitol was complete and occupied in 1910, it was believed to be commodious enough to house all the state departments and agencies. As soon as 1925, it was reported to be inadequate for needs. Wings and additions were discussed, and eventually the capitol annex was built on the south side of the capitol. This photograph from 1951 shows the building nearly complete. (Courtesy of Division of Historic Properties.)

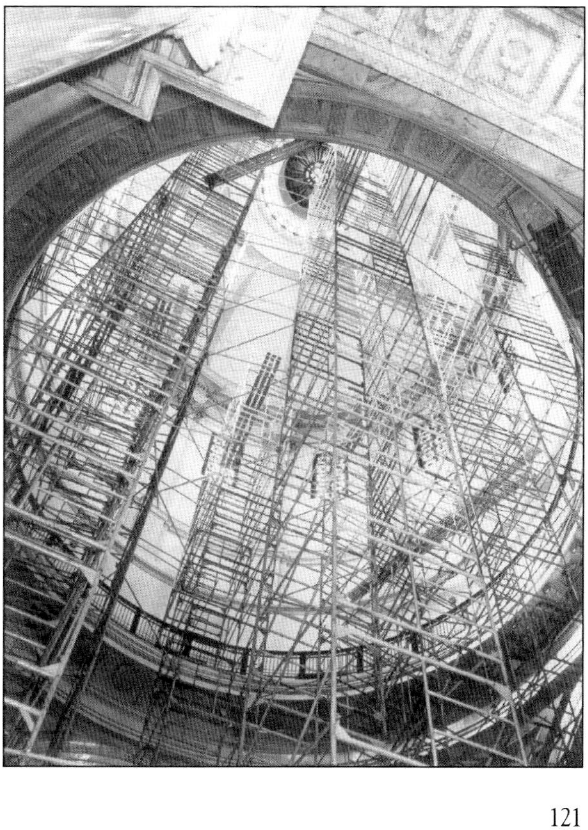

SCAFFOLDING IN THE ROTUNDA AROUND 1954. Scaffolding was set up in the capitol rotunda in 1953 for painting, cleaning, and maintenance work. In late 2009, scaffolding was put back in the rotunda for similar work, including energy-efficient lighting, in preparation for the capitol's 100th anniversary. (Courtesy of Division of Historic Properties.)

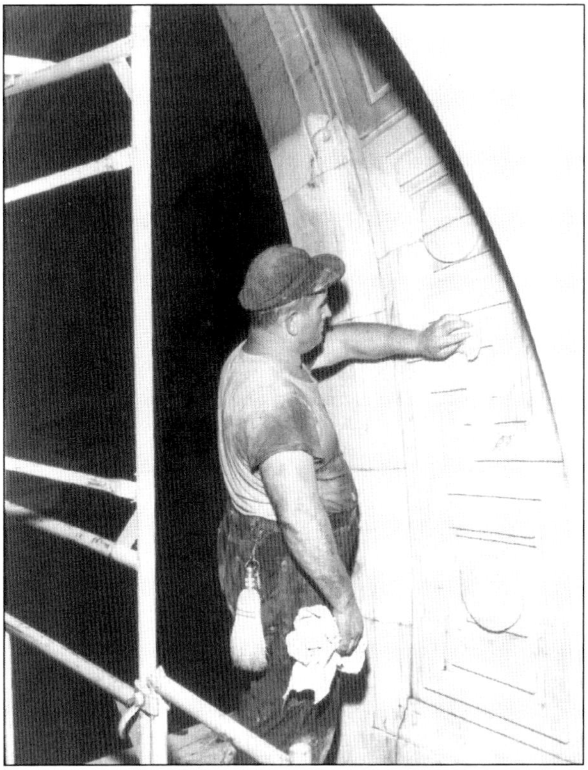

Cleaning Marble. Scaffolding was erected throughout the capitol in 1953 to access the marble walls for cleaning. The cleaning procedure included washing the stone with hot water, followed by an application of a cleaning solution. After rinsing the cleaner, the surface was polished with a dry cloth. The unidentified gentlemen in this 1954 photograph helped do the work.

Scaffolding in the Great Halls around 1954. This photograph shows the intricate web of scaffolding and ladders traversing the rotunda. The scaffolding erected in the rotunda in 2009 was even more intricate and included a stairway for access.

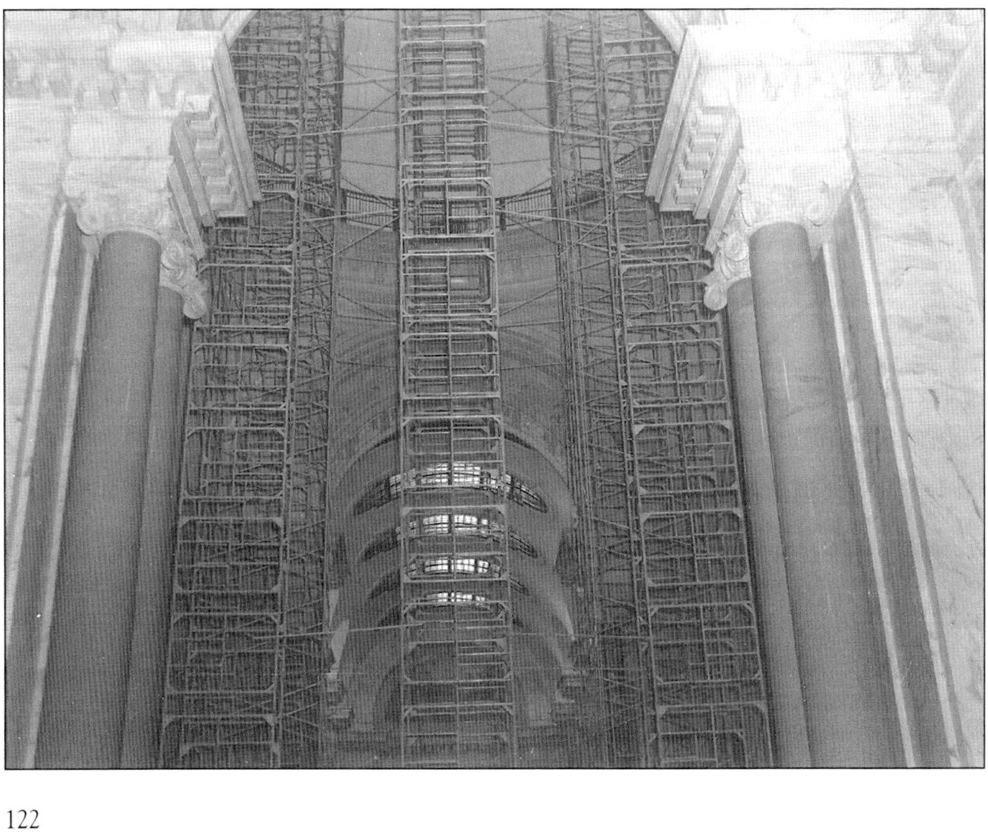

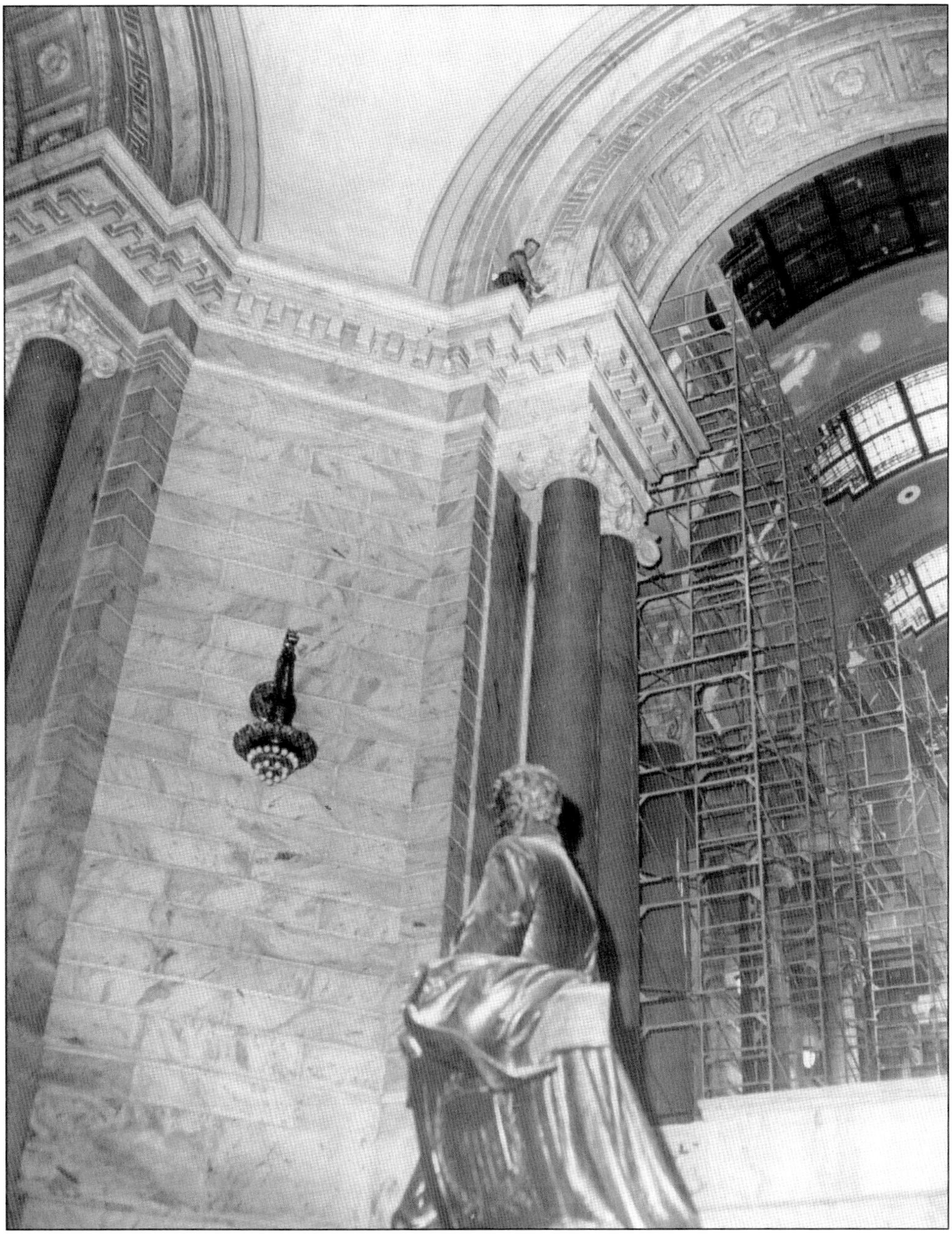

INTERIOR RENOVATION, 1953–1955. Renovation work began on December 1, 1953. Interior renovations included shifting office spaces, with several departments moved out of the capitol. The state education department and the agriculture department were moved across Frankfort to the state office building. The state treasurer had previously moved to the capitol annex. The governor and secretary of state offices were moved from the second floor to the first. The new governor's office was located in the space formerly occupied by the hall of fame, immediately south of the rotunda. The Kentucky Capitol Building was rededicated on November 17, 1955, with a ceremony led by Governor Wetherby.

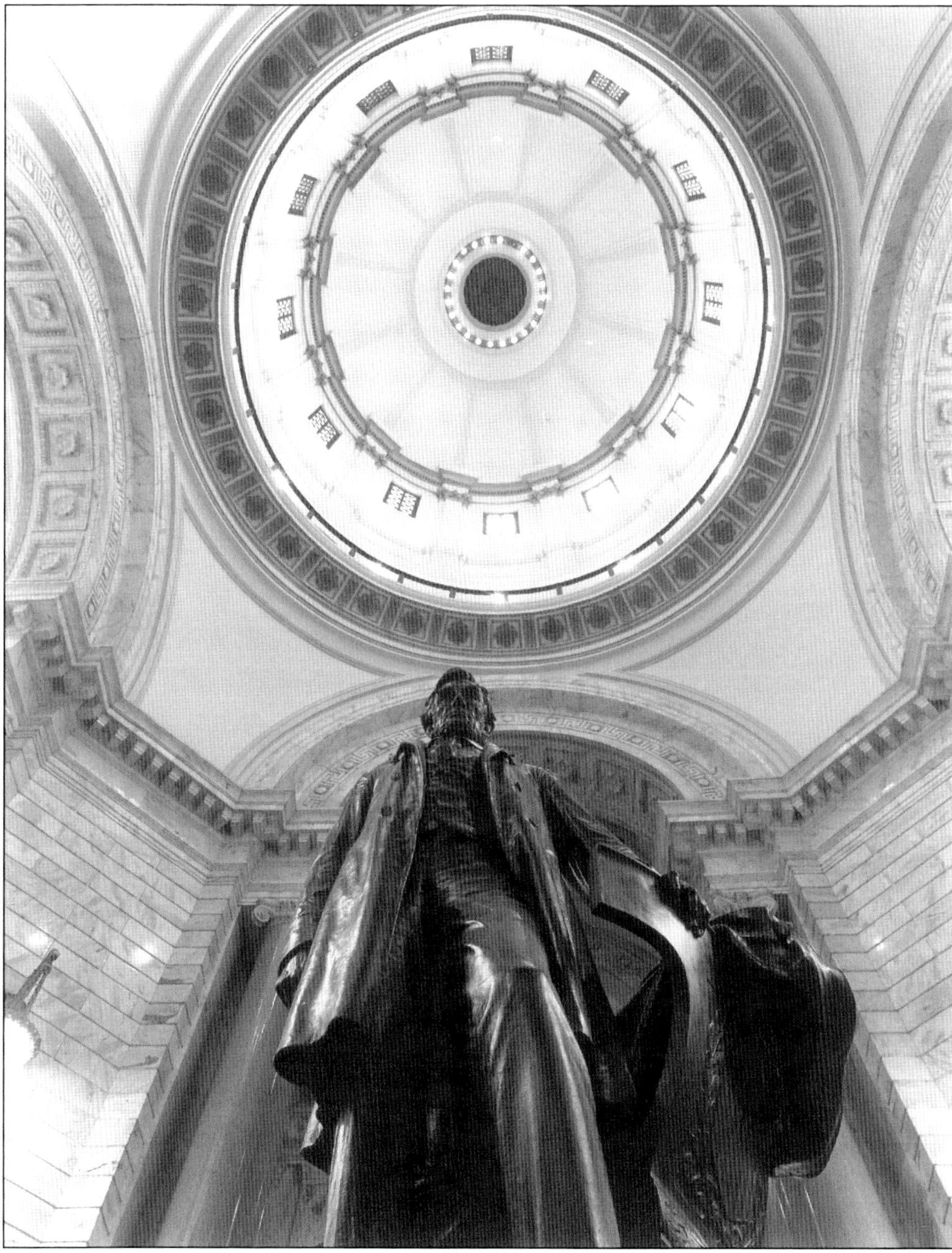

Pendentive Murals. In 1939, with the Commonwealth of Kentucky debt free, proposals were received for decorating the interior of the capitol building and specifically the pendentive areas of the rotunda. When the building was under construction in 1906, plans were discussed for mural decorations depicting Kentucky's rich heritage, but the plans were never implemented because of the state's financial situation. In 2009, this proposal was revived as the capitol centennial commission's legacy project, and due to a generous private donation by Marion and Terry Forcht of Corbin, Kentucky, it will be a reality in 2010.

KENTUCKY'S FLORAL CLOCK. On April 10, 1960, Gov. Bert Combs allotted $50,000 from the governor's contingency fund to build the floral clock on the capitol grounds. Inspired by a similar feature Combs had seen in Edinburgh, Scotland, it has survived early criticism to become one of the most significant tourist attractions and photograph opportunities in Frankfort. Pictured here, the capitol's floral clock is one of the largest clocks of its kind in the world.

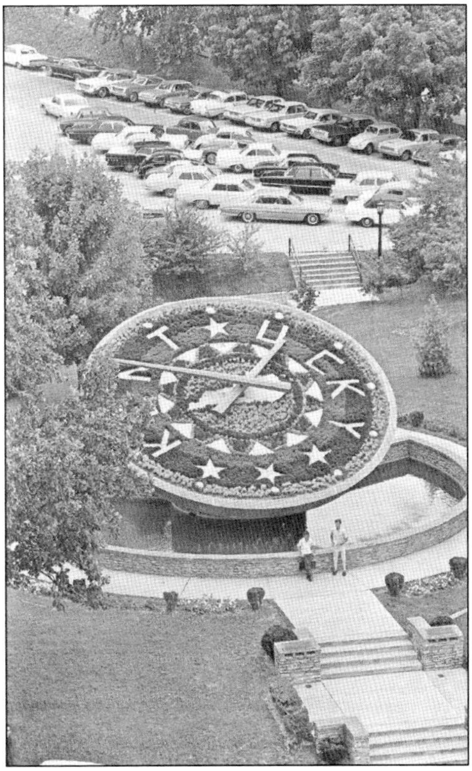

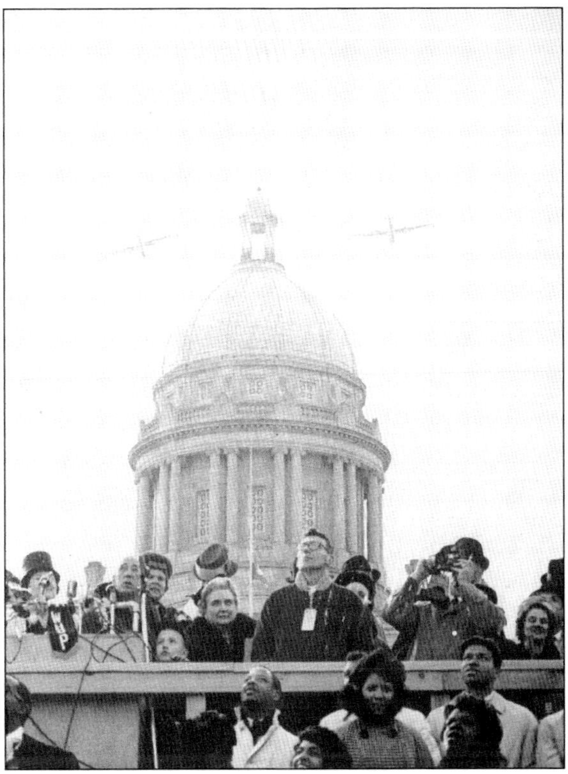

DOME WITH PLANES. This photograph of the capitol's dome, taken some time between 1960 and 1970 with military planes flying by on both sides, symbolizes the Kentucky State Capitol and its progress as the landmark building reaches its centennial anniversary.

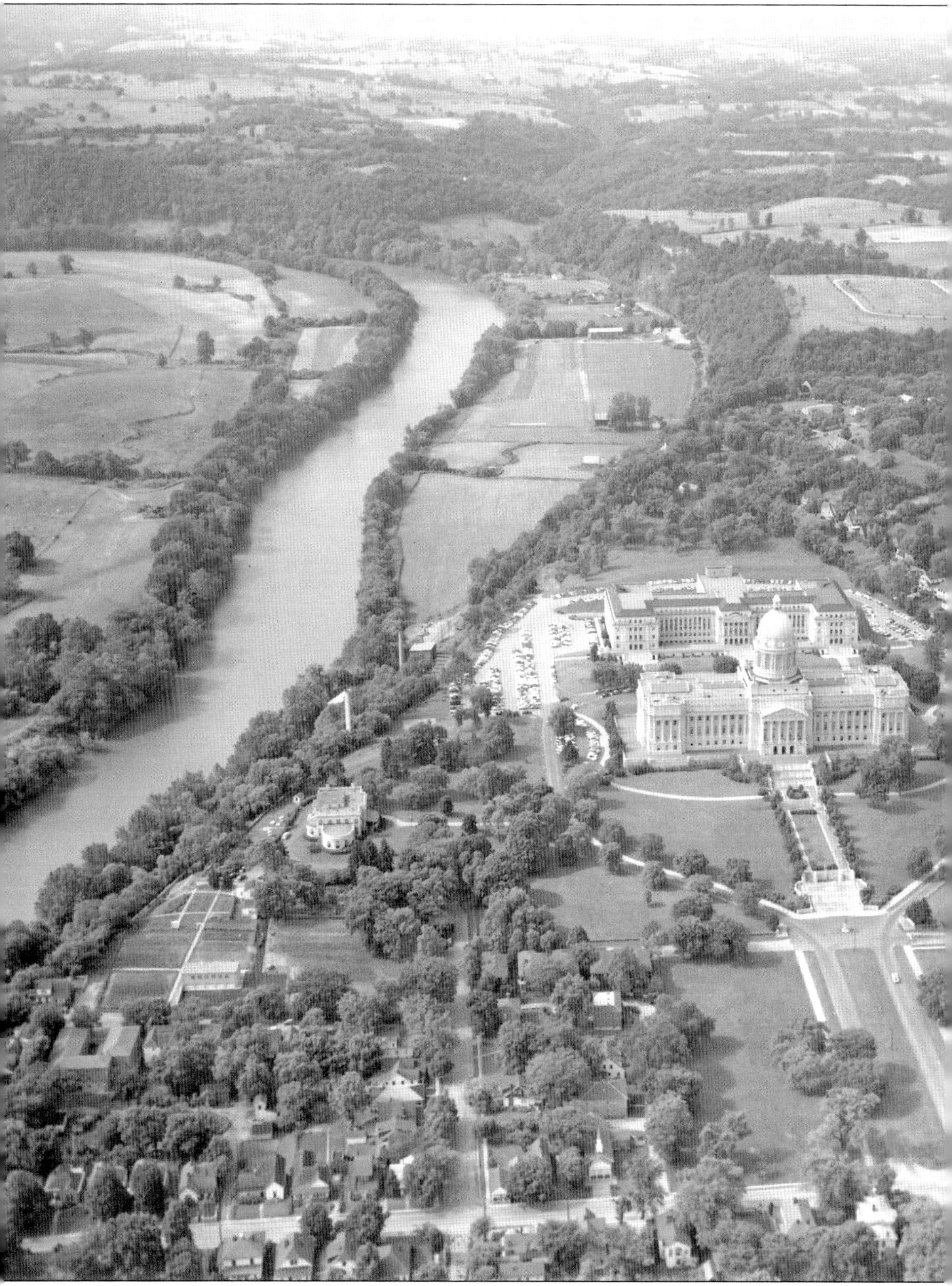

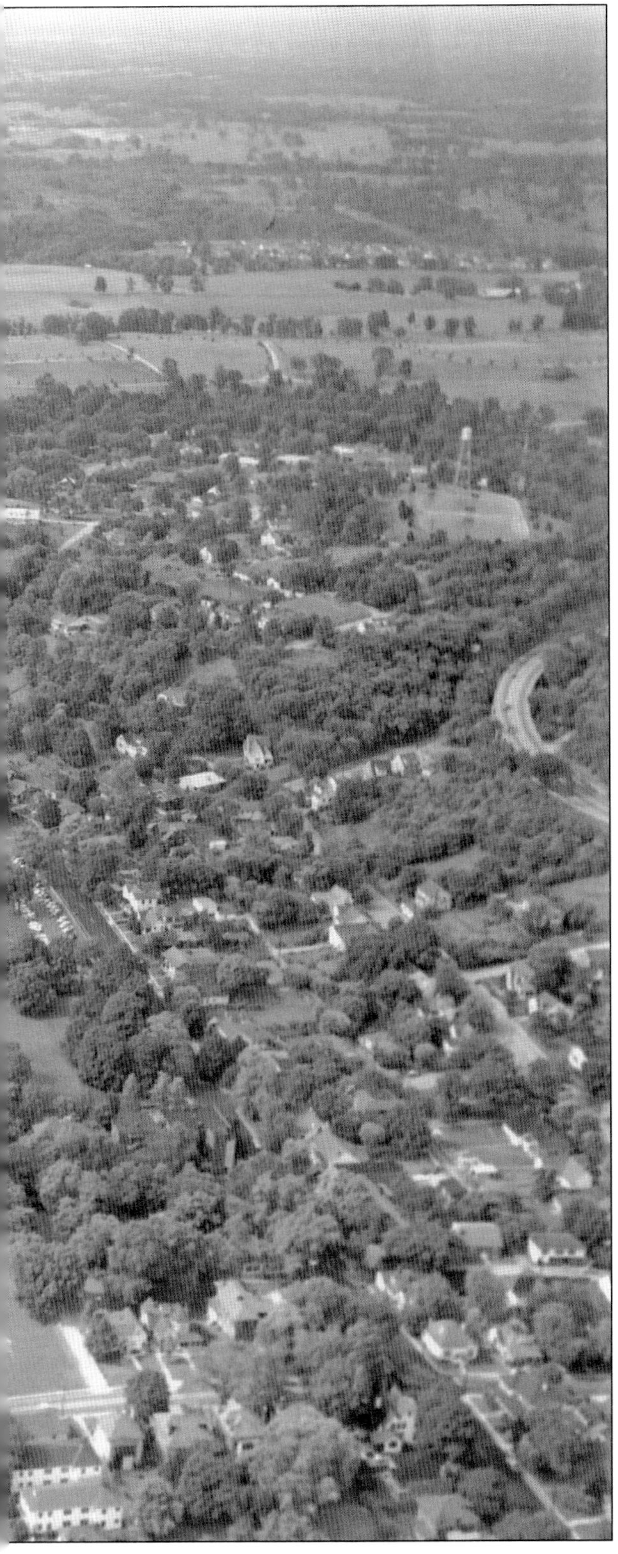

KENTUCKY STATE CAPITOL CAMPUS, 1950–1960. Taken just after the major renovations in the 1950s, this aerial image showcases the capitol campus in all its glory. The photograph is a fitting end to the book as a time-traveling journey from the cover image. As the Kentucky State Capitol prepares for its centennial anniversary in June 2010, it is appropriate to look back at its legacy in this forum. The Kentucky Division of Historic Properties' mission is to protect and preserve the integrity of the commonwealth's most important public building and its grounds for future generations to appreciate. (Courtesy of Division of Historic Properties.)